The World of
Elsie Jeanette Oxenham
and
Her Books

by

Monica Godfrey

Girls Gone By Publishers

Published by

Girls Gone By Publishers
4 Rock Terrace
Coleford
Bath
Somerset
BA3 4NF

First published 2003

Text © Monica Godfrey 2003
Design and Layout © Girls Gone By Publishers 2003

Typeset by Automated Systems, Somerset

Printed by Antony Rowe Ltd, Chippenham

ISBN 1-904417-15-9

Dedicated to the world-wide collectors
of books by Elsie Jeanette Oxenham.
Also to my patient family, particularly
my son Martin for his technical help.

Publishers' Note

Some of the illustrations in this book have been provided by the author; others are taken from our own collection; a large number were sent to us by Jane Webster (former editor of *The Abbey Gatehouse* in New Zealand) to whom we are extremely grateful. Where we have used illustrations from inside books we have indicated from which book each has come; it is quite possible that an illustration may also be found in another book from that indicated.

from *Girls of the Hamlet Club*

Elsie Jeanette Dunkerley (Oxenham) c 1922

Contents

INTRODUCTION

'The Challenge' (*Ven at Gregory's*)

Although the writer Elsie Jeanette Oxenham is remembered mainly for her Abbey books, one of the most fascinating aspects of her work lies in discovering just how far that series actually extended.

During her writing life, she produced several small sets of stories, each at first sight appearing to be about unrelated groups of teenage girls and young women. Yet by making characters move effortlessly from one book to another, she joined them together in many directions over more than fifty years, making a complicated web, the strands of which nearly all eventually led back to the Abbey and the fictional girls of her main series.

Elsie Jeanette Oxenham wrote her books over a far wider group of characters than any other writer in this category appears to have attempted although she probably had no intention of doing so when she began writing them. Right from the start of her career and before the Abbey series came into being, Elsie Oxenham linked

her earliest stories together by having certain characters common to more than one book although there were not always other obvious connections between them. Once she embarked on the Abbey series she produced complicated interweavings using characters or incidents from her earlier books, as well as those from subsequent stories and other smaller sets she was often writing concurrently.

The Abbey books, together with their related small groups

of connected stories, make a complicated canvas with a larger cast and backgrounds than is normally found in any series. This is partly why Elsie Jeanette Oxenham and her stories remain so popular although it is nearly one hundred years since her first book was published in 1907. No other author, apart from perhaps Elinor Brent-Dyer, appears to have done this on anything like the same scale, although many have written long series around the same characters while others such as Angela Thirkell and Mazo de la Roche have invented elaborate family cycles carrying them backwards and forwards through the generations.

Since there were and still are so many collectors interested in her and her work, a short and basic biography, *Elsie Jeanette Oxenham and Her Books*, was produced in 1979 giving brief details about her life and her writing. Ten years later *The Elsie Jeanette Oxenham Appreciation Society* was formed in Great Britain. Details of that and similar societies are given in Chapter 21. The first issue of their newsletter, *The Abbey Chronicle*, was sent to over sixty prospective members in May 1989. Membership doubled during the first few months and has increased steadily ever since.

This completely new edition of the first booklet about Elsie Jeanette Oxenham (or EJO as she is known amongst collectors) has been produced not only to show how far-reaching the Abbey series became but also to explain more about her as a person, how her background influenced her writing and how places which appealed to her were incorporated into her books. It has been written to answer the constant queries made by collectors and fans wanting to know more about their favourite author. EJO's enthusiasms outside her home enabled her to write about subjects, particularly English Folk Dancing and the American Camp Fire Movement, which hitherto had been unknown to many readers. Perhaps most important of all this will explain how much her varied interests provided the differing themes in her stories.

Chapter headings, sub-titles and other quotations are taken from the first editions of the books by Elsie Jeanette Oxenham. Quotations from all other books cited are from the first edition of each one unless stated otherwise. Many publishing companies have disappeared since her day while others over the years have 'lost all records'. Postcards and photographs are used with permission from their owners.

Monica Godfrey 2002

Dunkerley Family Tree

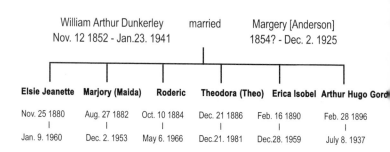

William Arthur Dunkerley   married   Margery [Anderson]
Nov. 12 1852 - Jan.23. 1941   1854? - Dec. 2. 1925

Elsie Jeanette	Marjory (Maida)	Roderic	Theodora (Theo)	Erica Isobel	Arthur Hugo Gord
Nov. 25 1880	Aug. 27 1882	Oct. 10 1884	Dec. 21 1886	Feb. 16 1890	Feb. 28 1896
|	|	|	|	|	|
Jan. 9. 1960	Dec. 2. 1953	May 6. 1966	Dec.21. 1981	Dec.28. 1959	July 8. 1937

The Dunkerley Family – (back) Elsie, William (JO), Maida
(front) Theo, Roderic, Madgie, Hugo, Erica

CHAPTER ONE

Home and Family
or 'The Friendly House' (*Jandy Mac Comes Back*)

'Of course this is home, and always will be! It's the happiest home any girl ever had; and I've been the luckiest girl. If I could say a fraction of what I feel, I'd make you understand.'
(*The Abbey Girls at Home*. 1929. p. 160.)

Many writers' first books are often based on real people or situations and the author Elsie Jeanette Oxenham was no exception. Her first published book, *Goblin Island* (1907) was written in the first person as by The Girl during a holiday in Scotland with her father The Author. The Author was based on Elsie's own father William

Elsie c. 1893

Elsie Jeanette Dunkerley c 1893

Dunkerley, who wrote as John Oxenham or simply as J. O., and the girl on herself. She described The Author's manuscripts as being decorated by drawings which was how her own father always ornamented his first drafts. The Girl (Jean) she wrote about in less detail, other than showing that she was writing a book in secret.

After leaving school Elsie became her father's assistant and, as well as typing his books, often went away with him in that capacity. In 1903 he wrote a booklet *The Very Short Memory of Mr Joseph Scorer And Other Seaside Experiences* about some family holidays and dedicated it: 'To Elsie who met most of these friends about the same time as I did—this little book.'

Scotland was a favourite holiday venue and when the children were small, their father thought nothing of sending them with their mother and nurse on the long train journey from London to Gourock (Scotland) after which they had to take a steamer across the Clyde before reaching his mother-in-law's holiday home, Avondale Lodge, in Dunoon. Short breaks were spent in Buckinghamshire and longer holidays in Sussex, other favourite places in those early days. Later they discovered the Channel Islands and Elsie's younger sister, Theo, remembered 'Our father took the three youngest for memorable holidays on Sark.' The family also began to go abroad, usually to France or Switzerland.

William Arthur Dunkerley married Margery Anderson at Afton Bank, Greenock, Scotland, on 6th June 1877. They first met in Manchester while she was on holiday there with Elizabeth, one of her many sisters. After a Highland

The house where Elsie Jeanette Dunkerley was born in 1880

honeymoon, the couple went to America where William was to start a new branch of his father's provision business. They settled in Orange, a small farming community some fifteen miles north-west of Manhattan. William travelled into New York, daily taking a ferry through the Narrows, a mile-wide passage with magnificent rocky cliffs edging the west shore of the Hudson. The business venture was not a success and by 1879 they were back in England where they lived at Gowanbrae, 3, Crosby Road, Southport. This was an ordinary double-fronted house with a small front garden actually in the village of Birkdale with,

Another view of the house where Elsie Jeanette Dunkerley was born in 1880

13

just a few houses away, the oldest thatched house in the area.

Soon after the birth there of Elsie Jeanette, their first living child, on November 25th 1880, William was asked if he would move to London to start a new branch of *The Detroit Free Press*, a paper on which he was already working. He agreed and, leaving his wife in Greenock with the baby, went to London where they joined him at Bedford Park in 1882. After Elsie there was a new baby approximately every two years, then they were more widely spaced until the last, Hugo, who arrived when she was sixteen.

From Bedford Park the family moved to Hanger Hill Farm House, Hanger Lane, Ealing (now part of London), then, liking the district of Ealing where they continued to stay, to Grove House, 105, The Grove. In 1900 they went to 15, Woodville Gardens which Theo Dunkerley told me was 'a late Victorian, double-fronted, narrowly detached house with a jolly little tower decorating one corner'. The great attraction for the children while living in Woodville Gardens was Ealing Cricket Park, as the bedroom shared by the two boys Roderic and Hugo overlooked the grounds and most Saturdays young friends were invited to sit on the Dunkerley garden wall to watch cricket matches. The girls were also interested in cricket to the extent that Elsie put accounts of matches into her early stories and also mentioned cricket in some Abbey books. Another highlight of watching was the fact that they actually saw W. G. Grace play there at least once. Many of the houses in that area have now been converted into flats, being large enough to accommodate more than one of today's smaller families. In 1913 the Dunkerleys moved to 2, Woodfield Road, until in 1922, partly for the sake of William Dunkerley's health, the parents and four girls left London for Sussex.

At Hanger Hill Farm House and before the arrival of Hugo in 1896, the children had their own garden plots. Theo remembered that 'the garden there was quite large as there were a tennis court, an orchard and a summer house; fruit bushes and walls against which were grown peaches and nectarines.' The children were encouraged to make their own amusements and use their imaginations and she also wrote that :

' ... the summer house was more often the settler's log hut, besieged by a furious foe, well armed with acorns from the large oak in the far corner of the garden. When he withdrew to replenish his stores of ammunition, it was a time-honoured ruse to squeeze through the narrow stained-glass lattice window, drop to the ground, and disappear in the bushes. And when the enemy's bombardment of your evacuated position began once more, you appeared as reinforcements and attacked him from the rear.'

Theo explained that the orchard could also be:

' ... a forest, where often the shadowy forms of dusky Redskins could be seen dodging among the trees, or worming their way through the long grass, and re-enacting scenes from the latest adventure story in the *Boys' Own Paper*.'

Ealing must have been a pleasant country-like place in which to live at the turn of the century. With the exception of Grove House all the Dunkerley homes were fairly isolated; there was a farm at the top of Hanger Lane and cows were driven to and from there every day. Yet they were near the tube line by which William Dunkerley travelled in and out of London and he made use of that to take members of the family to see anything of especial interest. From vantage points near their homes they could see across the Thames to Richmond, or northwards as far as the Chilterns. They travelled by the Great Western Railway to reach Buckinghamshire for days out, or even for short holidays visiting the beechwoods and villages.

Elsie described some of the areas local to their homes when she wrote *Finding Her Family* (1916):

'Her father has got us a permit for the Bird Sanctuary ... then set out by way of Hanger Hill, Alperton and the canal foot-path ... they had taken the other road, by the Brentham Estate and Perivale ... the wide valley of the Brent at their feet, and a long stretch of green country rising to the opposite hill, crowned by the Water Tower and the square spire of the Cuckoo Schools ... they wandered round the hill for a look at Harrow Church topping its opposite height and Wembley and Sudbury away to the east.'

Elsie even described suburban homes in great detail, based on the newly-built Brentham Estate when Hazel and Monica in that same book (p. 24) were shown walking home after visiting the Bird Sanctuary.

'... "I shall have cream-coloured curtains, quite plain." "I shall have a little green pattern on mine" and Monica glanced at the dainty windows they were passing. "Oh, will you? I shall have no railings to the garden, but just a loose chain, like that one over there. And I'll have my house red, with white woodwork." "Oh, *I* shan't!" said Monica as decisively as if she had intended to move in next week. "I shall have rough grey walls, like those, and dark brown wood, and a neat little brown wooden fence, and a tiled path."'

This was a great contrast to Hazel's first sight of Yorkshire on p. 50 when 'she stared out at the chimneys and steel works and the sky dark with smoke or reddened with the glare of furnaces, with amazement and some fear.' Then in Chapter VII on her arrival in Saltburn 'they went through the tunnel and across Milton Street with its shops, then turned down a road leading directly to the sea.'

That was followed by a description of the jewel and river names for the streets, all of which still exist other than Amethyst Street itself, which was made up for *Finding Her Family* and sited as if amidst the genuine jewel-named streets already there.

William Dunkerley continued his work on *The Detroit Free Press* until in 1892 he and Jerome K. Jerome introduced a monthly paper, *The Idler*. That wasn't very successful so the next year they embarked on a weekly paper instead named *Today*, which ran for nearly six years. During that time, William wrote many short stories and articles but, with the exception of one serial written as by Julian Ross, he used the pseudonym of John Oxenham, the name chosen deliberately by him from that character in Charles Kingsley's *Westward Ho!* Eventually he became so well known by those initials that *J. O.* was given as the title of the first book his younger daughter Erica wrote about him in 1942. His first novel, *God's Prisoner; the story of a crime, a punishment, a redemption*, was published in 1898 and followed the next year by *Rising Fortunes*; *the story of a man's beginnings*. At that stage William, as J. O., decided to work from home and he produced over forty novels before embarking on his more religious works. One novel was made into a film in 1922: the reference to *Maid of the Silver Sea* in the British Film Catalogue describes it as being the story of a silver mine in Sark and filmed there.

When they were small, his children were puzzled by the two names by which their father was known. So were some of their friends and one recalled many years later:

'I remember Olivia [Fowell] patiently explaining to me why and how John Oxenham managed to be married to Mrs Dunkerley and how Elsie Oxenham and Erica Dunkerley were sisters. In fact Mamma recounted that the first time Mr Oxenham and his daughter Erica came to our house, Erica told her that she had hastily enquired of her father as they rang the bell "Father, are we Oxenham or Dunkerley here?"'

It is clear from Erica's books on J.O. that in their early married life, Mrs Dunkerley had help in the house as was common for all but the very poorest people at the turn of the century until the war years. But in view of other things learnt from Erica's books about their father and from some aspects in Elsie's stories, there wasn't a lot of money to spare to start with so the Dunkerley girls were brought up to play their parts in helping about the house, leaving their brothers more time for studying.

That angle came into many of EJO's earlier stories when girls were shown as having to allow their brothers to take advantage of any educational prospects available if there wasn't enough money to educate their sisters to the same extent. That was made extremely clear in *The Junior Captain*, while another maxim of Elsie's was that in rich families, if there was no necessity for a girl to go out to work, she must not take a job from someone who needed it. At the same time, it was equally wrong for young women to sit at home joining in a mild social round; they must find voluntary or charity work to pass on all they had learnt from their education not only to try to help others, but to save their own self-respect.

Once Elsie was well established as a writer herself, Erica became their father's secretary and companion. She collaborated with him on many booklets and one book, but also had four novels published of her own. She was the only member of the family not to adopt either the names of Oxenham or Dunkerley automatically as an author, although she signed herself as Erica Oxenham when writing articles by herself, or joint items with her father. Resemblances to plots and settings may be seen in some of the books written by different members of the family. In one of her novels Erica had a young woman adopt an orphaned child being brought up in a large family, much as Eve Prideaux did in Elsie's *Troubles of Tazy*. The novel written jointly by Erica with her father, *The Lake of Dreams*, had the same background as his *God and Lady Margaret*, which is understandable as they spent many holidays in Talloires where both were set and the family knew the district particularly well. John Oxenham's *A Hazard in the Blue* used themes which EJO incorporated in her stories, including that of working girls invited to spend holidays in the country. Erica helped her father with his book *Out of the Body* which was completed only three weeks before his death on January 23rd 1941. The following year she wrote his biography *J. O.* then in 1946, *Scrapbook of J. O.*, a book with slightly more about the family.

Elsie's closest sister, Maida, who was always looked upon as being 'the useful one' by her brothers and sisters, helped Elsie with her proof-reading although, since that was something all the girls had learnt to do, Erica and Theo were able to proof-read EJO's final book *Two Queens at the Abbey* for her when she was in a nursing home. Theo's writing took the form of articles about her work, which were issued as a booklet. She was the only one of the four sisters who had a job as such; she described her working years thus: 'I was a reluctant Civil Servant for fourteen years and only once 'exploded' into print.'

Those years were spent in a Savings Bank in London where she helped to find 'tired typists' who might benefit from the generous holidays provided by Erica. This subject was used as a theme in several of EJO's books. Theo was remembered some seventy years later as having been '... the one who organised everything' while someone else described her as 'a wise and delightful lady.'

One of Theo's articles described how she felt when she received a box of spring flowers from a sheltered village in a southern county. Elsie portrayed Joy and Jen in the Abbey books providing for others once they realised just how bleak the lives of poorer people were and how cheering such boxes of flowers could be for those who knew nothing about the countryside. Theo wrote affectionately about holidays in Sark and about a sleepy little Welsh town from which she and a companion set out to 'walk and to revel in the scenery.'

After serving in World War I, first in the Argyll and Sutherland Highlanders, then the Royal Flying Corps, Hugo Dunkerley became a journalist, before becoming editor of *The Mombasa Times* in Kenya. He sent home copies of most of his writings for everyone there to read. The entire family was able to write though, even if only '... lengthy and voluminous letters to all and every possible friend or relation, at the least excuse' which was said by both Theo and EJO's great friend Doris Acland.

Hugo, the younger of the two boys and the baby of the family, went to a Quaker school near York. That, together with having Quaker cousins, gave Elsie the necessary details about their ideals and beliefs when she depicted Quakers in her books. However, thanks to J.O.'s interest in people and in all things appertaining to other religions, he would have

known as much about the Quakers as about other
denominations. He described them in *God and Lady Margaret*
as 'our friends the Quakers'.

Missionaries were also among William's friends and
throughout his life he kept up a large correspondence with
people of all faiths all over the world. He knew Katharine
Parr, the writer Beatrice Chase, a Roman Catholic, very well.
In fact they wrote books for and about each other (*My Lady of
the Moor* by John Oxenham, 1916, and *My Chief Knight* by
Beatrice Chase, 1943). There has been a theory that J.O.'s
book describing her way of life may well have driven
Katharine Parr/Beatrice Chase further towards devoting her
time to the Catholic Mission she had had built beside her
cottage on Dartmoor. William Dunkerley was once described
by a close friend as being a 'devout Congregationalist who had
great sympathy with the Roman Catholic Church.'
    Various friends and neighbours who knew the Dunkerleys

during their years in Ealing felt that 'the family was very much dominated by the brilliant and popular father' and that 'J.O. used to like an entourage of women around him.' This seems a little unexpected in view of the way he often went on long trips abroad by himself. Perhaps this was to get away from the feminism of his home if it ever palled, once both boys had left there. In her books about their father, Erica wrote that Hugo was lucky, in having been the child who was at home with his father, once J.O. gave up his previous work and concentrated on writing. Fortunately J.O. was able to spend a long and happy holiday in Africa with Hugo and his wife Prim, before Hugo's tragic death in an accident there in 1937. Hugo first met Prim when he was stationed at Seaton Carew in Co. Durham. None of the four Dunkerley girls married although both Roderic and Hugo did; Roderic was the only one to have children.

Roderic Dunkerley became a Congregational Minister and a writer, producing books of prayers for the young on his own, and also collaborating with his son Gregor or with his father on other books for children and many religious works. One of the former was written in the style of letters, each letter being just that but including a story with a moral, followed by games, puzzles or verses, some of which were provided by J.O. who would have been interested in such a project and done all he could to help. In collaboration they produced *First Prayers for Children*. Amongst Roderic's many other books were *Beyond the Gospels* and *At the House of the Interpreter*. One written with his son Gregor was *Prayer-Time in the Junior School*.

Dr Roderic Dunkerley had his first pastorate in 1909, in Colchester; after 1922 he became minister of a Congregational Church in Cambridge before moving to Gloucestershire. He went to Worthing on his retirement in 1958, having previously been Principal of Westhill Training College, Birmingham, for ten years.

Elsie's mother Mrs William Dunkerley (Madgie) did a great deal of welfare and charity work and was a keen supporter of the London Missionary Society. Erica helped with this more than the other girls, spending at least one day a week at an East End Mission helping in the crèche as well as with their girls' clubs. She wrote many articles about her experiences there, one of which related how two small children from a London slum had spent a week at the Dunkerley home. She wrote:

'You with cool, shady gardens, why not give a crèche baby a week's holiday in it this year? Let him roll on the grass, give him cooling foods and clean clothes and a bath every day and your enjoyment will be at least as great as his.'

Those particular children were a small brother and sister but it was obviously a source of concern that Erica couldn't provide the same holiday for all the children for whom she cared. Elsie also knew people living under the conditions shown in her story of *Muffins and Crumpets* as, before writing became her main occupation, she too helped her mother and sisters with their voluntary work. It was quite likely the experience they gained by helping with the Mission and people with large families which enabled Elsie and Erica to write books in which single women adopted children from overcrowded homes.

Perhaps it was their desire to help those less well catered for which gave the Dunkerley girls their wish to provide holiday homes for 'tired typists'. Typists weren't the only ones who benefited; shop assistants, teachers and war widows were amongst those given the chance. In time the two younger sisters bought a house at Bognor Regis which could be used to provide holidays for people who otherwise couldn't afford any kind of break, or experience the joy of getting away from town life for a few days. Erica and Theo did the work and catering involved there.

Mrs Dunkerley's father, William Anderson, married twice, so there were several step and half relations. He had four daughters by his first wife, then seven daughters and one son by his second wife. One of the half-sisters went abroad after her marriage; Jannet, the oldest of the second family, went to Canada, another girl to South Africa and it is thought the son Alec may have gone to America.

William Dunkerley's father, another William, had been a wholesale businessman in Manchester, hence the idea of sending his son to America to start a branch of the firm over there. William Dunkerley senior had three daughters before his son William Arthur, one of whom died as a child and only the eldest appears to have married.

Friends and relations of the Dunkerleys were often invited to spend holidays with them. Regular visitors to their home were the children of missionaries in Samoa, sent there for school holidays from their boarding schools. One can see that all EJO wrote about the Buchanan family in *Schoolgirls and Scouts* and her description of the feelings of Andrew and Maisie in *Rosaly's New School* once their missionary parents had returned to China, leaving the children behind, was the result of what she learnt by seeing and hearing various children who stayed with the Dunkerley family. The dedication in *Schoolgirls and Scouts* is: "To Mildred Elizabeth Hills and Gladys Mary Hills my friends from Samoa. 'Ma le Alofa!'" They and a brother were amongst those who spent time at the Dunkerley home. Later Gladys studied music and performed at concerts in Britain during World War I. Elsie explained to her friend Doris Acland, 'They were the daughters of Samoan missionaries, who spent their school holidays with us.' Thirty years later Elsie, continuing the family traditions, wrote to Doris that 'old friends turn up at holidays and must be entertained.'

Roderic's wife Daphne was another who as a girl at boarding school in Ealing spent holidays with the family. Perhaps watching that particular early friendship maturing into eventual marriage prompted Elsie to write about a boy and girl whose friendship whilst both were of school age progressed naturally towards matrimony. This was a theme she frequently used in her early stories.

CHAPTER TWO

Religion and Life-style
or 'The Text of the Sermon' (*The Girls of Gwynfa*)

Jen had glanced at the books on the table by Ann's bed and said "Were you reading your Bible? Is that how you always know what to think about everything, Nancy?"
(*The Abbey Girls Win Through.* 1928. p. 216.)

Knowing their father was hailed as a foremost writer of religious books as well as for his novels, brought up to believe in the traditional Scottish Sabbath of worship and rest, it's no wonder that four of the Dunkerley children became writers and that religion formed such an important part of the lives of all of them. A friend of the family wrote that 'the whole family shone with religious faith and a certainty of life in the next world.'

Some readers have thought it odd that Elsie didn't describe detailed Christmas celebrations in many of her stories. *Deb at School* contained a Christmas Pageant and in the remote connector *Peggy Makes Good,* Ven, Gard, Torkel and Svante spent an exciting Christmas at Barbara and Audrey's railway bungalow. Patch produced her twins at Christmas in *Song of the Abbey* (p. 228) but that timing had little to do with the story.

The fictitious Hall would have made a fascinating setting for Christmas with a tree and a large family gathering, while the Abbey against a background of snow would have looked quite spectacular. But with the Dunkerley Scottish upbringing, Christmas was not a time for parties, decorations, general jollifications and the holiday atmosphere of the present day. In any case, they would have been more inclined to welcome the New Year, rather than Christmas. That, for them, was a day on which to celebrate the birth of Christ by rejoicing in the event quietly, and going to church. Also it wouldn't have been normal for Elsie to have described any type of church service in her books; as Doris Acland explained to me:

'Elsie wasn't fond of weddings or funerals, looking on both as purely private functions for the people concerned. She only went into great detail about the clothes worn and the numbers of bridesmaids at any of the Abbey weddings to satisfy some of her younger readers who begged to be told about those smaller points.'

Sundays were always set aside for regular church attendance, prayer readings and hymn singing. Grandfather Dunkerley had been a church elder and his son (.J.O.) had taught in Sunday School as a youth. All four girls took Sunday School classes; Elsie had one before she was twenty. An early pupil remembered her as 'sedate and rather solemn, always quietly dressed. She used to tell us tales from *Parables from Nature* by Margaret Gatty.' (Originally published in 1855, with numerous subsequent editions.) That girl attended Elsie's classes for ten years, by which time she had become a 'sort of pupil teacher in the Sunday School.' She explained that her family, like the Dunkerleys when she first went to Elsie's class in 1901, was brought up:

'Strictly, eschewing everything like alcohol, smoking, playing cards, betting, sex or frivolity. With reading special books and wearing special clothes and going regularly to church on Sundays. Of course, there were no radio, cinema or television then and the theatre was frowned on and dancing taboo except the country dancing which Elsie loved so much and wrote so much

about until the day someone at last persuaded her to go and see a ballet, which was to appear in later books. Elsie seemed at that early time an ordinary person, kind, pleasant and serious.'

Nearly twenty-five years later, Elsie had a Bible Class at Shelley Road Congregational Church, Worthing, for older girls who provided the nucleus of the second Camp Fire she tried to start. During that time, she gave a copy of her book *The Abbey Girls in Town* to someone she had met through the church there with a note which said:

'May I give you a copy of this book? Partly because I am so grateful to you for your help on Sunday afternoons during the past year. But partly also because when I wrote it I was dealing with the problem we discussed on the way home last week - of the friend who "doesn't know she has said anything that could hurt". I thought it might interest you to have it in story form.'

That problem was obviously similar to the one between Mary-Dorothy and Joy in *The Abbey Girls in Town* when Joy took all the credit for the work Mary-Dorothy had done in organising a dancing display for Sir Andrew and Lady Marchwood. It has long been thought that some of the issues

26

EJO showed her fictional girls as having to struggle with might well have been based on her own experiences or else her sensitive observations of other people's difficulties, and that this is why she was able to write about them with such strong feeling.

Girls with their habits of developing mild fancies for older girls or women with stronger characters than their own may also have been drawn from life and Elsie's own experiences. Quite often in her books, pairs of girls are portrayed as having one looking up to the other. Mary-Dorothy is admired by Amy Prittle; Frances by Eve Prideaux; the Abbey May Queens by new juniors; and Ven by the schoolgirls, old and young, in both schools she attended while living with Gard and her family. Deb worships Chloe, then is adored in her turn by the juniors, and there are several other examples. EJO frequently pointed out in her books that as long as this hero-worship wasn't carried to extremes it was good for a slightly weaker character to try to model herself on someone deserving of admiration. She also indicated that this could result in difficult circumstances for those being admired, if they were not always able to deal with the situation sensibly.

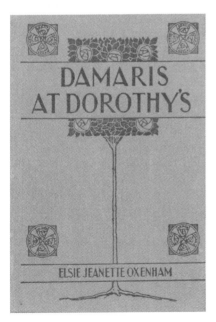

A regular saying of EJO's in her books was that 'to keep your friends you must learn to share them.' This was probably because she thought friendships were more sensible if extended over a wide range or perhaps she felt that twosomes were wrong if one of the pair was too intense. She also stressed the importance of loyalty, even in a situation where one friend felt let down by another. A good example of this is provided by Maribel and Phyllis in *Crisis in Camp Keema*, and another, though perhaps to a lesser degree, in *Damaris at Dorothy's*. In this book Rachel, at first, is completely unable to see, as everyone else does, anything wrong with Margery, but even after she is disillusioned she is still able to forgive and forget when Margery is in trouble. That was a theme which was repeated when Rosamund had her upset with Pat Mercer in *The Abbey Girls Win Through*.

Hero-worship is a feature of both *Debs* and also *Dorothy's Dilemma*, and *The Troubles of Tazy*. Of course, all cases were treated with great wisdom by EJO, her fictional girls being

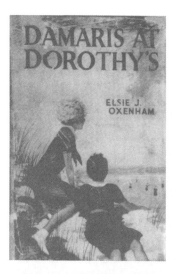

told that if they were looked up to by a weaker character, they should respect the fact and do their best to help the ineffectual person. At the same time they had to prove themselves worthy of the regard and to bear in mind that whatever the other girl's faults, these should be overlooked if her good qualities were deserving of true friendship. In this context it is interesting to note that the Camp Fire Handbooks, setting out the qualifications for would-be Guardians, include the following precept:

'A successful Guardian, while winning the girls' admiration and respect, guards against sentimentality and idolisation. She is not flattered by worshipful admiration, but knows how to turn it into healthy friendship.'

With the exceptions of Maidlin and her adoration of Joy in the Abbey stories and Astrid's wild jealousies in the Swiss ones, showing the stupidity of both girls when they carried their feelings to obsessive lengths, normally there was no hysterical nonsense between genuinely close friends in the stories. This theme of extremely close friendships features more prominently in the older books than in the Abbeys.

In *Finding Her Family* there was the trilogy of Audrey/ Brenda/Hazel with the loving care by Audrey for the younger girl she had thought was her sister, then the generous way in which Brenda and Hazel said she was still to regard Hazel in the same way, once they knew that Audrey wasn't really related to either of them. In the Abbey books there were Joan and Joy with the younger Jen, then Rosamund looking after Maidlin and, in the second generation, Littlejan and Jansy as well as Littlejan and Rosalind. The Swiss and Sussex sets showed Rena/Nancy then Rena/Elisabel; Karen/Tazy; Patience Joan/Barbara; Billy/Astrid - although Billy was far too long-suffering over Astrid's obsessional jealousy in the Swiss books. Then there was Tormentilla and the way she was friendly with Antonia and, eventually, Penelope, so they became a genuine three-some. These were all depicted as quite normal friendships but usually with one person clearly more level-headed than the other or others.

Another problematical angle EJO used in her stories was that of choice. That was displayed extremely strongly in *The Girls of the Hamlet Club* with Cicely and Margia both choosing what their consciences showed them was the right thing to do, followed in *The Abbey Girls* by Joan giving her chance of going to school to Joy, because Joy needed it more, lacked proper training with her music and was unable to work on her own as Joan could. Situations of that kind cropped up in other books: Angus and his conscience; Rosamund with her desire for a career but feeling she owed something to Joy for the years Joy had given her a home; Jandy Mac leaving Littlejan lying on the ground, but knowing it was more important to notify the police something was wrong.

Perhaps the best known situations of foregoing in the second generation Abbey books are in *An Abbey Champion* with Littlejan giving up her part in the Folk play to go into quarantine with Jansy through her illness, as well as previously having had to face up to telling Cicely what appeared to be wrong with the Hamlet Club. A small item of note arising from the Folk Play described in the books is that, when a version of the play was performed by Elsie's Camp Fire girls in public, the Jester, the part given to Littlejan in fiction, was played as the Fool by Margaret Bayne Todd, Elsie's Camp Fire member and young schoolgirl friend who was the part-model for Jen in the earliest Abbey books and one of her first Camp Fire Girls. In *The Abbey Girls in Town* Margaret Baynes Todd appeared as the tall schoolgirl Margaret with the long fair plaits, who met the Abbey Girls when they went to learn more about dancing at London Pyrotechnic.

The question of choice was something EJO used in *Finding Her Family* when Audrey had to decide if she could stop looking on Hazel as her sister and to ensure that Hazel went to her rightful home. This was a decision made harder by the knowledge that if she did so, only keeping in contact with her full brother, she would lose her own father and her half-brothers and sisters. Choice and duty were clearly portrayed in *Patience and Her Problems*. Patience Joan had to give up studying to become a medical missionary to care for the old grandmother who had brought her up after the death of her daughter, Patience Joan's mother. For a long time Patience Joan was completely unable to understand why the clear and strong desire for her career was being delayed. At the same time, she was clear-sighted enough to see that as well as it being her duty to care for her grandmother, it was a duty which must be carried out with love, willingness and without resentment. It took a long time for her to accept not only that there must be a reason to defer her training but that it was all a part of life's pattern and would eventually make her better fitted for her future work.

Despite proof that some of the situations in the book reflected genuine problems facing either EJO or someone close to her, not all such situations necessarily did. Doris Acland said that 'any good writer is more than capable of imagining himself or herself into difficult positions then writing vividly about the resultant situations from all angles.'

In most books of the time when Elsie was writing, religion was usually shown by others of those writing for girls by having the fictional characters saying their prayers regularly — or when in dire trouble — and preaching at their friends. In my opinion EJO's approach was much more sensible and tactful. Rather than making her characters try to influence or even force their friends into believing in God, then telling everyone they had become Christians and expecting them to follow their examples, she showed through her stories how they ran their own lives.

When Jen's father died in *Queen of the Abbey Girls* (p. 277) Jen was able to accept that 'if he's so sure he's going to something very good he can look forward happily. But we're going to lose him. Mother says it's up to us not to cloud his last months with thoughts of our loneliness.' After his death, Jen had a dream in which her father was walking along a road above and ahead of her, but once it was pointed out that they were both going along the same bits of road, knowing quite certainly that they'd meet again at the proper time, she was able to accept his death more easily. I think all of this — things shown as having happened to and been believed in by characters the readers looked upon almost as being real people — was far easier to accept than mere platitudes.

In *The Abbey Girls Win Through* (p. 50) when Jen's mother died unexpectedly just five months after her husband, Jen was told by Ann Rowney:

'Of *course* you'll see her again! And aren't you glad for her? She's gone to be with your father; she's only had to do without him for a few months. Now they're together again. Can't you be glad for them? Can't you see past yourself?'

Then Ann Rowney followed that with

'No-one is ever lonely who goes ahead. There's always somebody to meet everyone who goes. We're lonely, who are left behind; but we usually have friends.' This was a form of preaching, yes, but I think in a way which appeared to be based on experience and therefore was readily acceptable.

Many readers have admitted that they used EJO's principles and ideas all their lives with a selection of their comments, stating:

'My own philosophy has been shaped by absorbing the principles and aspirations of the central characters. I am sure that EJO must have had a great influence on many girls.'

'EJO has helped develop my life and given me good guide lines to live by, all based of course on her Christian background.'

'There is a spiritual level in the earlier books. The stress on asking for help and the importance of those who have, helping others.'

'In many ways EJO gave readers a code of conduct that I have constantly over the years thanked God for, and for her.'

'In a letter of sympathy I included the extract from *Queen of the Abbey Girls* where Jen describes the comforting dream of her father after his death. I learnt later how much it helped at the time.'

'EJO did a marvellous job in helping girls, with her own particular brand of philosophy.'

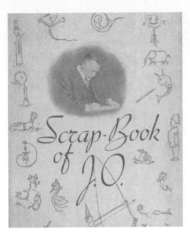

CHAPTER THREE

Literary Connections
or 'Old Friends and New' (*The New Abbey Girls*)

'Those lovely old books we found - could I look at them quietly, all by myself? You know I'll be careful. There's such a crowd round staring at them all the time. I thought perhaps while they're all busy I could have a go on my own. I want to see if I can read any of them, and to look at all the wee pictures in the borders.'
(*The Girls of the Abbey School.* 1921. p. 234.)

The Dunkerleys were all avid readers and, according to Theo, were:
'Always surrounded by masses of books of all sorts. In J.O.'s publishing days he would bring home a bundle of magazines every week; from *The Girls' Own Paper* for Elsie, down to *Little Dots* for Erica. Elsie was a tremendous reader - she seemed to read anything she could get hold of - girls' books of all kinds - and probably absorbed much from her wide reading and contacts with girls and young women. All of us went to the Ealing Public Library regularly. We galloped through books. Elsie kept a list of books she read, never less than three a week, and this didn't do

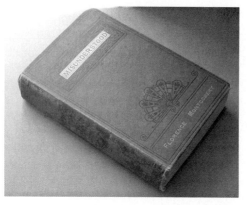

her already poor eyesight any good. Elsie was very studious and always carried off prizes. Whilst at *The Hawthorns* school she gained at least one prize for French.'

William Dunkerley collected biographies, travel books and the classics. He and his wife had retained many books from their young days and, as each child grew old enough, he or she built up his or her own library. During his time in Fleet Street, William provided books by his associates, including Conan Doyle and Kenneth Graham whose *Dream Days* (1899), was among those taken home for the family. From trips to America he returned with annuals such as *Harper's Young People* and *St Nicholas*, so the children became familiar with works by Frances Hodgson Burnett, Joel Chandler, Alice Hegan Rice and many more who were to become as popular in Great Britain as they already were in the United States. Among their books was a copy of *Misunderstood*, a real tear-jerker by Florence Montgomery, which, in view of the print size, can't have helped the young Elsie's eyesight. During the years the girls taught in Sunday Schools, they probably used *Moral Tales for Children*, another book by Mrs Montgomery, for some of their classes.

They were living through the golden age of books, so knew those by authors such as Grace Aguilar, Louisa Alcott, Susan Coolidge, Mrs Mansergh, L. T. Meade, L. M. Montgomery, the sisters Ethel and Lilian Turner and Charlotte Yonge. Many of their books were disposed of over the years so cannot all be checked, but when one thinks of more writers of that time, such as Rosa Nouchette Carey, Sarah Doudney, Evelyn Everett Green, George Henty, Percy Westerman and Emma

Worboise, a literary family must have read nearly everything possible and been familiar with works by writers whose books are still available as well as those by as many others now almost forgotten. Elsie adapted a version of Juliana Ewings' *The Peace Egg* in 1946, when she wrote *An Abbey Champion* and included a Folk Play, although by then she was familiar with variations of the theme and may well have incorporated other traditions in her version. She also used that play at a demonstration her Camp Fire Girls put on for wounded soldiers after World War I, as mentioned in Chapter 2.

Elsie was nearly sixteen when the *Books for the Bairns* were first published, but the Dunkerley children all bought those penny books as soon as they appeared. 'Between us, we had dozens of *Books for the Bairns*,' wrote Theo. Amongst the early titles were *Max and Moritz, Coal Munk Peter* and *Shock-Headed Peter*, folk-tale characters mentioned in EJO's *Captain of the Fifth* when Billy and Astrid were trying to work out which of the boys from St John's had been writing

Nancy Returns to St Bride's was dedicated to EJO

to them using those names. Years later Elsie built up a collection of completely different stories when she turned to detective fiction as a relaxation from her own writing. In *Deb of Sea House* Miss Willis remarked, 'I've been reading detective thrillers; have you? They're excellent for taking one's mind off one's problems.'

Her sister Theo reported that Elsie read:

'Louisa May Alcott, Mrs Marshall, L.T.Meade, Charles Kingsley, the *Katys* of course, Conan Doyle, Edna Lyall, Edward Lear, Henry Kingsley, Mrs Ewings, Mrs Molesworth, Andrew Lang and many, many more. We had all the annuals popular at the time as well as many American books and annuals. We had one American series, beginning with *Gypsy's Cousin Joy*. We devoured E. Nesbit's real life children's' books and many by the Australian Ethel Turner. Elsie turned to the Classics fairly early and the usual well known books of those days.'

The Dunkerley boys would have known about Frank Richards who was born just four years before Elsie and lived in Oak Street, near The Grove. Theo admitted 'I devoured my brothers' books, including those by Henty, Stables and many others.' Another writer who once lived not far away in Kings Road, Ealing, was Clare Mallory. Her books were published later, but she was another person who had lived in the same area and whose books Elsie would have enjoyed if she had known them, as they both used the themes of younger girls looking-up to older ones and of older girls being helpful to the younger girls.

A writer Elsie admired was Olivia Fowell and a collector wrote: 'As a child in Worthing, I met the Oxenham family through Olivia Fowell, who also wrote girls' school stories and was a friend of Elsie Oxenham's.' Olivia Fowell wrote books concentrating on girls in their teens, then their lives after leaving school, much as Elsie herself was to do a little later. She also had a few short school stories printed in annuals at the time Elsie was doing the same thing; she and EJO had short stories in the same annuals more than once.

Elsie began writing far earlier than most collectors realise; an unpublished manuscript found after her death is considered to have been written before her first published book. She was writing short stories in her late teens and submitting them to competitions where one was 'commended' as early as 1899. Four years later she won third prize in another one. In that same later competition Erica won a certificate for her entry in the thirteen-year-old age group.

Elsie's greatest writing friend, although she was five years younger than Elsie, was Dorita Fairlie Bruce. The two young women had a lot in common: Dorita's small brother, nine years younger than Dorita, was the same age as Hugo and Theo said the families knew each other quite well when they lived near the Dunkerleys in Ealing. That was after 1900 when the Dunkerley family moved to Woodville Grove. Dorita, when not at boarding school or spending holidays with her grandparents in Scotland, lived in Boileau Road, which was only just across Hangar Lane from the top end of Woodville

Grove.

They must have kept in touch after the Dunkerley family moved to Worthing as it was their later books they dedicated to each other. *Nancy Returns to St Brides* (1938) has 'To Elsie Jeanette Oxenham, who gave me no peace until Nancy returned to St Bride's.' *Secrets of the Abbey* (1939) is 'To Dorita Fairlie Bruce with thanks for all the pleasure her Dimsie, Prim and Nancy have given to me and so many others.'

Both Elsie and Dorita had Scottish ancestry and their forebears came from roughly the same area on the western coast of Scotland. They both enjoyed country dancing although Dorita — another writer usually referred to by her initials — wasn't as involved with that as EJO was to be throughout her life, and they were both associated with groups of young girls. Elsie had her dancing classes and was Guardian of a Camp Fire; Dorita was Guardian of a Girls' Guildry Corps.

Other writers of that era sometimes mentioned folk dancing in their books. Angela Brazil showed her girls doing country dancing in a few but she also used Camp Fire, notably in *For the Sake of the School* (1916) with some very peculiar ceremonies; for instance, the pinning on of material badges presented by the Guardian wearing her blue cycling costume while the girls were in school uniform instead of their gowns.

Elsie Oxenham knew Angela Brazil as well as several other women writing at the same time (another was Evelyn Smith), but Angela Brazil was born in 1869 so, being over ten years older than Elsie and with books published well before Elsie's

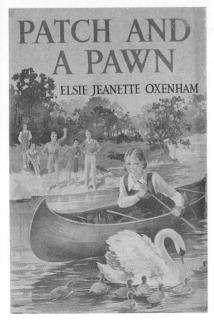

PATCH AND A PAWN

ELSIE JEANETTE OXENHAM

first ones, they may not have had a lot in common other than the fact that they were both writing for girls. They wrote quite different types and styles of stories, though.

Elsie Jeanette Oxenham and Dorita Fairlie Bruce both used local legends and names in some of their fiction. When writing books set in Scotland, their backgrounds nearly overlapped as amongst other places they both sited stories in the area around Loch Long. The *Goblin Island* group by EJO was located as if in the Morven Peninsula, with fictionalised names to places within there. She used the Rosneath Peninsula and Loch Long for others, including *Patch and a Pawn* and *The Secrets of Vairy*. Some books by DFB were set on the opposite side of Loch Long, while most of her Nancy stories were mainly on and around the river Clyde, which both women knew well.

Above all, the pattern of the writings of Elsie Jeanette Oxenham and Dorita Fairlie Bruce was slightly similar. They each wrote historical novels; those by EJO set in Wales, DFB's in Scotland. Both were followed by modern stories in which characters from their previous stories were portrayed as ancestors. They wrote about girls at different and unrelated schools with characters common to more than one group, thus linking the sets together. Their short stories were often about girls at their fictional schools and were sometimes used in annuals, although EJO wrote very few short stories in comparison with DFB.

Dorita Fairlie Bruce's early books such as the Dimsies and Springdales were set emphatically in the enclosed worlds of boarding school, which she had experienced herself, but the Nancys were portrayed as half boarding school and half day school. Her Sally trilogy had girls boarding in local homes much as Elsie Oxenham had done with the girls in her main Swiss and Sussex stories, while in EJO's Abbey series Miss Macey's day school with just twenty boarders only formed a very small part of the background to the books. In answer to queries, Elsie always replied, 'It was not Wycombe Abbey which is a boarding school; it was a big day school the Abbey Girls went to.' But other than stating that the girls went to school on weekdays or had homework to do, describing the Coronations which were held in the big school hall as well as at Broadway End for small private ceremonies, and mentioning a few meetings held at school, dancing evenings, or lunch-time talks, EJO didn't make her Abbey School often figure as a background.

However, and although she only went to small private schools herself with no actual experience of boarding schools, Elsie used them, or half and half, for the settings of many of her earlier stories. The books set in Sussex were placed firmly inside schools which often contained a mixture of day-girls and boarders. Some of the pupils in *Two Form Captains*, the first of the Swiss group, had to live in various houses in the vicinity instead of being genuine boarders. The same applied to *The School Without a Name*, one of the Sussex groups which when newly built had to rely on boarding in private homes those girls destined to be boarders until dormitory accommodation could be provided.

A favourite theme of Elsie's in her early school stories was to send a child to one for the opposite sex. In the three *Torment* books Tormentil Grant attended a school for boys when, due to the lack of male teaching staff during World War I, her sister Dorothy taught at a boys' boarding school in Wales, taking Tormentilla with her to join their classes. *At School With the Roundheads* depicted three girl cousins spending holiday time at a boys' school where the aunt of the sisters,

SEVEN SCAMPS

Jenny and Nesta, was housekeeper. They stayed there after that holiday because of an outbreak of scarlet fever at their own school and in time joined the boys for lessons. In *Rosaly's New School* the headmistress's young nephew had to spend a term in her care due to his delicacy and the absence of his parents, so attended classes with the girls.

Not quite in the same category, the Swiss schools were for boys and girls in separate buildings with a limited amount of interconnection for concerts, church services, cricket matches and combined picnics. The fictional schools of St Mary's and St John's had been founded for the sake of children whose parents or close relations were at a nearby sanatorium.

Apart from Dorita Fairlie Bruce and the authors within her own family, the only other writer to whom Elsie dedicated one of her books was Elinor Brent-Dyer. (The last of the 'Big Three' as they are known collectively and the other one known by her initials.) That was a reciprocal gesture after Elinor's *Seven Scamps* had been dedicated 'To Elsie Jeanette Oxenham, whose friendship and books have given me so much pleasure and to whom I owe so much.' At the time Elsie wrote to her friend Doris Acland that 'I shall have to dedicate one to her because she's just done one to me, but I don't like her book much.' Yet when they gave each other copies of their books years later, the inscribed messages were quite affectionate. 'To Elinor with all good wishes from Elsie Jeanette Oxenham' for instance. More of those inscribed books have appeared since Elsie Oxenham's death than any which had been given to her by Brent-Dyer. Unfortunately, some years after the deaths of both women, it was requested by one of her publishers that the books written by Brent-Dyer and given by her to Elsie should be returned to them.

Both *Maidlins, Secrets of the Abbey, Joy's New Adventure, The Crisis in Camp Keema, Schoolgirl Jen at the Abbey* and *Selma at the Abbey* were given by EJO to Elinor Brent-Dyer. Oddly, in view of her early feelings about the way the school/sanatorium aspect had been copied, that last was inscribed 'With love from Elsie J. Oxenham 1952.' An early book of Elinor Brent-Dyer's, given to Elinor by her step-father, was a copy of Elsie's *The Girls of Gwynfa*. EBD had nearly every book by EJO, though, and not only collected them all her life but frequently mentioned them in her own stories. After EBD's death in 1969 the majority of her Oxenham books were donated to Reading University.

Most signed books by Elsie Oxenham to have been traced are quite formal even if the message is affectionate e.g. 'To Miss B. and Miss G. with love from Elsie Jeanette Oxenham' and 'To my Dutch friend, Jo H. with love', then her own name in full. That is hardly surprising, since during her life time the automatic use of Christian names was not usual. Others with no name were merely inscribed 'Yours sincerely' followed by Elsie's signature.

Any early slight coolness towards Elinor Brent-Dyer on Elsie's part was understandable. Although the close link between the school and sanatorium of EBD's Chalet books wasn't stressed unduly until after her first few had been published, Elsie had used that theme in books written years before they met and long before publication of Brent-Dyer's *The School at the Chalet* in 1925. Their first meeting was through a dancing group at Farnham, Surrey, when Elsie was already well established with thirty books to her credit while Elinor had only just started writing for publication. However, although Elinor knew Elsie's books and owned the majority, she seems to have remained serenely unconscious all her life of the fact she had copied Elsie's original idea of a school in the Alps for children who had relatives at a nearby

The SCHOOL at the CHALET

ELINOR M BRENT-DYER

sanatorium.

When a book using exact wording and themes from several books by Dorita Fairlie Bruce appeared, Elsie was almost more disgusted than her friend, complaining bitterly about the blatant copying of entire paragraphs, names and incidents and, as many other readers did, wrote to the publisher, but to little avail. A collector who used to visit EJO found a copy of the book, *Hilary's Difficult Term* (1949) by Daphne Ramart in a bookshop in Worthing but when she gave it to Elsie and asked what she thought about it Elsie merely said,

'Fancy finding that awful book here in Worthing. Although it is wicked as a piece of plagiarism, I'm glad to have it as a curiosity.'

Imitation was something about which she became annoyed, so she must have been irritated, at least, by EBD's copying when the Chalet School stories were linked to a sanatorium.

Neither Elsie, Dorita nor Elinor wrote too well about love and romance although they all put marriages and subsequent children into their stories. DFB was the only one sensible enough not to give her heroines unlikely sized families but it has to be accepted that by providing their heroines with large families, EJO and EBD were both ensuring more young girls coming along to be given the parts in the next generations of their prospective books.

CHAPTER FOUR

Elsie Oxenham As A Person and Over the Years
or 'Two Kinds of Eyes' (*The Two Form Captains*)

The Writing Person moved up three chairs and took the one next to
her. Her tunic was brown, and she had wrapped a brown knitted coat
round her shoulders.
(*The Abbey Girls Again.* 1924. p.96.)

Elsie Oxenham put a lot of herself, even if unconsciously,
into certain of her characters. The fictional Karen Wilson, in
The Two Form Captains, The Abbey Girls Go Back to School
and others, was given very bad eye-sight, which meant she
had to wear thick glasses and was unable to take part in games
or do anything arduous. Eventually Elsie had to give up the
folk dancing she loved lest the exertion damaged her eyes
any further. In later years her sight became very bad and her
sister Theo told me:

'She had to wear thick glasses and see her oculist regularly
and she wasn't allowed to do any strenuous dancing once the
trouble was diagnosed. She used to bend double over her writing
and Erica thought that this habit partly caused the state her spine

was in - it was some kind of spinal trouble which was connected with her last illness.'

Reading the Swiss books, one can visualise the young Elsie as being very like Karen as a person, not only in having similar physical traits. Shy and short-sighted but also full of insight, that rare ability to see beyond the superficial and into people's characters. A dancer who met her briefly at a dance party in Brighton when Elsie was middle-aged, apparently thought her 'a rather dull spinster who only came to life in her books.' It is tempting to wonder what Elsie, taking mental note of characteristics as she must have done with many people she met, would have thought of that person in her turn, after such a short encounter.

Karen was also portrayed as having Elsie's brown hair with reddy tints. In her fifties, Elsie was described by people who met her as having 'auburn hair, sprinkled with grey; pale skin with freckles, very Scottish-looking'. This sounds like an older version of Betty McLean in *The Abbey Girls At Home* where she was shown as 'Betty, just twenty-one, had soft red hair plaited round her head and a fair freckled skin, and was as Scottish in her type and colouring as she was in her accent and her shy, reserved nature.' Or Libby and Tibby in *The School of Ups and Downs* 'with the golden-red hair and delicate skin so typical of real Scottish girls, and big brown eyes and freckles.' Libby was also shown as being shy, quiet and very reserved, as most people found Elsie herself.

A picture of Elsie Dunkerley as a young woman showed her with wavy hair parted in the centre and a plait wound around her head; in others she had a top bun, to which style she reverted towards the end of her life. Yet as a girl her hair was short; fair with a fringe as Samanthy was said to have had in *The School of Ups and Downs* and Annabel in *A School Camp Fire*. Maida was the only one of the four Dunkerley sisters who had long hair as a child, which was unusual in an era when girls were brought up knowing that they would have to grow their hair long, ready to put it up as soon as they were old enough. The frontispiece in one of their father's early books is of a young woman who looks much as Elsie did at the time when that book was published and which was said could have been of her, except that it is most unlikely she would have consented to pose for such a picture. She disliked having her photograph taken and, although several remain of her Camp Fire Girls on their assorted group holidays and weekends, their Guardian was rarely included in them.

A close friend described her as having a 'curiously curly, well-defined mouth — almost a scornful mouth'. She was generally spoken of as being slight in build with big eyes behind thick spectacles. She gave the impression to nearly everyone who met her of being 'quiet and shy', 'reticent and modest', 'kindly and pleasant', 'amusing and kind'. Her voice was described as 'pleasant with a hint of a Scottish accent' though she had 'an abrupt and incisive way of speaking.' She was also said to be 'complex and full of contradictions'. On the surface she appeared to be reserved and rather cold and dry, but Doris Acland said:

'That was just the superficial Scottish manner with mere acquaintances. She was extremely warm-hearted and emotional, compassionate and very understanding about tangled-up characteristics in other people, exceptionally modest about her own achievements but definite and rather autocratic if she felt she was the object of unjust criticism. Her sense of humour was very hearty and her artistic responses were surprisingly responsive to fresh demands when she was the age when people often sit back and stick to old impressions.'

From her middle-age she was described by many people as 'an extremely lonely person apart from Maida' and although after their parents had died there was a certain amount of

Libby and Tib crept near among the bushes.

from *The School of Ups and Downs*

visiting between their two homes 'the pairs of sisters were never very close'. That was understandable when they were children with several years between each pair, but normally age differences tend to diminish as people grow older. To her nephews and niece she appeared as a busy but detached personality. She reckoned to write a complete chapter of any book at a sitting and on visits the nephews and niece were warned to keep reasonably quiet if their aunt was 'upstairs working', as she usually was, either writing or correcting proofs. The latter became a task she disliked more and more as she grew older, largely thanks to her worsening eye-sight. In 1946 she wrote to Doris Acland, 'I'm trying to get a bit rested before the proofs come, as I always find the concentration a strain.' Then to her four years later, 'It seems silly to register proofs but it would just about kill me if I had to read them all through again!'

In view of her father's abilities and popularity, the religious books he and Roderic wrote, Hugo being an editor and Erica producing four adult novels, the fact that Elsie's books were regarded as being 'only for girls' meant that they tended to be looked upon slightly disparagingly as unimportant, trivial and insignificant in comparison, an attitude which, sadly, continues to the present day in some circles. The fact that she produced nearly ninety long books in just over fifty years tends to be ignored, as does the way they were collected with enormous enthusiasm from their first appearances and are still sought, almost more eagerly now, nearly a century later.

Her isolation was very evident in letters written to her few close friends and to some of those collectors she met over the years. Little personal information was ever included or offered in her letters and, even if direct questions were asked, answers were basic with no elaboration whatsoever. There were no mentions of family group visits or outings and for many years Elsie rarely went on holiday with anyone other than one or both parents unless she took her Camp Fire girls away for semi-working week-ends.

EJO was always much loved by her Camp Fire Girls, one of whom wrote 'how nice it was to have someone like Elsie, writing new books all the time.' Elsie and Margaret Bayne Todd, whom EJO seems to have looked upon as a younger sister, stayed at least once at Roderic's home when they went to an early E.F.D.S. School near there. She frequently attended concerts in Worthing by herself, so her love of music doesn't seem to have been shared with anyone within the family, although her father enjoyed listening to the wireless.

There has been speculation about why, after the death of their mother, William Dunkerley/John Oxenham didn't live with Elsie and Maida, rather than with Erica and Theo. As the elder pair of sisters, in those days they would automatically have been expected to care for any remaining parent who was left alone. By that time, though, EJO was an extremely hard-working person and well organised with her own career which meant writing (or that dreaded proof-reading) for a set length of time most days. Maida, who was described over those years by all who knew her as 'lovingly supportive', helped all she could and acted as home-maker for herself and her busy sister as well as helping

from *The Tuck-Shop Girl*

49

Elsie with proof-reading, so wouldn't have had a lot of time to look after their father as well.

In any case, by then Erica, her own books regardless, was acting as secretary to their father who would have wanted her to be on the spot whenever they wrote any joint items. It had long been accepted that she was his companion whenever he wanted to travel anywhere. An instance before the family moved to Worthing came soon after the end of World War I when John Oxenham and Erica went to Yorkshire together. The result of that trip was a booklet *Bricks Without Straw - How Fame Came to Copmanthorpe,* written jointly about the building of an Institute for a village not far from York. Interestingly, in view of EJO's coming involvement with the E.F.D.S., the first activity indulged in by the entire village was the crowning of a May Queen, along with a Maypole and country dancing when the new Institute was opened.

Erica also regularly accompanied their father on his frequent holidays to Talloires, leaving Theo behind to look after their home. So the question of where William Dunkerley should live was simply one of convenience in several directions rather than anything to do with who was expected to care for him once he was a widower.

Elsie was methodical with her work and, although details were all clear in her mind, she took the time and trouble to make charts of relationships within her fictional families to ensure she made no mistakes. A classic example is the family trees she made for the Kane offshoots, to ensure that the tiny suspicion of illegitimacy in *Secrets of Vairy* was, in its historic time, perfectly legal in view of the elaborate way she had worked it all out, then going on to add the fact that Rosalin might, over the years, have been connected very remotely to Janice Fraser/MacDonald. This makes it interesting to speculate whether, given time, Elsie would have enlarged on that angle and tied Jandy Mac in more with the Kane family through that possible link. It was something she had hinted at faintly in *Schooldays at the Abbey,* although in that story, Janice merely said (p. 118) her grandpa Fraser 'was the factor for the Earl of Kentisbury' and on the next page that while in

Scotland she had seen some of the Kane family. 'There's a dear little girl about two, with dark curly hair; and a fat fair baby boy, who is the heir to the title after Lord Verriton.' That is a small point towards something else in EJO's mind, which could have been shown to happen, had she written all the stories she wanted to and had planned.

Elsie always managed to see both sides of complex situations and to have the ability to work out and to help with problems. In 1935 one of her young correspondents wrote to her describing in great detail how, giving no notice or an address, she had walked out of a job where she was treated very unfairly, and had gone to another town where she found herself a room and a much better position. She finished the letter by saying it had 'all been a big adventure.' 'Yes, it was a big adventure,' Elsie wrote in return, 'but did you stop to think how worried your family and your employer would be about your disappearance?' This was something a sixteen-year-old hadn't stopped to consider in those days, but proved that, while EJO was able to see how and why the young girl had been driven to act as she had done and could sympathise with the cause, she could also point out tactfully from a more mature age that it had been done the wrong way, resulting in concern to others.

On a lighter note, a collector who visited her in the mid-1940s and had been invited to Inverkip for tea wrote many years later relating that EJO went to the station with her afterwards. When the train came in, EJO walked to a smoking compartment and told the young woman 'with a delightful twinkle in her eyes' that now she could enjoy a cigarette. Cigarettes hadn't been mentioned at all during the visit and the visitor certainly hadn't admitted to being a smoker.

During her lifetime, EJO must have seen an extraordinary number of changes. Clothes, for instance: as a girl she would have worn the (then) traditional layers of underclothing and, with two younger brothers, she would have known all about the shortening of clothes for small boys when they discarded their petticoats, as was shown in *Patience Joan, Outsider* for Jockie. By 1910, when she was approaching thirty, dresses were still worn long. So was hair, which was put up as soon as girls left school — sometimes sooner if they were staying on after they had reached the age of eighteen — while hats were large and ornate. No lady would have gone out without wearing a hat and gloves. 'I didn't expect to go visiting, so I came away in my oldest, most comfortable hat, which ought to have been given a holiday long ago. But I had got fond of it, so I stuck to it' she wrote to Ribby, the Camp Fire mascot.

Costumes were popular for walking out and would have suited the Dunkerley girls. In the very few photographs of Elsie and her sisters taken then, they were shown wearing long skirts and blouses rather than dresses. It was an era when clothes varied greatly for women according to the age of the wearer; styles in annuals and journals were usually quoted as being 'for children', 'for walking out', 'for the older woman', 'for evening wear', or 'for the matron'.

All her life Elsie enjoyed walking for which she would have worn a shorter skirt than otherwise, but with a hat and gloves (unless in the country) until after World War I when the formal essentials of what ladies were expected to wear were relaxed somewhat. During the 1930s, going out in Worthing, she wore either 'tweeds with a hat and flat walking shoes or, on warm days, a patterned dress, a light summer coat and a straw hat.' Prior to that date and for the long walks Elsie took with her Camp Fire Girls, 'woollen stockings and no petticoats' as well as shorter skirts were advised in articles about appropriate clothing for those planning country walks.

During their years in Ealing, the four Dunkerley sisters, Elsie, Marjorie (Maida), Theo and Erica attended private schools where uniforms weren't compulsory. Uniforms weren't worn automatically by the girls in the schools about which EJO wrote before 1920. The subject was mooted in *Girls of the Hamlet Club* (1914) but when that book was written, at Miss Macey's school the girls wore what their parents could afford, hence Cicely being described as arriving on her first day with an expensive Liberty scarf wrapped around her hat, while Miriam had to give priority to thick boots for walking before she could consider a warm coat. The Robins and Brownies of *The School of Ups and Downs* had their red jerseys or their brown tunics; regulation dresses were described in the Swiss books and *Damaris at Dorothy's,* while most of Elsie's younger schoolgirls in her books wore gym. tunics from choice if there was no set uniform.

Illustrations in the very early books usually showed the younger girls in tunics and Tormentil in *The School Torment* chose to wear 'the shortest of blue gym. tunics with girdle and white sleeves, her legs looking abnormally long and her hair shorter than ever.' When she went for her first bicycle ride with some of the boys, she added 'her green tam with its gold badge, pushed well to the back of her head, and a white sweater identical with theirs over her very short blue tunic.' Thora from the Swiss stories was described in *The Captain of the Fifth* (1922) as wearing 'a white, shady St Mary's hat with the blue school band, the blue school frock with neat white collar and cuffs, and the long smooth plait the regulations demanded.'

Poor Pip in *Damaris at Dorothy's* was horrified when she thought that her green dress was the wrong colour on first seeing Roberta (p. 16) wearing a dress of the same pattern as her own, with a wide white collar, but in blue, while Pip's was green. It wasn't until Patsy explained 'Green's all right. You needn't look so tragic. We wear either blue or green. Some girls keep to one colour, but others have both green and blue frocks' that Pip was able to relax. In *Rachel in the Abbey* there was trouble at school when the new headmistress insisted that the older girls wore skirts and blouses instead of tunics, although no change was made for the juniors.

Houses would have been lit by gas when EJO was a girl.

from *Girls of the Hamlet Club*

Transport was by horse and carriage or, as she experienced living in London, by underground or tram. That was the same in most of the big towns and cities, when new railway lines were gradually being opened to link main cities together.

Elsie lived through two wars while of an age to be affected by them and narrowly escaped being caught in an air raid when she and her Camp Fire Girls were out one evening for 'a moonlight walk across the fields to a tiny old church beyond a little stream and narrow bridge.' Afterwards they were very glad they had gone home just then for half an hour later 'the German aeroplanes came, and the guns began to roar, and shrapnel began to fall, and one of the guns was quite close to the little church by the bridge.' On another occasion:

'The guns got nearer and nearer, but I was in here, very warm and determined not to budge. Then - something began, apparently in our back garden; I know I jumped about a foot in bed. I heard all the others talking out in the passage, and presently Edward's Bestest Lady came into mine too, and said very emphatically 'I don't care where I go, but I'm not going to stop alone.' I said 'righto, sit on my bed'; all right for me, for I was inside, cuddling my hot water bottle. She went out to find someone more comforting, and I thought if it was really as exciting as it sounded, I should be missing something if I stopped in bed alone. She was wearing her best Sunday coat with a big fur collar, so we all said she'd look nice when she - I mean her corpse, you know, - was carried out. Father and Mother stopped in bed, which was the only sensible thing to do. All five of us got on the big bed in the next room! We all sat there and talked, and those really awful cracks went on overhead ... We hauled him [Little Grey] in and carried him to join the five ladies on the bed! I can tell you he was surprised; never in his life had he seen such a thing before. He walked round and looked at everybody, and clawed the down quilt, and sang till he nearly drowned the guns. ... Every now and then the firing would die down, and somebody would say it was getting over and we'd better go back to bed, then it always broke out again, so that remark was howled down whenever it began. I was the last offender, for when I had said it, and by so doing restarted the raid, we were more careful, and only put it like this. 'It really does seem to be what you mustn't say you think it is.' But at last I decided that it really was what I mustn't say what I thought it was, so I cleared off to my bed and bottle and I suppose in time the rest did too. The Bestest Lady says the bugles went about 1.30; she was awake, as she was having trouble with Grey.'

(From a letter to Ribby, about whom more is written in Chapter 7.)

Elsie obviously thought marriage the ideal for her fictional women, unless they were writers, but although overly grateful to her father for the help stressed in her dedications, she doesn't seem to have been drawn towards marriage itself. In fact, she doesn't seem to think much of men generally, as she wrote in *A Fiddler for the*

from *The Captain of the Fifth*

Abbey (p. 18) about Gilbert that 'Like any other man, he sees only as far as the end of his own nose.' Perhaps it's no wonder none of the Dunkerley girls married as they didn't seem enthused by some aspects of marriage and married life. Elsie made the remark ascribed to her above, while Theo wrote in her *Bank Notes* (p. 28) after a time of stress at work 'we wish we had seen it coming in time to get a transfer to East Africa, or endure the hardships of emigration or even marriage. Anything, rather than this.'

Whatever her personal feelings, future marriages were implied in several of EJO's books, particularly the earlier ones with Karen and Rennie being the most obvious partners even while they were still at school. Rena and Lisabel married the boys they had known from their early teens but a lot of other romances were hinted at, mainly Lucinda/Svante, Nesta/Charlie, Hazel/Osmond as examples. The Abbey Girls were older and into their twenties by the time they met whoever Elsie had planned them to marry, yet she reverted to a young marriage for Littlejan at the end of the series as well as constant hints that Jansy and Dickon were likely to marry eventually.

After Elsie's death, Doris Acland explained some of Elsie's ideas on the subject of marriage.

'The husbands were made shadowy background creatures because Elsie wanted to write about her girls and although necessary, the husbands bored her. It was probably a sign of the times when she produced Sir Konrad 'fancying' Jansy. With the exception of Dick Jessop, it was usually a case of settling for the first and only male the Abbey Girls met. Consequently, most of the male characters appear to have been brought in purely as a convenience and as prospective fathers for the next generation, although they had their places in the stories in some cases. Andrew to show how Joy reacted to him initially. Then allowing him to be killed after the honeymoon. Or Ken almost giving his life to save that of a child, showing Jen how much he mattered, then providing an excuse to remove Jen from the scene which in turn led to bringing Joan back to the Abbey as EJO was frequently asked to do.'

CHAPTER FIVE

Origins of the Camp Fire Movement
or 'CFG' (*The School Without a Name*)

'Her black hair was plaited in two long ropes, which hung over her shoulders nearly to her knees, and across her forehead she wore a curious band woven of gaily coloured beads. Her dress was a long, straight gown of khaki-yellow material, with brown leather fringe round the hem and on the arms; her lower arms, and neck were bare. On her feet were moccasins of soft brown leather, with designs in beadwork upon them. Round her neck and hanging on her breast were chains of coloured beads, which swayed and jingled as she walked. On her dress were curious designs, flowers and circles, which looked as if they must have meanings.' (*A School Camp Fire*. 1917. p. 172)

The Camp Fire Movement, one of Elsie Oxenham's interests, was first considered, then conceived, during the summer and autumn of 1911 in America where a Dr. Gulick and his wife held a private camp named Wohelo for their daughters and their friends. The name was made from the words WOrk/HEalth/LOve for the watchword of their proposed Camp Fire organisation. Once the details had been finalised, they 'gave the Movement to the public' on March 17th 1912. The first two Camp Fires in Great Britain were 'affiliated to American Headquarters' in 1914. The *Council of the Camp Fire Girls of the British Isles* was formed in 1921.

Handbooks were soon produced giving details about procedures, clothes, symbols, names with their meanings, rituals and everything involved with the organisation. The first American Handbook

Moccasins made by British Camp Fire Girls as a wedding gift for Princess Mary

was issued in 1912 and by the 1920s copies of *British Camp Fire Girls* and *Camp Fire Girls, Supplement for the British Isles* were also available. In 1961 a book entitled *WO-HE-LO, the Story of Camp Fire Girls 1910 - 1960* compiled by Helen Buckler, Mary Fiedler and Martha Allen was published in New York.

Dues [subscriptions] in the early years were $1 per year (2/6 in Great Britain) and the girls weren't supposed to work towards Honours before they had paid that fee. They were expected to make their own gowns from regulation khaki drill, finished at the bottom with a leather fringe which had to be seven inches from the ground. The Guardian had to make hers within two months. All the materials were available from Headquarters, an early branch of which in England was in Birkenhead.

Underneath they were required to wear 'no petticoat, but dark bloomers or knickerbockers with dark stockings and either moccasins or dark shoes' (1922). Otherwise, the girls wore a white middy (blouse or jumper), a blue skirt and a red tie for meetings or in camp. Another Handbook written by Ruth Clark or Minobi (of the Glad Heart), entitled *Camp Fire Training for Girls*, suggested 'a tussore-coloured middy jumper, dark brown skirt, tie and hat'. This sounds far more appropriate for Camp Fire colours than the white, red and blue outfit.

Having decided on her Camp Fire name, each girl made, designed and adorned her gown with the appropriate symbols for that chosen name and also made herself a headband of

bead-work on a small hand loom, ready to wear for ceremonial meetings. She was not allowed to wear her gown at meetings until she became a Wood Gatherer.

Their other requirements were similar to the ideals of the Girl Guides and the earlier Girl Scouts. Honour Beads were given instead of badges but the work for both was very similar with Health, Home and Nature, taking precedence and a variety of sub-

British Camp Fire Girl weaving symbols in raffia

divisions such as Child Care, Laundry and Cooking for Home Craft, and Gardening and Bird-identification under Nature. Just as the Guides could achieve their All-Round Cord once a set number of badges had been added, the Camp Fire Girls could claim a Big Honour, a large wooden bead in its matching colour, for any complete group of Honours they had gained.

Unlike the Guides with their Patrol Leaders, Patrol Seconds and small groups of girls in their care, Camp Fire

Girls merely moved upwards as they achieved their different ranks of Wood Gatherer, Fire Maker and Torch Bearer. Honours always counted towards those but were not enough on their own; the girls had to prove to their Guardian they were capable, ready and prepared for the different ranks, as well as having attained the required number and variety of Honour Beads. A Torch Bearer had to prove her ability to care for others and to lead groups of younger girls. Trail Bearer is a recent innovation.

Law of Camp Fire Girls

The Blue Birds were for girls under the age of twelve years and their small groups were often run by the older Camp Fire girls working towards becoming Fire Makers or Torch Bearers under the supervision of their Guardian. The watchword of the Blue Birds is Sihegro, from SIng/HElp/GROw and their name, given to the first group formed in America in 1912, was inspired by the Maeterlinck Blue Bird of Happiness. They too chose new names but more usually as groups of birds, flowers and similar items related to nature rather than the individual ones of older girls, although the single name of Uda was given to EJO's 'littlest Blue Bird' in *Camp Watéwin*. Uda, as an adult, appeared as Miss Helen the Camp Fire Guardian in *The School of Ups and Downs* and *Patience Joan, Outsider,* still with the name of Uda or Firefly.

Dr Luther and Mrs Charlotte Gulick (founder of Camp Fire)

Ceremonial Dress

Once the Camp Fire Movement became more widely known in America, books taking Camp Fire as their theme began to be written for girls. Most of them weren't very appropriate with little in their contents about Camp Fire as such. *The Camp Fire Girls at Camp Keewayadin* by Hildegarde Frey, who was perhaps one of the better known of the American Camp Fire writers, contained a certain amount about their activities. The Camp Fire leader in her books was Nyoda of the Winnebagos; the girls of that fictional Camp included Hinpoha, Sawah, Migwan, Veronica, Nakwis and Medmangi. However, not all her books were strictly Camp Fire even though centred around the Winnebagos, as the majority were no more than stories of the holidays taken by the group and the slightly unlikely adventures they had during each one.

A Campfire Girl's First Council Fire

Camp Fire Girls are taught weaving

by Jane Stewart, another of the better-known writers, included 'My name is Wanaka - that is, my Camp Fire name; we are Manasquan Camp Fire Girls' but apart from the inclusion of the girls singing *Wohelo for Aye* and the occasional use of Indian names it was similarly nothing more than one of a run of rather unlikely stories for older girls. The illustrations of their covers and dustwrappers were accurate, usually showing girls sitting around camp fires wearing middy outfits plus, in at least one instance, their ceremonial bead headbands. *A Campfire Girl's Happiness* had an attractive and correct dustwrapper showing girls in middy clothes with one of the group wearing her ceremonial gown and her headband.

The Jane Stewart stories comprised a series, the main theme of which was of a girl being kidnapped, one in particular trying to help her, the other Camp Fire girls befriending the pair, and thrills and rescues along the way. It is unfortunate that on the whole those books weren't very good as they must have given a rather poor impression of Camp Fire to any girls — or their parents — who read them, with the authors giving prominence to the thefts, near-drownings and other unlikely hazards suffered by the girls instead of enlarging upon their aims and ideals, and making them family or school type stories showing perhaps a little of their ceremonial meetings and more of their ideals and their work. That also applies to the majority of books purporting to be related to or about Camp Fire. However, the fact that activities were often shown taking place outdoors, camping or on holiday gave the authors a larger scope in which to portray their improbable themes than stories which otherwise could only have been about schoolgirls and probably set in school term times.

Each genuine Camp Fire had a Count, Record, Memory or Log book. Those were to keep accounts of each member with her chosen name and any Honours and ranks she attained. Outings, walks and extra meetings were written in each one, together with the date. Months were given Indian names such as *The Month of the Long Night Moon, The Month of the*

THE WOOD GATHERER'S DESIRE

As fagots are brought from the forest firmly held by the sinews which bind them, I will cleave to my Camp Fire sisters wherever, whenever I find them.

I will strive to grow strong like the pine tree, to be pure in my deepest desire; to be true to the truth that is in me and follow the Law of the Fire."

THE FIRE MAKER'S DESIRE

As fuel is brought to the fire so I purpose to bring my strength my ambition my heart's desire my joy and my sorrow to the fire of humankind. For I will tend as my fathers have tended and my father's fathers since time began the fire that is called the love of man for man the love of man for God.
JOHN COLLIER

Thunder Moon, *The Month of the Snow Moon* and other relevant titles.

Wood Gatherers are entitled to wear a ring which is silver with a bundle of sticks (faggots spelt with only one 'g' in America) to represent a group bound together in friendship. At her initiation the Guardian places the ring on the finger of the new member, then says:

'As Guardian of the Fire, I place on the little finger of your left hand, this ring, with its fagot of seven twigs, symbolic of the Law of the Fire, which you have expressed your desire to follow, and with the three circles on either side, symbolic of the three parts of the watchword of this organisation, Work, Health and Love.'

On moving up a step to the next grade, Fire Makers are given a bracelet with the word *Wohelo* engraved around it. Torch Bearers have a pin or brooch designed as four parts of a circle showing fire, lightning, a pine tree and the wearer's

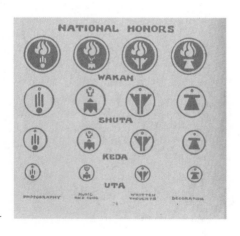

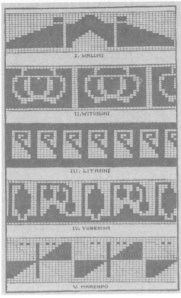

Names, Symbols and Headbands

own chosen symbol. In each case the presentation is made by the Guardian, with a similar ritual but with different wording for each rank. In more recent years a custom has arisen of giving each new Torch Bearer a candlestick. The Trail Seeker's rank wasn't added until 1936; their badge depicts a flame and a path.

Many rituals are associated with the Camp Fire ceremonies but have dwindled or altered over the years. In the early days a typical Council Fire Meeting could open with the Guardian reciting *The Sacrament of Fire* by John Oxenham. Lighting the candles or the fire at the start of each meeting was done by three girls each of whom lit a candle, at the same time saying the ritual for her share of the ceremony. The first is always 'I light the light of Work, for Wohelo means Work'. The girl then said the verse for Work.

'We glorify work, because through work we are free. We work to win, to conquer, to be masters. We work for the joy of the working and because we are free. Wohelo means work.'

That was followed by the other girls lighting the lights of Health and Love in turn with the words: 'I light the light of Health for Wohelo means health', then 'I light the light of Love for Wohelo means love'. After she lights the candle, each girl says the verse related to her particular word.

'We hold onto health, because through health we serve and are happy. In caring for the health and beauty of our persons we are caring for the very shrine of the Great Spirit. Wohelo means health.'

65

SYMBOLS AND INSIGNIA

Membership Ring

Fire Maker's Bracelet

Torch Bearer's Pin

Fire Maker

Torch Bearer

Wood Gatherer

Guardian's Pin

Symbols and Insignia

'We love Love for love is life, and light and joy and sweetness, and love is comradeship and motherhood and fatherhood, and all dear kinship. Love is the joy of service so deep that self is forgotten. Wohelo means love.'

Fifteen years later, that last saying had been changed to:

'We light the light of love, for love is comradeship and motherhood and fatherhood, and all dear kinship. Love is the joy of service. So deep that self is forgotten. Wohelo means love.'

Fire-lighting was also ceremonial, the materials for the fire being brought in by the Wood Gatherers and arranged by the Fire Makers. A Torch Bearer or the Guardian actually lit the fire while the girls either sang a song such as *Burn Fire, Burn* or the group said their *Ode to Fire*. Whether they chose to sing or not was clearly indicated by EJO in her book *The Camp Fire Torment* with the younger girls choosing to sing with actions, which the older girls didn't want to do, considering it too childish.

In more recent years, ending meetings is given a reverse of the opening, with three girls chosen to extinguish the candles. This time the girl says 'I extinguish the light of Work' (or Health or Love). Then kneeling she does so, before standing and reciting the correct verse; in the case of Health: 'Wohelo means health. And the flame that we lighted may its message leave with us.'

A message of beauty
And of health to be treasured.
Go we forth then with gladness
To show unto others
What Camp Fire has taught us.
The keen joy of living.
(Alice Batchelder 1936)

Other Camp Fire Ritual Verses include:

The Wood Gatherer's Desire
As Faggots are brought from the forest
Firmly held by the sinews which bind them,
I will cleave to my Camp Fire Sisters
Wherever, whenever I find them.
I will strive to grow strong like the pine tree,
To be pure in my deepest desire;
To be true to the truth that is in me
And follow the Law of the Fire.

The Fire Maker's Desire (John Collier)
As Fuel is brought to the fire
So I purpose to bring
My strength, My Ambition

My Heart's desire, My Joy
And my sorrow
To the fire,
Of humankind.
For I will tend
As my fathers have tended
And my father's fathers
Since time began
The fire that is called
The love of man for man
The love of man for God.

The Trail Seeker's Desire (Theodore Harper 1936)
I desire
To seek the way
That shall become
A delight to my feet,
For it will bring me to
the fire of human kindness
Lighted by those
Who have gone before me
On the Camp Fire trail.

The Torch Bearer's Desire   (1912)
That light which has been given to me
I desire to pass undimmed to others.

The Blue Bird Wish (Theodore Harper 1938)
To have fun,
To learn to make beautiful things,
To remember to finish what I begin,
To want to keep my temper most of the time.
To go to interesting places,
To know about trees and flowers and birds,
To make friends.

68

CHAPTER SIX

Elsie's Camp Fire
or 'The Sign of Fire' (*A School Camp Fire*)

Hearing that the Guides had made custard and cakes and biscuits and scones for supper the night before, Aurora and Tamakwa and Opechee promptly banished these from their menu. 'We must be original! We won't do any baking except the dumplings. The Guides never thought of those! We'll make pancakes!' said Dawn. 'I love pancakes!' (*Patience Joan, Outsider.* 1923. p. 197.)

The Camp Fire Movement, which had begun in America in 1911, was of great importance to Elsie. She ran a Camp Fire in Ealing (*Camp Watéwin* The Camp of Those Who Conquer) made up of girls who went to her church or her classes there, and from local families. The Bayne Todd family attended the same Congregational Church in Ealing and the families became friendly enough for Margaret to go away on holiday with Elsie.

Margaret remembered Elsie as 'cheerful though reserved' and thinks she was the favourite of J. O. Margaret wrote to me that:

'She [Elsie] was almost maternal with 'her' girls, anxious for them to do well. She was also always self-effacing. With them and via the slight mystery of the Camp Fire perhaps, she was able to express herself in a way that would not have been possible at home.'

Elsie (2nd from left) with some of her Camp Fire girls c 1919

Elsie added to her original Camp Fire girls over the years as the first ones left when they became too old to belong and younger ones were introduced. There was at least one Blue Bird amongst her earliest girls: Uda the Firefly, as mentioned in chapter 5. That child was obviously the later inspiration for Helen Robinson or Uda the first Guardian in *The School of Ups and Downs*, then in *Patience Joan, Outsider*. Having much younger girls coming along in the Camp Fire helped EJO make her letters suitable for a child of Ribby's age when

MAIDLIN BEARS THE TORCH

ELSIE JEANETTE OXENHAM

she wrote to him during those years.

Camp Fire meetings invariably began with a poem by J.O. 'Kneel always when you light a fire ...' which was quoted in all the Camp Fire Handbooks of that era. The supplement to *The Camp Fire Girls for the British Isles* 1922 showed Elsie's name amongst their Executive Committee members. Another name was that of a friend of hers, Muriel Wynzar, a Guide Officer and on the Committee in that capacity until her death in the late 1970s, by which time she had collected all the main Abbey books and their close connectors. She could have been an early member of *Camp Watéwin* then, when the Camp Fire Movement became less popular in Britain, like Maribel in *Crisis in Camp Keema* but for different reasons, transferred to the Girl Guides.

Camp Watéwin existed from 1916 to 1922 and in the Minute Books are records of all their meetings. Dates there are given as *the Month of the Crescent Moon*, *the Month of the Harvest Moon*, *the Month of the Windy Moon*, and similar Camp Fire expressions. The names of some of Elsie's first Camp Fire Girls at one meeting were: Enid Razzell, Elsie Sates, Catherine and Janet Millar, Doris Newsome, Edith and Agnes Evans, Florence West, Doreen and Bernice Weight, Stella Perry and Gladys Kingswell. Their chosen names all appear too and show for those who know the books how Elsie used them and the characteristics of her own girls, in her early Sussex stories. Below is the list of names and meanings selected by Elsie's first Camp Fire Girls as they were portrayed in EJO's book *A School Camp Fire*.

Name	Meaning	Symbol
Wenonah	Eldest daughter	Pansies for thoughts
Daisy	Innocence	
Minnehaha	Laughing Water	Cheerfulness, a sun
Heather	Covering unsightliness	
Esperanza	Hope	
Olive	Bringing Peace	Olive branch/dove
Iris	Hopefulness	
Mavis	Gladness	Thrush
Pamela	Bringing music	Harp
Mnanka	Working cheerfully	Spider's web
Tanpa	Uprightness	Silver Birch
Uda	Doing kindnesses	Firefly
Romany	Gypsy life	Tents
Renee	Queenly	Crown
Rosemary	Remembrance	

From that book (p. 225) :

'Phyllis chose the Indian word Mnanka meaning 'I weave' for her name, with a spider as her symbol to stand for industry. Irene Smith, adapting the meaning of her own name, became Olive and took the symbol of peace, a dove with an olive-leaf. Her sister Violet, not having much originality, copied her method, took a violet, meaning modesty, for her symbol and, turning her name into Greek, became Ianthe. Others were Ivy, meaning fidelity, and Daisy, standing for innocence; while Clare, the most musical girl in the Lower School, adopted a harp as crest, and became Pamela.'

As those earliest Camp Fire Girls left *Camp Watéwin*, new ones joined who took these names: Ayshe, Ansudi, Aurora, Watanopa, Kokoko, Thistle, Monadamin, Clover, Tiamalia, Bernice, Esperance, Kim, Hilda.

Thistle was chosen by Margaret Bayne Todd once she became a Camp Fire girl, showing independence ('No-one meddles with me') while Aurora ('The Dawn/Herald of Sunshine and Light') had a rising sun for her symbol. In later books, Elsie worked from the *Camp Fire Handbook* to find names for characters in her stories instead of using those selected by the girls of her own Camp Fire. She herself adopted the name of Wenonah, the Eldest Daughter. Mary Manners, who picked Wenonah in *A School Camp Fire,* the first book in which EJO portrayed Camp Fire, was given pansies for her symbol to show that an eldest daughter has to be thoughtful. Elsie put pansies into a lot of her books, reminding her readers that 'pansies are for thoughts'. She was fully aware of the position of an older girl in any family and remarks given to various of her characters may well have

indicated her own feelings, viz. Marion telling Rena and Nancy in *A Go-Ahead Schoolgirl* (p. 154) 'All I can do is to wait and look on and be ready if she ever asks me for help. I think elder sisters often have to be content with that! I know they need a lot of patience sometimes!' Yet the younger Moll Sanderson, who was described in *The School Without a Name* as 'never being without some kids tacked on to her' said on p. 31, 'It's a frightful fag always having to look after kids.'

EJO was fond of pansies although they were sometimes associated with sadness in her stories as when Rosamund in *The Abbey Girls on Trial,* thinking Joy wouldn't let her start the shop she yearned to run, was shown dead-heading pansies in the Abbey garden. They were always depicted as having grown in the Abbots' garden at Grace Dieu Abbey. A very old explanation of the word suggests it was a corruption of pensive.

from *The School Without a Name*

Elsie sometimes took her Camp Fire Girls away for short holidays even after she had moved from Ealing. During 1923 they went to Goring-by-Sea where they stayed at a bungalow in Sea Lane. In 1925 it was to Cambridge where they spent much of their time punting on the river. As by then she was living in Sussex, joint outings can't have been easy to plan but other venues included Bognor Regis, Clapham Woods and Pagham (over Easter 1923), and at least once to Chichester.

Elsie wrote an account for *The Christian World* of an outing when she booked a small school in Hertfordshire for an Easter weekend. There were twelve of the girls; 'ten aged between sixteen and eighteen and two younger ones.' They 'shared beds, hair ribbons and coats, did all the cooking and cleaning between them.' Some of them walked fourteen miles on the Bank Holiday when they went to Tewin which was approximately seven miles from Stevenage and would have made an ideal round trip when they wanted a walk of that length with which to earn Honours. They went to Knebworth House, to church on the Sunday; they made the apple-pie beds which Elsie put into her books, played cricket, danced, had nightly sing-songs and, before their holiday ended, held a Camp Fire Meeting round their council fire. 'Everyone reported it one of the jolliest meetings ever held in three years of camp fire life, and one of the happiest evenings of a very successful holiday.

from
Patience Joan, Outsider

74

The girls proved capable cooks and worthy camp fire maidens; the Guardian never cooked once, and departed as ignorant of the ways of the coal range as she arrived. But the girls knew all about it, and meals were ample and well cooked and even occasional failures disappeared, and caused no ill effects.'

They visited the Wymondleys too; Great and Little Wymondley both have 'some lovely old buildings, although a lot have been destroyed.' A description of Wymondley Priory states that the pond there was the original stew-pond of the monks until the Dissolution and was a point Elsie could have remembered when she wrote about the fish stream at Cleeve Abbey/Gracedieu in her Abbey books. There had been an Augustinian Priory at Little Wymondley; Cardinal Wolsey entertained Henry VIII in a great house on the site of which now stands Delamere House. At Little Wymondley there was a barn about one hundred feet long and nearby there had been a monastery or priory. These were, again, items which Elsie could have remembered and used in her later stories.

When Elsie described any such surroundings her pen became as evocative as when she wrote about her beloved beech woods in the Abbey books. In that particular holiday account were: 'woods starred with wind flowers ... trees hung with streamers of budding honeysuckle ... hawthorns wore filmy green veils ... buds reaching eagerly for the Good Friday sun ...'

For normal indoor meetings, the girls usually 'clustered round a scarlet night-light embedded in a bundle of twigs and lit candles' rather than round an open fire. There were occasional extra meetings such as the first birthday of *Camp Watéwin* on February 25th 1917 for which they held a

Camp Fire Supper with all the food provided by themselves. John Oxenham was invited towards the end, to admire the candle-lit table. For their second birthday they held a small party with the resultant entry in the Minute Books of 'the second birthday of the Bestest Camp Fire Girls', which expression ties in with phrases used by EJO and Ribby and the fact that the handwritten inscription in a copy of *A Go-Ahead Schoolgirl* bought second-hand in 1971 reads 'To Nancy, from her bestest little friend' making it sound as if it might have been given to one of EJO's own Camp Fire Girls by another. The copy of *The School of Ups and Downs* bought from the same source contained a newspaper account of the death of Ribby. The hand-written inscription in that book reads: 'With 'bestest love' to Nancy from Uncle Bernard, Xmas 1918.'

Some meetings were given special themes such as Egyptian, Red Indian (which was on the sixth day of the Grass Moon) when the girls would have dressed appropriately or provided food in accordance with the custom of whatever was the subject. On *the eighth day of the Rose Moon* they were invited to a Garden Meeting in Conifer Crest off Montpelier Road, where their hostess provided lemon drinks and biscuits. A dance practice was held at West Ealing Congregational Church on *the second night of the Hunger Moon*, an evening attended by E.F.D.S. member Helen Kennedy.

In October 1917 they 'went for a moonlight walk through Pitshanger Park, across Perivale Fields then back through Pitshanger Park again.' One summer outing they made was to Kew Gardens. In 1916 they held a Hallowe'en meeting when they speared apples from a tub as well as playing other traditional games. Two years later they put on a Pageant for wounded soldiers in Ealing and in 1920 they gave a display of folk dancing there. It was also 1920 when they performed the Folk Play at the Congregational Church in Ealing; the one taken from the version in Juliana Ewings' version in *The Peace Egg* ending with 'We learnt a rapper sword dance for the finale.'

Business meetings were those at which members of the

Camp Fire and Guardian showed work they had done towards the gaining of Honours. Minutes of earlier meetings were read, candles were lit, then the new Honours distributed after which there were discussions about dates and arrangements for further meetings, entertainments or outings. The second parts of meetings were much more informal.

One entry in the Camp Fire Minutes Books states that: 'Our Guardian has been to a summer School for Folk Dancers at Cheltenham', then that 'Miss Dunkerley has visited Gloucester Cathedral and Tewkesbury Abbey.' Both events were fully described in *The Abbey Girls Go Back to School*. Elsie was referred to as Miss Dunkerley or Guardian throughout the Minute Books, rather than Wenonah, and never by her Christian name. The entries in the Minute Books are nearly all in her own handwriting even though many of them were obviously copied from items the girls had written themselves. However, in *A School Camp Fire* the Guardian, Iris, referring to the work one of the girls had read out during their meeting, said 'We must have these copied into our new minute-book', so presumably normal practice was for all entries to be in the Guardian's hand.

Many of Elsie's books include various aspects of crafts and cookery but it is clear that she wasn't allowed to do a great deal in the way of either. In any case, with her bad sight any close work was definitely forbidden which is unfortunate as she was obviously interested in many aspects associated with crafts such as the carvings and pictures sold by Rosamund, the Pixie's handwoven dresses, home-made sweets made and sold by Prue and her aunts in *The Tuck-Shop Girl* and the way Joy was shown providing craft centres in her village. However, EJO made her own Camp Fire dress and gained Honour Beads for knitting; she had knitted socks for Hugo during World War I when he first joined up as a soldier. After he transferred to the Royal Flying Corps, she wrote to Ribby the Camp mascot: 'When my flying brother went up to nearly 19,000 feet the other day, his eyelashes etc. were frozen! You should see his flying boots; leather - up to his hips - and all sheepskin inside! All woolly'.

She made scones or gingerbread to take to meetings for her Camp Fire Girls to sample, also home-made jams. Food was often mentioned in her books, particularly the earlier ones. She was interested in their regional variations in the same way she always was with the altered dances from different areas. In some cases the backgrounds from which her characters came showed how some of them had never been expected to do anything domestic to help in their homes, for example, Dorothy-Anne and Katharine in *A School Camp Fire* (p. 78) not knowing for how long to boil eggs.

It must be said that most of the food mentioned in her books was typical of what might have been provided for dormitory feasts, snacks after dancing classes, or as suitable picnic foods, rather than for actual meals. In *The Tuckshop Girl* Prue provided a picnic for Jock and Jinty of:

'"Bottle of lemonade and one horn mug. ... Good for Prue!" ... and he opened the tin box. "Sandwiches of potted meat, kept jolly and fresh." "Jelly cookies! Oh, now nice of her. How did she know I loved them!" "D'you mean those buns with jam in? Scones, home-made cake, two bars of chocolate. What have you got there?" Jinty had dived into the box with a squeal of delight. She held up a tiny pot of jam. "To eat with the scones! ... Strawberry jam - and here's a wee spoon to spread it with! She thinks of everything. It's a beautiful tea."' (*The Tuck-Shop Girl*. p. 96)

All of this came over in the books as with the cream buns and jam tarts at Jacky-boy's or at dancing weekends about which type more was written than about the necessary leg of mutton in *Patience Joan, Outsider* when the Guides and Camp Fire took charge of the house during the absence of Patience's

THE
TUCK-SHOP GIRL

By
ELSIE OXENHAM

grandmother. It is also clear from that particular book how much Elsie knew about housekeeping and cleaning.

On leaving London, Elsie tried to begin another Camp Fire but '... Worthing was very much geared towards Guides and it didn't last long there.' Initially she gave two or three talks to the Camp Fire already run in Worthing by Miss Jessie Cropper who, as Elsie had done, taught her girls country and sword dancing. More of EJO's books were published during the next few years than before, so perhaps it was as well she had more time to spare for writing than she had had during the latter years in Ealing.

The differences between Camp Fire and Guiding were portrayed very effectively in many of her books. She admired the Girl Guides, but Doris Acland stated that 'their military style didn't appeal to her' and some of the things she showed them as doing, such as drilling in camp, have been queried as not having been part of the Guide Movement at the published dates of the books. But that leads to another point altogether: no one knows when EJO actually wrote her books and, had it been years before their publication, the events and expressions she used would have been perfectly correct at the time when they were written.

After drill and the use of the name Corporal had been questioned, both of which Elsie put into books published during the decade 1910-1920, it was pointed out that, in the very early days of Guiding, both were perfectly normal. In fact, the rank of Corporal was used in some Guide companies right into the 1940s, while a few Guiders continued to include drill as a regular part of their meetings, fifty years later.

It was during the years of *Camp Watéwin* when Elsie

discovered Ribby (Wriggles) who was included as a character in the tales set in the *Rocklands* era and about whom more is written in chapter 7. Once Elsie knew Ribby, *Camp Watéwin* adopted the delicate little invalid as their mascot. The girls wrote to him, found small toys and games he could handle while lying flat on his back, then added details about those and about the letters exchanged between him and them to their Minutes Books.

Elsie's Camp Fire Certificates are retained in her old home, along with her ring, bracelet, brooch and Guardian's pin, first editions of her books and the original framed pictures as shown on her dustwrappers. Sadly, her Camp Fire gown and bead headband have vanished but those made and owned by Margaret Bayne Todd were given to the Dunkerley family when she returned the Minute Books to Elsie's niece. Until then the Minute Books had been in Margaret's possession for over thirty years, having been given to Margaret for safe keeping by Theo Dunkerley after Elsie's death when no one in the family wanted them, the same way that nobody at that time wanted her photographs of Cleeve Abbey.

CHAPTER SEVEN

Ribby/Ribbie/Wriggles
or 'The Fairy Prince' (*The Conquest of Christina*)

Prince Ribbie lay there in the shade of the sycamore, the fierce sunshine broken into flecks of light and shade by the big leaves, the moor wind blowing right across him. He wore a little cream knitted coat, and spread over him was a cream-coloured rug the Queen of the Castle had made for him with her own hands. His hair against the white pillow was just the same creamy colour, but his cheeks were red and his big blue eyes were very bright.

'It was a surprise for you, so that you could finish the story,' Bear explained to the Witch.

So that was how Ribbie celebrated the fact that he was eight years and three hundred and sixty-four days old!

(*Ribbie's Book*. 1917-1919.)

Wriggles, who appeared in EJO's stories about Rocklands: *Jen of the Abbey School*, *A Go-Ahead Schoolgirl* and *Tickles*, and was mentioned very briefly in *Rosamund's Victory* (p.50), was Reginald Willis Wilson, known to his family as Ribby or Ribbie, a name taken from his favourite book by Beatrix

81

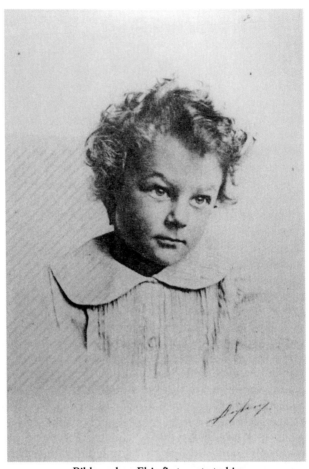
Ribby, when Elsie first wrote to him

Potter, *The Pie and the Patty Pan*.

A London violinist, Miss Olive Watt, who knew the Dunkerleys in Ealing, used to entertain Ribby by playing the violin to him during her visits to relations near Sheffield who were friendly with the Wilson family. It was she who told Elsie Oxenham how much the small invalid had enjoyed reading her *The Tuck-shop Girl, Rosaly's New School* and *At School With the Roundheads*.

On learning that Ribby had to lie flat on his back all the time and was permanently confined to bed, Elsie began writing to him regularly. Eventually she collected all his and her letters and made them into a book. The publisher to whom she offered the collection rejected it, on the grounds it was for too young an age group and too personal to be of general interest. Perhaps that was sensible; it *is* a young book in some ways, but not when one realises that Ribby, aged eight, was only a little boy at the start of their correspondence, and clearly an extremely intelligent child. Or if considering it as suitable reading for other young children who might also have to spend their time in bed during long illnesses.

The original manuscript is in the possession of the daughter of Ribby's nurse Violet Ellis ('Bear' or Eddie) and takes the form of letters mainly written between The Witch (EJO), The Enchanted Prince (Ribby), Little Grey (Maida's cat), and a variety of pet animals and toys.

The reason Violet Ellis was known to Ribby as Bear was because he was so fond of teddy bears and thought that 'a bear is the nicest thing in the world.' One of his small sisters was unable to say Violet's surname except as Eddie, which became the name the others in the family used for Violet.

The manuscript opens with a supposed witch who sits weaving her spells [stories].

'Once upon a time there was a Witch ... [complete with a description of the Witch and the fact that she had a cat (Grey Edward)] ... and he wore a red leather collar with a big bell, to frighten away the birds, and a round silver medal hanging under his chin. On the medal were the words 'Sir Edward Grey', and his address. But his long name often got shortened into Grey Edward, or even Grey, or Little Grey. By degrees he collected quite a number of other names, till his full name was so long that only the initials could be written on a postcard!'

There are interesting references throughout the manuscript to not only Ribby's toys and animals but members of the Dunkerley family and Elsie's Camp Fire Girls. The latter adopted Ribby as their mascot and did all they could, as Elsie was already doing, to brighten his life by writing to him, sending him small gifts, and any crafts they thought he could do, lying on his back.

The letters make fascinating reading and give another insight into Elsie Oxenham as a person.

'The Witch used to spend all day weaving webs. When she had finished a web she would dress one of her children in it, and send her away out into the world. She had heaps of children, all girls! A queer thing was that when her children went away from her, they never came back ... sometimes they made friends out in the world and these friends told the Witch how they were getting on, and in that way she made new friends too; but more often she never heard any more about her children once they had gone away from her.

'One day three of her children had an adventure. There was Jinty who was a Mischief and wore a bright green dress; and Polly, who was great friends with all the boys, and wore a deep blue dress; and Rosaly who was just an ordinary little girl who made norful ugly faces, and her dress was bluey green. These three went away together, ever so far, across wild lonely country, all bare moors and deep valleys, until they came to a cold little grey village perched high up in the wind. And here, just outside the village and all among big trees,

they found an enchanted castle. It was enchanted because of the Prince who lived in it. They flew in at one of the windows and sat on his bed, and made friends with him and that is how this story began. The little Prince's name meant that he was a King, but he was only eight years old, so as yet of course he was only a Prince. He had been enchanted by a wicked fairy godmother, so that all day long and every day he had to lie flat on his back in his bedroom. Nobody could undo the enchantment, though the

Wise Men said he might perhaps grow out of it some day.'

His sisters said Ribby was the most clever of their family and he seems to have been a very talented child. Even in the books in which he appeared as a character he was shown as being able to do wonderful hand-work: embroidery, bead-work, knitting, plain sewing — he made clothes for his family of teddy bears — and other light-weight crafts. When EJO first visited him, he had embroidered a table centre for her.

Ribby was born on May 31st 1909 at Parson Cross House in Ecclesfield and first wrote to EJO soon after his eighth birthday. Eventually she spent a holiday in the Peak District and while there went to see him. The following year she was invited by the Queen [Ribby's mother] to spend a week in their home, the house named Waldershaigh. In Elsie's description of that first visit in her manuscript, it can be seen as the background for *A Go-ahead Schoolgirl* and Rocklands School as all her descriptions of the area and the interior of the house were so accurate.

'We have found a cottage halfway up a cliff, but there is no sea at the bottom, only a river and woods and fields and trees and a village and an old stone bridge and dusty white road. A very steep lane climbs straight up the cliff till you come to a few cottages, and that is our village. If you go on still higher up, you come to The Edge and there you find The Moor, and rocks and miles of heather, and little paths, and one big white road running straight to - where?'

Elsie hadn't told Ribby she would be in the vicinity; merely

"TICKLES" OR. THE SCHOOL THAT WAS DIFFERENT

OXENHAM

"Tickles" is a charming character who thinks for herself, and does not take part in the unfortunate school food. All girls will read her adventures at school with great pleasure.

ELSIE JEANETTE OXENHAM

that she was having a holiday as 'even Witches need a change sometimes.' Once Bear and the Queen had said it wouldn't be too tiring for Ribby, she went for that memorable first visit. She found:

'A big old grey house, with long windows, and a long carriage-drive through the trees, and a great door. Inside the big square hall looked almost like a museum, with curiosities of all kinds, and beautiful old china and silver and carvings, and the walls crowded right up to the roof with pictures, many of them paintings of the Prince's grandfathers and great-grandfathers. Upstairs she found two nurseries; the outer one a big sunny room with wide windows, and filled with all the dolls Margaret and the others had played with. A bookcase full of fascinating books - girls' books, boys' books, children's books - all kinds of books!'

But once inside the inner nursery she saw:

'... quite clearly, just one thing - a Guardian Angel in a white dress, with pretty red hair sitting on the edge of a little white bed, and holding the hand of a tiny white boy. He was tiny because he was so thin and white; that was the enchantment of course, but the Witch was not sure that he would not have been quite big if she had seen the whole of him standing up. But she only saw his face, and that was very very white, and so thin that she said to the Guardian Angel, 'May I kiss him?' - because she really felt as if the kiss might go right through onto the pillow! But Bear said she might kiss him quite safely, and nothing unpleasant happened to the kiss though she felt as if she must hardly touch him, for fear he should fade away altogether while she looked at him. He had rings of pale yellow hair and big shy eyes, and he looked as if he was not quite sure what a Witch who wrote books would be like, nor how he ought to speak to her. So Bear held his one hand but he stretched out the other to the Witch and smiled a shy little smile. And he never said a word.'

It was after that visit that the Witch, in her position as their Guardian, told her Camp Fire Girls about Ribby; their first joint effort to amuse him was to send him postcards:

'Yesterday I had postcards from Minnehaha, Mavis, Romany, Aurora and Edward and today from Wenonah, Uda, Tanpa, Stella, Heather, Clover, Hilda, Kokokoho, Mnanka and Renee. I am just delighted with them, you see it came as such a hugeous surprise.'

Anyone might wonder how, with her busy life, Elsie Oxenham made time to write to Ribby as frequently and regularly as she did. She was settled with her writing career, was attending dance classes and running her Camp Fire, and the correspondence began in the middle of a war at a time when she must have been concerned about that and the fates of her brothers and their friends. But once started, she didn't stop. At the same time, she worked out as many ways as possible to make Ribby laugh and to give him something fresh to think about.

The first family of animals EJO sent him was bears she had brought home from Switzerland. They were soon followed by amusing toys, such as a doll which couldn't fall over, the Three Wise Monkeys and assorted sized rabbits and chickens. Later during their correspondence Ribby, having made Miss

Molly, his favourite bear, a completely new outfit, had the bright idea of packing her up and sending her to have a holiday in London where she was taken shopping and to meet the Camp Fire girls, who ' all took it in turn to nurse her all evening.'

If the Witch 'happened' to forget to cover her typewriter, Grey Edward decided he would use it.

'Well now, somebody has been typing an article, and if she hasn't been and gone and left the typewriter uncovered ever since yesterday!' as he wrote to one of the cats in the Enchanted Palace. 'I like to sit out on the front path where I can hear what people say as they pass the house ... people say 'what a beautiful cat.' Really and truly that's why I sit there, just to hear people say that; but I'm not at all conceited really.'

Later Grey Edward reported :

'I was starving; you see there's nothing to eat in my dug-out and the rain comes through the roof. But my Bestest Lady was just norful good to me and gave me my dinner and warmed me, and let me choose my piece of cake at tea before any of the ladies had theirs. I like my Bestest Lady best. Did you know I had learnt French at school? Vraiment! Oui, oui, certainement! Oh, la-la! la-la - as my Mam'selle used to say.'

Ribby replied to that with:

'Have you heard any more loud thunderings lately? We really are surprised at you liking to stay out all night, but as you are now a Special Constable, we suppose you think it your duty? Still we never heard of a S.C. having a dug-out before! and wonder if you are allowed to entertain your lady friends there? But you are clever to know French! Perhaps you too will have a surprise one of these days! Au revoir, mon cher Edward! Tout à vous.'

Letters flew between London and The Enchanted Palace almost daily. Ribby received others written not only by Elsie and individuals among her Camp Fire Girls, but from Elsie's brother Hugo in France, together with a photograph of him in his flying gear. The toys and animals during this time began to marry, usually when EJO discovered a new toy which she thought would make a wife, husband or child for the families of which she already knew so much.

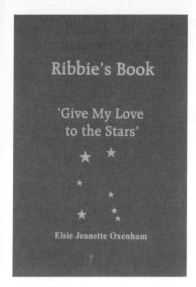

Ribbie's Book

'Give My Love
to the Stars'

Elsie Jeanette Oxenham

An idea EJO had to help keep Ribby amused through a dreary winter during which he had measles to contend with as well, was to give him a half-way birthday.

'You are going to have a half-time birthday on November 30th, your 8½ birthday, see?'

When Ribby wrote after that extra birthday, it was with a letter to thank her for the Chinese ornaments she had sent him; his other letter was:

'Dear Camp Fire girls, Thank you all very much for the pretty postcards and good wishes you sent me on my 8½ birthday, it was more norfully kind of you. Yes! I really am a lucky boy to have two birthdays in one year. I got a scrumptious lot of presents and postcards. I had another pleasant surprise this morning - a letter from Hugo, in France; wasn't that just norfully kind of him? I DO think the Witch has just the kindest family I know! I say, I know all about your ceremonial meetings, honours and mottos. If I were a girl, I should like to join.'

The letters give a fascinating insight into how a busy person spent such a lot of time trying to amuse one small boy and how intelligently he responded. Ribby wrote to her with puzzles he had worked out or in cryptic codes, as well as sometimes in French or Welsh. Elsie always felt that his nurse's devoted attention had a lot to do with his attitude and how fortunate it was that Violet Ellis was able to help him develop his many skills. Violet in her turn was so fond of Ribby that she deferred her wedding so she could stay with him as long as he needed her. As a wedding present Elsie gave Violet a copy of *A Go-ahead Schoolgirl*, which was dedicated to them both:

Dedicated with much love and all best wishes
to Reginald W. Wilson ('Ribby')
and
Violet A. Ellis ('Bear')
The 'Wriggles' and 'Eddy' of this story.

Every year the Wilson family rented a house at
Scarborough for ten weeks. They took Violet with them as
Ribby's nurse, as well as some of their domestic staff, while
Ribby's father, a solicitor, joined them whenever he could.
Violet used to take Ribby, in his invalid carriage, to listen to
the music played daily at the Spa. Ribby was always interested
in music and composed some when he was only seven years
old. One day a lullaby Ribby had written was included in their
repertoire, having been orchestrated by Quentin, the son of
the conductor Alick Maclean. A newspaper account reported
that: 'A gifted crippled child had composed a melody ... the
child died shortly after and his mother said it had been the
happiest day in his life; she sent each member of the orchestra
a gold tie pin.'

Ribby's Grave

Ribby died at Waldershaigh when he was ten and a half years old of 'tuberculosis of the spine, tubercular peritonitis and exhaustion' with Violet beside him. On his gravestone is a carved bunch of violets, because of her. The news reached Elsie on a day when she had a Camp Fire meeting which she managed to complete before telling the girls of his death.

Violet's husband died quite young as a result of his time during the war, leaving her with a daughter, Margaret, then aged two. Ribby's father offered Violet and the little girl a home. Many years later her daughter, in a letter to Olga Lock-Kendell, reported that Violet:

'... spent most of her time sewing - she was a skilled needlewoman - (she made dresses for the young ladies, uniforms for the maids, loose covers for the furniture and kept the household linen in good order). My life was bound up with the Wilsons for about eight years.'

The copy of *The School of Ups and Downs* mentioned in Chapter 6 contains a newspaper cutting which reads:

'WILSON - On 11th December, at Waldershaigh, Bolsterstone, after a long illness. Reginald Willis (Ribby) aged 10½ years, second son of Rex and Gladys Wilson.'

Underneath someone had added by hand:

'1919, Bolsterstone, near Deepcar station, G.C.R., near Sheffield.'

Olga Lock-Kendell, the first researcher of the Elsie Oxenham Society in the UK, traced the original manuscript of *Ribbie's Book* which the daughter of Ribbie's nurse still owns. With permission from the daughter Margaret Perry, Olga Lock-Kendell and Ruth Allen, the present editor of *The Abbey Chronicle*, published a selection of the letters which had been written by EJO and Ribbie during the short period before his death. The resultant book, *Give My Love to the Stars*, is available from *The Abbey Chronicle*.

Apart from the letter written by Margaret Perry, the quotations in this chapter have all been taken from the original manuscript *Ribbie's Book,* rather than from *Give My Love to the Stars.*

CHAPTER EIGHT

The English Folk Dance and Song Society
or 'The Moonlight Dance' (*Girls of the Hamlet Club*)

Soldier's Joy appealed to the Club and became a favourite at once. Tazy followed up her success with *The Alderman's Hat* which was nearly the riot that had been predicted. She calmed the class with *The Dressed Ship*; and then everybody found seats, on the floor, if necessary, and ate biscuits and drank milk and talked.
(*An Abbey Champion* 1946 p. 155.)

Elsie Jeanette Oxenham had always been enthusiastic about English music and dancing so must have been delighted during the years she lived in Ealing to discover the English Folk Dance Society. Thanks to the efforts of Cecil Sharp many of its songs and dances had been revived before she was aware of its existence. He became the Society's Director and had had his first book of traditional songs *A Book of British Songs for Home and School* published as early as 1902. His first book of folk dances had come out in 1906 when he was asked to suggest songs and dances suitable for a working girls' club to perform in public. Although initially pleased to help them to the extent that a later book of newly discovered morris music he had traced was dedicated: 'To our friends and pupils, the members of the Esperance Girls' Club', Cecil Sharp gradually became concerned about the standard and teaching of the club. Eventually staff and students from the Chelsea Physical Training College formed themselves into the Folk Dance Society which became the nucleus of the English Folk Dance Society, founded officially in December 1911. Their first Summer School was held at Stratford-on-Avon in 1912 and Stratford was the first place where regular Holiday Courses were held.

The Esperance Club, which was intended as a club for working class girls, ran from 1895 until 1914. In 1905, Mary Neal, one of the two women running the club, had visited Cecil Sharp to ask if folk songs were suitable for working girls; he, not surprisingly, had said that they were, so she began teaching them to her girls. It wasn't long before she and the girls thought that their next step should be to find dances to match the songs. Morris dancing came first, country dances next, then sword dances, and the girls learnt enough to be able to dance in public later that year with Cecil Sharp himself giving an introductory talk to the audience.

from *The Abbey Girls*

The Esperance girls were soon demonstrating dancing all over Great Britain and progressed to teaching as well, but at the same time Cecil Sharp began to feel concern about the standard of their dancing. Unfortunately, the resultant differences of opinion between Cecil Sharp and Mary Neal became known to the public as both of them were giving interviews to newspapers expressing their views; this split helped lead to the eventual formation of the English Folk

Dance Society. Miss Neal once wrote an article entitled *May Day Revels and the Morris Dance* describing both as being 'a modern revival'. She included details about the old dancing giving dates ranging from 1557 and ending with:

'... the life of those glorious days is to be once more in our midst ... those who have never seen the traditional dances of England will have an opportunity of seeing them danced by the Esperance Guild of Morris Dancers.'

In 1912 a male side of the newly formed E.F.D.S. danced in public for the first time at the Savoy Theatre in London. Those same few men used to go with Cecil Sharp most weekends to demonstrate the dances when and wherever he gave lectures. Sadly, four of those men were killed in 1916; one was Perceval Lucas whose brother the writer E.V. Lucas (Edward Verrall Lucas), helped Cecil Sharp by writing down the words of the

from *An Abbey Champion*

songs they heard as they travelled around the country together, collecting details of old songs and dances. In his book *London Lavender* (1912, 11th edition) E.V.Lucas wrote about having met a gentleman (Cecil Sharp) who was searching for old English songs and dances. E.V. Lucas, although admitting he was no musician, offered to help with the work by writing down the music as it was discovered.

A group of folk dancers formed in Scarborough in 1913 and Cecil Sharp took a team of dancers from London to their first meeting. The first two years at Scarborough classes were taken by a Miss Roberts, until she was asked by Cecil Sharp to accompany him to America. She was followed in Scarborough by Gladys Hall, who continued teaching there for forty-eight years during which time she taught dancing all over Yorkshire as well. She passed the teaching on to one of her young male dancers and by their eightieth anniversary, those were the only three teachers there had ever been in the Scarborough branch, an enviable record.

Scarborough was one of the places to which the E.F.D.S. member, whom EJO put into her books as the Pixie, went to judge dancing. It would be nice to think that the time referred to in *Jen of the Abbey School,* when the Pixie managed to spend a night at Rocklands on her way back to London, was based on one of those genuine occasions. It seems quite likely that it was as the two women had become friendly by then and EJO would have been interested

from *Secrets of the Abbey* (in *Little Folks 1921*)

in places where the dancing was popular enough to justify holding a competition. Also by that time she had established the fact in her books that Jen's home was in Yorkshire so it was quite probable the competition described in *Jen of the Abbey School* was based on an actual event.

In 1914 Cecil Sharp went to America where he concentrated on tracing and recording music and dances from the Appalachian Mountains, but he also collected songs, tunes and dances from other areas, many of which are now well known in Britain. It is largely due to his efforts that American folk music and dancing as well as the traditional British dancesare so popular these days. After his death, annual festivals of folk dance were given in London to which dancers from abroad were invited to participate, while teams from Great Britain were asked to reciprocate by demonstrating their dances in other countries. All of this led to the first International Festival being held in London in 1935.

THE ABBEY GIRLS
GO BACK TO SCHOOL

Elsie J.
Oxenham

Author of
The Abbey Girls.

The "Abbey Girls" Series   of School Stories.

Elsie had always liked traditional songs and sea shanties enough to include their words in her early books. Her very first published story (*Goblin Island* p. 45) had the children singing in the evenings on their island. 'We'll sing all the songs in Malcolm's song-book - the songs they sing at college. We'll choose the very silliest ones we know, and they'll make us laugh, and then we shall all feel better.'

At School With the Roundheads (p. 303), as well as having a lot of songs throughout the book, included some unexpected dancing at the end of term concert.

'Then the curtains were drawn, and the girls stood there, one at each side of the platform, facing each other, Jenny in white, Polly in her pink frock, each wearing a cotton sun-bonnet, and holding a white handkerchief in each hand. The boys stared, wide-eyed and expectant. Mr Pearson played a lively air, a morris jig, *Princess Royal*, as the programme announced, and still the girls stood waiting, till on the last beat Polly gave a little jump and then danced forward, her handkerchiefs waving, flapping, circling her head and down again, bells jingling below her knees, approaching the passive Jenny who stood watching her, a tinge of colour in her face. When Polly had danced forward and back again to her place, it was Jenny's turn to repeat the movement, and so they went through the dance, each waiting her turn till the other was finishing, and starting her dance with the quaint little jump on the last beat of the air.'

Perhaps those were small indications of Elsie's interest leading towards the Hamlet Club dancing in her later Abbey books. As soon as she learnt of its existence, she joined the

from *The Girls of the Abbey School*

English Folk Dance Society (E.F.D.S.), eagerly attending classes, vacation schools and parties and taking part in as many of their activities as she could. She was said by Margaret Bayne Todd to have had a 'passionate interest in the E.F.D.S. and she bravely wore a gym slip of very decent dimensions, well below her knees.' A photograph thought to have been taken by EJO but not credited is included in the book *Cecil Sharp* by A. H. Fox Strangways in collaboration with Maud Karpeles 1933, and shows Cecil Sharp playing the piano for an outdoor Demonstration at Stratford-on-Avon in 1919. In 1932 the English Folk Dance Society amalgamated with the Folk Song Society to become the English Folk Dance and Song Society, or E.F.D.S.S.

When Doris Acland was taken by Elsie to watch classes, she said that Elsie 'sang prettily and used to sit on the platform, singing away with the others'. She also reported that 'like Jen she could get only one note from her Basque pipe, but could play many tunes on her morris one'. It is unlikely Elsie would have participated in making apple-pie beds or the pillow fights she described so often in her earlier stories, but they were an accepted part of the vacation schools in those days. When she went to their E.F.D.S. vacation schools, the schoolgirl (Margaret Bayne Todd) she took with her said that the atmosphere was 'total magic for Elsie because she had never been to a very big school or a boarding school.' As well as describing such incidents in her Abbey books, EJO had used similar ones in *Expelled from School* (1919) where, rather strangely, they were depicted as taking place in a hotel with a complete lack of concern about the disturbance to any other guests.

Her Camp Fire girls were taught to dance by Elsie and one of her Camp Fire Girls remembered EJO teaching them sword dancing. However, on attending proper classes EJO learnt at once they were all wrong. In *The Abbey Girls Go Back to School,* which is the most factual of her books, using real people, incidents and locations more than in any of her others, she deliberately wrote about the mistakes made by her own girls. Then in *The New Abbey Girls* (p. 235) Maidlin,

Joy, Jen and Jack were told by The Writing Person 'we tried it in our dining room first, and nearly smashed the electric light.' That referred to the dining room at 20, Farncombe Road, Worthing, where the Dunkerley family had moved to in 1922. A member of those classes wrote that 'the dining room was certainly large enough for a short longways set. The room contained a dining table with six seats along each side and two carvers.'

Classes in Worthing were started in 1924 and held at Orchard House 'later purchased by Miss Hilda Wood so the E.F.D.S. had a permanent place in which to meet. One large room was the club room, big enough for a small number of dancers. Guiders and doctors' wives helped with the teaching.' Some of those Guiders and teachers went with EJO to at least one E.F.D.S. Summer School in Cambridge in the early 1920s.

Other classes took place at Storrington, a village north of Worthing. There, they were usually held in the hall of a house called *Idlehurst,* but occasionally and when permitted by the weather, the class was taught in the garden of *Holly Cottage* further along West Street.

One correspondent wrote: 'I was in the Congregational Rangers 1927 - 1929. Elsie Oxenham took us all through our Bible Class at the Congregational Hall, also a Country Dance Club for us. We all thought a lot of her.'

from *The Abbey Girls Go Back to School*

Outside school hours during the 1940s, Elsie taught Country Dancing at Worthing High School for Girls.

After Elsie's death, an obituary in a Worthing paper stated that:

'She founded the first Worthing Club in 1924 and from then on did much to encourage interest in the district, organising talks, demonstrations and local dancing weeks and teaching newly formed clubs in the surrounding area.'

EJO took Margaret Bayne Todd, who was still at school then, with her to classes in Chelsea. They went together to Folk Dance Schools, including those in Cambridge. Margaret wrote that 'passion for senior girls and staff was familiar to me, but Elsie adored it all. To be a girl in a girls' school setting.' That atmosphere obviously gave her the feel of a boarding school and could also have showed her how some girls were prone to hero-worship others. That angle was put into *The Abbey Girls Go Back to School* when Madam was shown to have made such an impression on Cicely.

Elsie was The Writing Person in the Abbey books and everything attributed to her in the texts of those was true. It is safe to accept that all the tiny vignettes of young widows or of various working girls attending classes were factual and based on people she knew slightly through meeting them at any classes she went to as well. Her statement to the Pixie about having written so many words in the train and being told she had 'made her fare' was also correct.

The Miss Newcastle of *The Abbey Girls Go Back to*

from *The Abbey Girls*

100

School was another person slightly disguised in the books; her real name was Catherine Ord. Elsie gave her a copy of that book and, inside it wrote: 'To Catherine Ord, "Miss Newcastle". With love from Elsie Jeanette Oxenham. Cheltenham 1922.' Another book given to Miss Newcastle had the same wording but arranged differently: 'Cheltenham 1922, 'To Catherine Ord, "Miss Newcastle" with love from Jean. (Elsie Jeanette Oxenham).'

The year after publication of *The Abbey Girls Go Back to School,* Elsie must have been delighted by *Peeps at English Folk Dances* by Violet Alford which supplied much information about early dancing. Elsie once wrote a series in four parts about folk-dancing, probably originally in a Christian newspaper. They were written under headings as follows:

1. Folk Dancing as well as introducing the subject, compared the different types (country/sword/morris) and also told about her own early experiences.

2. Our Folk-Dance Parties described some classes, what clothes were usually worn, a little about 'the beautiful meaningful points of the dances' then ended describing a party EJO had attended, which had finished with a demonstration of *The Horn Dance of Abbot's Bromley.*

3. Holiday Schools began with a detailed account of one EJO went to at Cheltenham, but added 'These schools are held every holiday - Christmas, Easter, August - at different places all over the country' then explained more about the origins and traditions behind the dancing.

4. Variations of the Dance. This chapter told about dancing, as taught to 'The Tommies' during World War I but then the variations of steps and music, according to the district from which each evolved. For instance, of *Shepherd's Hey* she wrote "You learn it as an Ilmington dance, with stick-tapping and the funny hey; presently you come across it with Bampton arm-waves and back-steps. Then you find it is also a Headington solo jig, with hand-clapping, and then it turns up as a Badby dance, with sticks again, but quite different sticks. And last of all it is a Fieldtown dance, with handkerchiefs, as in Bampton, but no other likeness, either in tune or dance.'

She followed that by writing, 'Each time the tune has some fascinating little variation peculiar to its own village.' Her conclusion took the form of a postscript suggesting that:

'If you want a very jolly Christmas present, a book of delightful coloured pictures of the English Folk Dances has just been published, called *Mr North's Maggot.* There are pictures of sword dances, morris jigs and several of country dances and they are drawn by an artist who knows ALL about country dancing. The book costs 10/6 so if you can get anybody to treat you to one this Christmas, you must write to me and I will tell the artist to send you one.'

Later those articles were reprinted as a complete long item in *Every Girl's Annual* 1923. The artist who wrote and illustrated *Mr North's Maggot* was Stanley North, husband of Helen Kennedy North, the Madam of Elsie's books. There is a copy of the original in the Ralph Vaughan Williams Memorial Library at Cecil Sharp House. The manuscript on which he was said to have been working when Joy and Jen visited Madam in her new flat soon after their marriage could have been a version of *Aucassan and Nicolette,* another of the books he illustrated.

'Joy and Jen and Maidlin stood and looked at the wonderful hand-wrought books, an old French love-poem, which the artist-husband of their loved Madam laid before them.' Then Jen admired his work by saying, ' "It's like the work of the old monks, who lived in cells and cloisters, and had no time for outside, but only lived to make beautiful things." '

Other writers of that era sometimes mentioned folk dancing in their books for girls. Winifred Norling in *The Leader of the Rebels* (Sampson Low 1936) at a school display had each class dancing: country, Morris 'with staves', Running Set for the twelve-year olds, one solo jig and The Horn Dance of Abbat's Bromley (normally referred to as Abbot's Bromley). More authentic descriptions were included in books by Brent-Dyer and Fairlie Bruce, but once dancing was included in school curricula, several writers of the era tended to mention it in school stories for girls.

CHAPTER NINE

Real People
or 'Making Friends' (*Patch and a Pawn*)

But there is one very interesting thing about nearly all these people! If you talk to them long, you find they have 'girls' in the background. You hear about 'my girls' or 'my children.' Sometimes it's the children in their day-school classes; most of them are teachers, of course. But very often it's big girls, Guides, or a club, or Guildry girls to whom they're teaching folk-dancing in the evenings, mostly just for the love of it. They nearly all do it.
(*The New Abbey Girls*. 1923. p. 233.)

Elsie used many of the E.F.D.S. staff in her early Abbey books. At first there were no objections, but there was an obvious stop to the practice after *The Abbey Girls at Home*, a book of which EJO said, 'I always rather liked it myself!' But the Pixie, who made her first appearance in *The Abbey Girls Go Back to School* (p. 152), when given a copy, told EJO she 'couldn't get on with it.'

There have been many theories about why she stopped using E.F.D.S. people in her books; this change came at much the same time as the move by the Dunkerley family to Worthing. Either some of the staff were reluctant to be portrayed in Elsie's fictionalised-but-based-on-fact manner and let this be known, or the fictional Abbey characters had too many other occupations to attend classes, or Elsie realised that now Folk Dancing was no longer the main factor in her life, there was less need to write about it and its people. A likely solution could simply be that it was no longer as easy for EJO to attend classes from Sussex as when she lived in Ealing so she saw less of their staff. Also, once in Worthing she became involved in starting and teaching dancing classes locally, so would not have had time to attend many elsewhere as well. It is unlikely there was any real coolness between Elsie and the E.F.D.S. members, particularly as she continued to attend vacation schools and weekend classes whenever possible.

Cecil Sharp died in 1924 and, in view of his work over the years, his memorial took the form of a building in London named Cecil Sharp House which became the Headquarters of the Society. In 1993 a tapestry of embroidered squares, each made by a member of the [retitled] E.F.D.S.S. demonstrating various aspects of dancing, was unveiled there in the presence of the late Princess Margaret. One of those squares, based on a picture by Arthur Dixon for the first edition of EJO's *The Abbey Girls*, was stitched by Gillian Jackson, a member of Oxenham Societies, who also belongs to the E.F.D.S.S. The Australian Society did a similar scheme by asking members of the Abbey societies all over the world to embroider squares which were then sewn together. That second time Gillian provided an E.F.D.S.S. badge as would have been worn by

THE
ABBEY GIRLS
AT HOME

ELSIE J.
OXENHAM

COLLINS

dancers when they had attained their Advanced Certificates, and surrounded it with forget-me-nots for all the past Abbey Queens. Since its completion, the resultant form of a hanging banner has been taken to be displayed at the Australian national weekends. It is interesting to see the different angles chosen and worked by individuals.

Another theory about why there was less mention of E.F.D.S.S. people is simply that as related in *The Abbey Girls at Home* (p.235) when Mary-Dorothy told Jen that she had realised that Folk Dancing wasn't the only thing in the world and that others were of equal, if not more importance, perhaps EJO had reached the same conclusion. She had been over-enthusiastic with her first discovery of dancing being beauty personified and progressed naturally over the years to the fact that to be wrapped up in a single hobby, almost to the exclusion of anything else, wasn't as essential as she had first thought.

'There are more important things, *real* things. You're

105

feeling without quite realising it, that you'll have other things to do and that dancing will have to be kept in its proper place; that it can't be as important to you as it has been, and as it still is to Maidlin and Pat.' *(Abbey Girls at Home* p235)

At the same time in subsequent stories, various characters actually stated that with their growing families they had less time and opportunity to attend classes so, although they did that whenever possible, the fictional people were no longer depicted as being in such close touch with the E.F.D.S.S. staff as they had been in the earlier books.

Madam was obviously an idol to Elsie, but it is evident that they also became friends as one cannot imagine E.F.D.S.S. members inviting everyone from their classes to their homes. Elsie would not and could not have written about Madam's flat if she hadn't been there. The same applies to the flat the Pixie shared with two other working women as described in *The New Abbey Girls*. The surnames of the two others were accurate because, unless she gave them nicknames, Elsie did not normally invent names when describing real people. Doris Acland told enquirers that 'anyone given a nickname was a person EJO actually knew.'

Keenie was Miss Keen while The Prophet was Cecil Sharp; the Director/Joshua Douglas Kennedy and Madam was Helen Kennedy North. The most notable real people about whom Elsie wrote were those of the early E.F.D.S. and others mentioned in relation to dancing. Included in that group were Miss Newcastle (Catherine Ord) head of folk dancing in her home town, The Pixie (Daisy Daking), Mrs Joshua (the other Helen Kennedy), the Dear Little Robin (May Gadd), The Little Page (Maud Karpeles) and the Fiddler (Elsie Avril). One nickname not used in the books, was Sinner for Marjorie Sinclair. Elsie would have known Lavender Jones, one of the young women taught to dance by Cecil Sharp who became another of his travelling teachers. They always had to take the clothes needed for up to a week away, Morris sticks, swords, folk song books and the music needed, and carry all those on their train journeys, then stay wherever accommodation could be found and teach in whatever rooms

were provided.

Everything written in the books about Madam and the Pixie was factual. Madam had been one of the staff members who went to France in the 1914 war to teach the soldiers dancing and who worked towards their rehabilitation by the same method. The Pixie had also been in France, helping the soldiers over there and yes, she owned a caravan which was settled permanently in a Surrey field, as described in *Queen of the Abbey Girls*, where she entertained friends, including members of the Kibboo Kift, an organisation with which she was involved.

One of the Pixie's diaries, written in 1914 and amongst those kept at Cecil Sharp House, related how she and some friends went on a caravan tour through and around Oxford, not knowing that in a matter of weeks war would be declared and that most of the young men they knew would be killed.

Daisy Daking, the Pixie in the books, had a sister who died within a week of having given birth to a son. After unhappy years for the little boy with a stepmother, then in a children's home, the Pixie became his legal guardian and he lived with friends of hers in Oxfordshire. In view of all Elsie wrote about the Pixie's character, no one can understand how she could have committed suicide in May 1942, at which time she was the Superintendent of a hostel in London. Possibilities for the reasons she died as she did include the rejection of a book she had written on psychology. That seems unlikely, though, since two others she had written had both been published: *Feed My Sheep* and *Jungian Psychology and Modern Spiritual Thought*. The more likely reason is because her offers to work with the troops in World War II were refused. If she felt she was no longer wanted to do the type of work she had done

Cecil Sharp in his Library

during World War I so usefully, she could have felt she had nothing to live for as, whatever else she did, she had always been totally wrapped up in folk dancing.

The Pixie was four years younger than Elsie, having been born in 1884. That seems a little peculiar when realising how much Elsie in the form of The Writing Person was depicted as looking up to the Pixie as a fount of wisdom just as the first Abbey Girls were shown as doing during their early years. She was named Daisy Caroline but known by either name. She was teaching dancing before 1914 and in 1917 was a member of a Concert Party which went to France, to teach folk dancing to the troops. After the war, she continued to teach but also took a job in a shop in London's West End. That would have been designing dresses for Liberty's since Elsie put that store in more than one of her books as well as describing the Pixie designing a dress for Ruth and mentioning others of the workers.

Madam was a sister of Douglas Kennedy who appeared in *The Abbey Girls Go Back to School* as Joshua and who succeeded Cecil Sharp as Director of the E.F.D.S.S. She married Stanley North, an artist and picture-restorer. Amongst others he maintained the King's pictures at Windsor,

Sandringham and London. He and his wife were later divorced and Madam went to South Africa where she taught and examined folk dancing as she had done since the end of the first world war. Later she returned to England where she died at Tunbridge Wells in 1975. Stanley North also did illustrations for folk dance and other books.

A dancer who knew most of the E.F.D.S.S. people during the 1930s reported that:

'Marjorie Sinclair (the tall fair girl in blue of the books) was a very good teacher. Maud Karpeles (The Little Page) was concentrating by then entirely on folk music research which she did almost to the day of her death at the age of ninety. Elsie Avril was The Fiddler. The Kennedys, Douglas and Helen were very much in command. He, I liked very much; she was almost unbalanced about the dancing - it was almost a religion to her.'

This last reference is strange since originally Madam hadn't cared much for some of the dancing, as shown in an issue of the E.F.D.S. magazine in 1917 where she admitted that on her first introduction to Morris Dancing and until she learnt the history and reasons for the movements, she disliked it enough to avoid those classes.

Another dancer from even further back wasn't at all impressed by Douglas Kennedy who, once he was fully in charge, 'wouldn't give paid work of teaching to anyone unless it was to one of 'his young ladies'.' That dancer wrote that:

'Vaughan Williams was our greatest treat. He'd sit down at the piano, teach us how Folk songs should be sung. Quite an experience. The Pixie was a darling. Her work was nothing to sneer about; it meant constant hard work, self-giving to others, thought for others, self-sacrifice when she was tired out and others needed her strength and vitality. During World War II we were teaching dancing down in the Tube Shelters but The Pixie had already taught it in places like Holloway prison.'

The dulcitone played by Gail in *Rosamund's Tuck-Shop* was genuinely based on one played for classes and parties and is the kind of item Elsie would have tucked away in her mind until she could use it in a story. The zither Joy used is another matter entirely. After playing it in the Abbey and at her coronation it only reappeared in *The Abbey Girls Play Up* very briefly, then vanished from the books not to be mentioned again. This is a pity, as it had been such a useful item to carry around while creating music. Was it relegated because once Joy was having music lessons at school, she wasn't allowed to invent her own tunes unless at the piano? And where did it come from in the first place? Was it an instrument which had been brought from abroad at some stage by Elsie herself or anyone she knew, which she thought would make a nice item to include in her stories? John Ruskin had a Zythern at his home by Lake Coniston so it could just have been something about which EJO knew and thought would fit nicely into a book.

As well as portraying genuine dancers in her books, Elsie used other people with whom she was in close touch. It has been shown in Chapter 6 that the characters in her early books were given the Camp Fire names her own Camp Fire Girls had chosen and she would also have used them as models for her early imaginary schoolgirl Camp Fire Members, the way she took Margaret in *The Abbey Girls in Town* from Margaret Bayne Todd who had been an early model for Jen as a schoolgirl.

Madam with Roger

When Joy took Maidlin to London to meet her lawyer and to buy the child some better quality clothes, then rounded off the trip by taking her to watch a class (*The New Abbey Girls*), Maidlin told Joy all she had learnt from The Writing Person about some of the

Country Dancing by E.F.D.S. Team
in the Cheltenham College Cricket Field

dancers. Ally and Olly were sisters Elsie knew whose names would have amused her in view of her fondness for nicknames. Others would have been the right ages for Elsie to have taken them as models for future books.

She put a lot of herself into Mary-Dorothy and later Rachel Ellerton, both of whom were depicted as unmarried writers of books for girls. Mary-Dorothy was asked to teach in Sunday School as Elsie had done for most of her early life before she changed to Bible Classes, and it is safe to assume that Elsie went through those same initial misgivings, particularly since she would have been much younger than Mary-Dorothy was when she was asked to take a class in *The Abbey Girls Play Up*.

As well as using genuine sites, Elsie sometimes gave place names to her characters: Charlie Bassenthwaite — Lake Bassenthwaite. The Tarring sisters and their aunt — Tarring, a pretty village near Worthing. Quellyn is the name of a beautiful lake in Wales (Llyn Cwellyn) but that name was used deliberately to link Robin with the Abbey crowd. While

111

writing *New Girls at Wood End* EJO wrote to Doris Acland 'I was so glad to find Robin in the story. It's pleasant to meet an old friend.' That she had hoped to bring Robin back had already been shown by her references to the Quellyn pictures in books written after *The Girl Who Wouldn't Make Friends*. It has been suggested that the fictional Robert Quellyn, Robin's godfather who left her his home for her mother's sake, might have been based on a genuine artist, Christopher Williams, who drew pictures from the *Mabinogian* and was popular around the time when Elsie visited North Wales and could have been thinking of ideas for that story.

Cats described in her books were all ones she knew. There were usually dogs at home in her early days 'J.O. always had a dog' but she was 'passionately attached to cats and talked and wrote about them.' If there were horses in her books, they were illustrated on purpose to attract those girls who were particularly horse-minded as 'EJO thought them rather lovely creatures'. In *The Abbey Girls Play Up* was a description of the white animals at Marchwood Manor. Doris Acland explained that:

If there were horses …

'Although the Abbey twins had Tunnel for a short period, he didn't last long, neither did the white dog Jen had during the time when everything at Marchwood Manor was deliberately chosen to be white or yellow. There may not have been many dogs in the Abbey books because of the cats which were always in the Abbey as, to EJO, the cats would have had preference always. And she tried to get cats into most of her stories.'

There were 'the striped mother-cat, who had been the school

kitten, but had lost her position by producing a miniature of herself during the holidays' (*Damaris Dances*); Tib from the very first book *Goblin Island;* the Pouffe, based on one of the family cats and described in *Elsa Puts Things Right* then again in *Margery Meets the Roses*; Rachel's Miss Nigger and the Angel (*Guardians of the Abbey*); Quinty and Quentin (*Pernel Wins*); Ambrose pictured playing with the little 'strippit cat' (Minette) in the book of pictures given to Jen when she saved Lavinia from a falling tree. Not forgetting the Mother Superior and the Curate of the first Abbey stories, nor Kitty-sweet on being ... 'startled out of one at least of her nine lives at sight of his [Nicholas] moving brush, sprang back quite two feet in one big leap, and stood arching her small back and spitting in terror' (*Finding Her Family*) and many more, all of which had parts to play in the books. An amazing number of fans nowadays tend to give names they associate with EJO's characters to their pet animals; Tazy, Abigail/Abby/Abbey, Jenny-Wren, Minette, Ambrose/Amber, Min/Mor, Jandy-Mac and even Minou and the Minimacs.

Doris Acland was able to pass on the information that during the 1930s EJO had:

'... an elderly mother cat named Little Miss and of course, there were always new kittens. One especial favourite was Peter who is actually described as the Pouffe in the *Margery* stories. The publisher's reader originally objected to all the cat-bits in *Margery Meets the Roses*; she felt that cats were doubtless nice creatures, but there was altogether too much about this one in the story. In the end however it was left in. That reader also objected to Margery as being 'too romantic'! As Elsie said, if girls couldn't have romance when they were girls, when could they have it? It was their birthright.'

This is another indication that EJO was writing for older girls than is generally accepted and that girls to her did not mean young ones.

Grey Edward is perhaps the most famous of the cats Elsie put in her stories and everything he was shown as doing was based on reality. Elsie wrote a lot about him to Ribby in *Ribby's Book* including the fact that he was actually Maida's and had been brought home as a kitten:

' ... inside her jacket when he was only 6 weeks old - not even in a basket, and he was terribly afraid whenever a motor passed, and tried to climb up her shoulder as if he thought he would be safer if he could get down her back. I think he has never quite forgotten that she took care of him that day, and even now, if he seems sound asleep when she comes in at the front door, he lifts his head and listens. He doesn't need to hear her voice - he just knows her step'.

Another cat which Ribby was told about soon after Grey Edward joined the household, was 'a little black kitten-puss come to live with us, so I have christened him General Smuts. I don't see why Little Grey should be the only one with a swanky name.'

Grey Edward was really named Sir Edward Grey, but eventually had a collection of alternatives, Little Grey being the most usual. 'He was a beautiful cat: he was a silver, grey cat, rather small, with regular dark rings round each leg, like striped stockings, several dark necklaces round his breast, and long dark stripes down his back.'

The episode in *The School of Ups and Downs* when Grey Edward was shown coming into camp, soaking wet, after being out in the rain most of the night, was based on a genuine night. 'I was the very wettest cat you can ever have dreamt of. Every single hair on me was sticking to the next one'.

As well as occasionally giving characters names of her own relations, EJO's very early stories usually included a Katharine and Dorothy and much later a Katharine reappeared when given to Katharine Marchwood. Elsie sometimes repeated names in her books, duplicating them for girls who had nothing to do with each other, e.g. Rhoda in

Jen of the Abbey School while another Rhoda turned up in *Rosamund's Tuckshop* as a Kane cousin. There were Dorothy Nairn in *A School Camp Fire*, Dorothy Cheney and Dorothy Bayne in *Dorothy's Dilemma* and Dorothy Field in *Two Form Captains*. Most readers know about Avice who became Cicely's sister-in-law; less well known is Avice in *Damaris Dances*.

Many of those were likely to have been included at the request of girls Elsie knew who wanted their names put into her books. *Damaris Dances* had a Margery who wasn't the same as the girl of that name in *Margery Meets the Roses*. There are other duplicated names throughout the stories which lead readers to wonder if Elsie perhaps began by meaning a girl with a certain name to take part in another book at a later date. Using names again was something John Oxenham tended to do too; using different versions and spellings. A favourite of his was Margaret, probably because of his wife.

Cleeve Abbey Gateway

CHAPTER TEN

The Abbey
or 'The Valley of Flowers' (*The Captain of the Fifth*)

They faced a square green lawn. On each side were long gray buildings, richly ornamented windows, ancient doorways leading to winding stone passages or up flights of irregular steps. To the left stretched the cloisters, their roof upheld by old oak beams, long narrow windows with richly moulded arches allowing views of the green inner lawn.
(*The Abbey Girls*. 1920. p. 14.)

Although the abbey of the series was shown as being situated on the borders of Buckinghamshire and Oxfordshire, Cleeve Abbey in Somerset was the model described by Elsie Oxenham. When people asked her about the changed position she explained in letters:

'Although I based my abbey of Grace Dieu on Cleeve Abbey which is in the village of Washford, near Watchet, I moved it to Buckinghamshire to link up with the Hamlet Club girls. All the underground parts are made up, of course.'

Cleeve Abbey was founded for an order of Cistercian monks at the end of the 12th century. 1186—1198 are the dates given in various charters but 1198 has been suggested as being the year when the main buildings were started with more durable materials than the earlier ones, which would have been made of no more than wattle, mud or wood. The Abbey was dedicated to the Blessed Virgin and named Vallis Flora — the Roadwater Valley used to be known as the Vallis Florida of the monks — but soon became known as Cleeve Abbey after the village of Cleeve a mile away. Over the years, that village gradually changed to its present name of Old Cleeve. The Luttrell Arms in Dunster was once a residence for the abbots of Cleeve and there is a building there known as the Nunnery which they may have used as a guest house for pilgrims.

At Blue Anchor on the coast the monks had a Lady Chapel with a hospice for pilgrims together with a plot for a graveyard, but, after being damaged by rain and cliff falls, the chapel was rebuilt at Chapel Cleeve in 1455. Some four centuries later a private house was built there incorporating part of the remains of Chapel Cleeve. That house still retains some stained glass windows as well as a small well in its grounds.

A cobbled path, known as the Monks' Path, led from the Abbey to one of their monastic granges named Chapel Cleeve, which was for travellers. Another path led to an ancient pilgrims' hostel. Parts of these old paths still exist: beside the railway tunnel in the village of Washford is a flight of shallow stone steps which leads up to the fields with a path across it leading towards the coast. At the top of the rise are fragments of a cross which once marked the way to Old Cleeve Church. More steps may be found in the village of Old Cleeve which are reached via a steep, rocky and damp lane at the end of which is another flight of stone steps with a wooden gate at the top; beyond that is a flat stretch of cobblestones before a further lot of stone steps leading to another field path. The remains of yet another stone cross may still be seen at the side of a road in the area, dating from the days when it was used as a wayside shrine.

An old path, known as the Black Monks' Path, was said to be haunted by a monk in a black habit, although those of the Abbey wore white. 'They were Cistercians! Coarse white woollen

Cleeve Abbey General View (modern)

robes with a black head-dress' as Joan told the girls from Wycombe in *The Abbey Girls* (p. 18). The local police sergeant, Charles Clapp, used to relate that he had 'experienced a feeling of not being alone in the garden drive' of Cleeve Abbey. His daughter Cleeva Clapp wrote in her booklet *Cleeve Abbey As I See It* 'at times there is a strong feeling of unseen power.'

After the Dissolution of 1535, and the last monks vacated the Abbey in the spring of 1537, the buildings fell into ruins until a great house was established there using some of the original walls and the frater became the main hall of that house. Later the Abbey was used as a farm when, although a lot of damage was done to it, some of the general neglect may have helped towards preservation of the remaining walls. The rampant ivy protected parts of the walls from the worst onslaughts of the weather while for centuries the painting of the Crucifixion at one end of the refectory was covered and protected by a curtain of thick ivy. The layers of straw and dung did the same to the old tiled floors; while the grass growing everywhere outside did its share in covering and protecting what little was left of the foundations.

At the time of the Dissolution the King's receiver, Sir Thomas Arundell, (an interesting name in view of the fact that Arundel Castle was another site used by Elsie Oxenham in her books) wrote to Thomas Cromwell:

'Riding down to Cornwall and passing the monastery of Clyffe*, hearing such lamentations for the dissolution thereof ... I beg on behalf of the honest gentlemen of that quarter that the house may stand. In it are seventeen priests of honest life who keep hospitality to the good of the country.'

(*Highways and Byways of Somerset* 1924. p. 374.)

* The old name used was also sometimes written as Clyve.

Early prints and pictures of the Abbey show some of the changes over the years; at one time the entire building was almost completely covered with ivy. Others show trees growing against or even in some cases out of the walls; there were piles of stone and rubble inside the cells; tiles were missing from the roofs; there were clumps of ferns nearly everywhere; the refectory was almost hidden under its coating of ivy and a stone byre had been built inside the day room. The buildings were surrounded by broken fencing; grass behind the chapter house was waist-high and many of the walls had been scratched and defiled.

The roof of the dormitory gradually fell in when the buildings became used as a farm; the cloisters were made into two tiny cottages for workers; the garth became the main farmyard with a low wall built right across it; most of the monks' cells were turned into storage rooms or byres and some were used for keeping hay, apples and other produce. Part of the gatehouse

Old Cleeve - The Monks' Steps (modern)

Washford - The Monks' Steps (modern)

was widened to allow access for farm wagons. The people who lived there during the years as farmers occupied the rooms which had once been the abbots' lodge.

Included in early Guide Books of Cleeve Abbey is a picture of an old engraving attributed to T. Bonner c. 1790. A print of that same picture is described as 'Belonging to Sir James Langham Bart. To whom this Plate is inscribed by his Obliged Servant, J.Collinson.' The picture is not strictly true to the lay-out of the buildings: the refectory is shown accurately, but there is another small building in front of the abbots' lodge which may have been added to the building during the time when it was used as a Great House. The wall of the cloisters shows none of its old windows with their elaborate tracery and pillars; they could have been covered by an inner wall with plainer windows. The other side shown on the print has no sign of the chapter house entrance with its small windows on either side. The entire fourth wall is missing completely, presumably removed by the artist to show the others more clearly. Sheep, lying or grazing in the foreground are included on the print.

When the Dunster estate was inherited by Mr Luttrell in 1875, he bought the Abbey lands and set about the preservation and restoration of the buildings. The main archaeologist to inspect the ruins for him was the Reverend Mackenzie E. Walcott, B.D., F.S.A.. who, fortunately, wrote at least two accounts (1876 and 1915) about his investigations. In his undated *Memorials of the Cistercian Abbey of S. Mary Old Cleeve,* all the discoveries he and a Mr C. Samson, an

The Rose Window c 1910

architect from Taunton, had made, were fully described:

' ... modern walls, huge ancient fragments of rubble toppled over a hard road ... A sycamore grows out of the midst of an octagonal basement, which may have supported the cross round which the annual wool-fair was held.'

In *Memorials of the Cistercian Abbey of S. Mary,* Reverend Walcott gave measurements of parts of the Abbey and listed some of the discoveries such as loose tiles, pieces of glass, fragments from the old pillars, remains of the bell tower (he wrote that there would have been two bells there, not weighing more than 50lb as 'that was all that one monk could toll single-handed', and 'a canister of lead with a cross on the lid ... and

The Day Room c 1910

near it a solitary gargoyle.' He went on to describe the original
use of each room or cell in the Abbey, giving their individual
dimensions and adding details of the doors and windows with
their dates and architecture.

Reverend Walcott thought that the painted chamber might
once have been a buttery. He described it saying of the main
picture: 'It represents S.Thecla, at the right is S. Margaret and
on the left S. Katherine. Angels hover above.' Other sources
spell the name of that last as St. Catherine and Thecla as
Thekla. He explained the painting which was discovered at
the east end of the refectory as 'a distemper painting of the
Rood, Mary and John.'

He suggested that the Abbot's second room may have held
his bed. Another idea was that the second room could have
been occupied by each abbot's servant or chaplain. Little is
normally written anywhere about the calefactory, but the
Reverend Walcott described it as 'having windows looking out
upon the pleasant flowers and sweet smelling herbs, the humming
bee hives and green hedges of the abbots' garden.' Nothing
remains of the abbots' garden now and what would have been
grown there before the dissolution can only be identified from

general reference books. Probably there would have been a lawn with medicinal herbs as well as others for flavouring foods: vegetables, salad crops, edible and scented flowers, fruit trees, vines, bee hives and perhaps one or more dovecotes.

The Slype c 1910

In the account of the Reverend Walcott's findings from a paper (dated 1875) he read at a meeting held for the Royal Institute of British Architects in 1876, which included plans made by Mr Samson of the Abbey lay-out, he spoke in greater detail about pigs and calves having been kept in the cloisters and sacristy, carts and lumber in the chapter-house, hides being cured in the parlour, chaff and grain stored in various other places, whilst a cider-press had been built extending through a hole made in the floor of the refectory. There were pig-styes, a duck-pond to the north and there had once been moats to protect the Home Park, but they had been filled in by the 1870s.

He quoted from an even earlier account that 'the garth was half-covered with a loathsome ooze of dung and filth.' This was probably taken from an early report of 1794, which was quoted by him 'as the old homilist wrote two hundred years ago':

123

' ... the church is occupied by a shed for horses and cows ... the refectory is converted into a granary ... on the west were the cells of the monks, now stables to the adjoining farmhouse. All lay uncomely and fulsomely, defiled with rain and weather, with dung and other filthiness as it is foul and lamentable to behold, in many places in this country.'

In her books, Elsie Oxenham repeated a selection of the above facts by giving them to her fictional character of Joan Shirley to relate while showing Sir Antony over the Abbey in chapter XXII of *The Abbey Girls*. Not knowing the Abbey belonged to him, Joan said how grateful she was to Sir Antony. 'He saved it, you know.' Sir Antony asked her to describe it as it had been and was told:

'It was used as farm buildings, and the place was thick with dirt, and sheds, and things. There was a wall across the cloister garth, and fruit and hay were stored in the rooms, just as if they'd been barns. Think of the day-room used for straw, and the chapter-house for keeping apples! It seems sacrilege to me.'

Then Joan went on to say:

'He [Sir Antony] cleaned it all up, and made it as much as possible as it used to be, and now he takes the very greatest care of it. He has an expert come down from London regularly to be sure it's all right.'

Reverend Walcott wrote that although no traces of them were left, there would have been stables, a bake-house, brew-house, forge and similar out-buildings near the site of the lay-brothers rooms. All those would have been in the entrance court between the gate-house and the actual Abbey. A weekly market was held there as well as annual fairs on certain feast or saints' days.

The gate-house itself, which had one of two original walnut trees and a giant sycamore beside it, would have had a small dormitory in the upper story to be used as a guest-house. An opening on the ground floor was the means by which bread and ale could be given by the porter to travellers and, at night, there would have been an oil lamp kept burning there. The statues flanking the Rood had disappeared by 1886 as had the one on the other side of the gate-house below St Mary with her Child, where there should have been a figure of a kneeling abbot or monk.

Traces of a cemetery were discovered[1] on the north side of the old church. The chapter-house once had a bay, extending below the muniment-room but that had to be replaced by a dry stone wall. The abbots had been buried either under that floor or the cloister garth and there had been a fountain on the garth. An interesting fact is that the Reverend Walcott dated the origins of the Abbey even more precisely than the generalisation normally made of 'about 1188' by stating it was begun on June 24th of that year.

Details discovered in various documents included that:

'At the Dissolution of the late Abbey of Cleeve together with edifices, dovecots, stables, barns, gardens, a meadow ... plus the Chapel of the Blessed Virgin Mary of Clyve, belonging and appertaining to the said late monastery was rented by one Anthony Bustered, for a rent of £423.2.8.'

An account of Cleeve Abbey written in 1923 in *Country Life* by Christopher Bussey, beautifully illustrated and with the addition of two plans, gave a date for the erection of the market cross as being 1466. A particularly interesting explanation was given in that article about the old infirmary, gleaned from details learnt directly from Mr Luttrell. It appears that a Sir William Hope had once excavated a grassed area near the original monks' kitchen where traces of the infirmary were discovered with the remains of a chapel at one end. Further work was carried out on the kitchen area after 1960 but as far as can be ascertained, nothing was discovered of any other foundations or remains.

Although mention is made in assorted old guide books of an infirmary, stables, a guest house and the cellarer's range, a cider or wine press, nothing remains of those today. But Elsie Oxenham knew about the infirmary site as in *The Abbey Girls* she wrote that Joan 'pointed out the site of the old infirmary, where once had stood a long hall filled with beds, and opening into a little chapel.'

Similarly EJO described the abbots' garden with Joan working there (*The Abbey Girls*) as:

A grave (modern)

'... a tiny place, but now as gay with roses and lilies as the gardener's care could make it, and probably in much the same state as when the white-robed monks looked out from their labours in calefactory, garde-robe, or day-room - unless, indeed, their strict ideals had led them to banish flowers and grow chiefly herbs, which she thought possible. Perhaps, however, their well-known love for nature had led them to be broad-minded in this respect. Joan busied herself cutting off faded pansies and tying up sweet peas ...'

There used to be a Home-park which now is just a field. At one time the lay brothers' building, which shared the same wall as the outer wall of the cloisters, had an upper storey. That would have been used for the accommodation of guests as well as the Gatehouse dormitory and, if so, would have been very convenient for anyone who went to the markets held at Cleeve who wanted there to stay overnight.

The monks owned five granges or farms in the area, other chapels and at least one mill, possibly two. One mill is just a little further along the road from the Abbey; the main part is now a house, but there had been a water pond (which has been filled in) served by the monks' fish stream, and a water

126

wheel which has also gone, but the hoppers and crushers could still be seen there in 1990. Most of the granges these days have been converted and are occupied as private houses or farms.

A chapel some seven miles away is now part of a working farm but there is a separate building behind the farmhouse; an older chapel in a cobbled yard made of the same stones as the Abbey, its beams blackened by age. Two rooms were added to that farm in 1626. By the middle of the eighteenth century, the farm had become something of a mission centre and its chapel was served by Benedictine monks.

Blue Anchor Bay was once known as Cleeve Bay and old maps show Chapel Cleeve, Cleeve Hill and even a Cleeve Bay Villa in the area. The small town of Monksilver is reputed to have connections with Cleeve Abbey, the most visible being an inscription over the door of a big country house there [Combe Sydenham] which in translation, says 'Gate Open Be to all grateful souls'. This is remarkably like the one over the gatehouse at Cleeve Abbey, which is usually translated as 'Gate Open Be, to all men free.' Recent restoration work at Combe Sydenham exposed a tiled floor in the Great Hall, almost identical with the tiled floors at Cleeve. The one at

The Chapter House c 1910

127

Combe Sydenham has been covered by a new floor with just a few pieces of the original tiles kept on display.

The abbot's lodge, the part of the Cleeve Abbey used during the years of occupation as a farmhouse, was restored and opened to the public in 1991. Notices were added at the same time giving the names and explanation of what each area of the Abbey had been used for. Figures of monks have been placed in one of the new rooms so visitors may see the type of clothes worn by them. Artefacts are on display in a large glass-fronted case as each visitor enters that part of the Abbey. The room at the top, next to the painted chamber and known as the abbots' chamber, is where the various abbots slept in later years; much earlier they would have shared the dormitory with the monks.

Books on the history of monasteries in Great Britain abound, and for several years Cleeve Abbey was used as the model for lectures given by Bristol University, being near enough for students to be taken on guided tours of a typical abbey. Cleeve Abbey was chosen as being a site representative of the late twelfth century, although at that time not much more would have been there than the foundations of the original church with somewhere for the monks and lay brothers to live and worship whilst carrying out their building work.

The monks were known to have chosen their sites with a view to the future and permanency and it wasn't until the bad flooding of 1993-1994 that Cleeve Abbey suffered from a new problem. The amount of water which poured down from the Brendon Hills covered the entire site to a depth of three feet in the sacristy. It was feared that constantly being covered by that amount of flood water would have a detrimental effect on the tiles, ruining the glaze and patterns. Fortunately the water receded quickly so that those and the remaining floor tiles in other parts of the Abbey weren't unduly endangered after all.

[1]Reverend Walcott. *Memorials of the Cistercian Abbey of S. Mary, Old Cleeve.*

Cleeve Abbey Chapter House.

CHAPTER ELEVEN

Caretakers of the Abbey
or 'The Abbey Sanctuary' (*The Abbey Girls*)

'What about the Abbey? Mary-Dorothy's forgotten, but it's after ten and this is Saturday. There may be troops of tourists here at any moment, and there's no time to fetch anybody. You and I must be the caretakers for today, and show the Americans round. Are you game?' (*Guardians of the Abbey*. 1950. p. 55.)

Elsie and her mother were staying with cousins at Weston-super-Mare when they first learnt of and visited Cleeve Abbey in Somerset. Elsie was so attracted by the ruins that she decided to use them in her next book. Afterwards she told people, 'The door was opened by a girl with a very pretty voice. That gave me the first idea for my story.'

That girl was Frances, a grand-daughter of Charles Clapp who, with his family, had been the first person to occupy the Abbey after its long use as a farm. Frances lived there from 1909 until her marriage ten years later, helping her aunt Cleeva, particularly after the death of Charles Clapp who had

Cleeva Clapp c 1895

been in charge for nearly forty years. When Mr Luttrell decided to open Cleeve Abbey to the public, he had provided accommodation there for a custodian: Charles Clapp with his wife and family. In 1877, when a daughter was born in the Abbey to Sergeant and Mrs Clapp, Mrs Luttrell decreed that 'the child must be called Cleeva with the 'a' because of the Abbey.'

Cleeva Pevensa Clapp, becoming the custodian after her father, lived in the Abbey all her life until she retired to a cottage in the village. She died in April 1955. Although not very old when her mother died, as the youngest daughter of a large family, she was the one who stayed there, helping with the Abbey and caring for their father until his death in 1913.

Cleeva was quite a character, especially in her later years. She was very tall and walked with a stick with which she used to threaten small boys from the village when they went scrumping for apples in the Abbey grounds. She often walked around with a parrot sitting on her shoulder; the parrot's cage hung on the Abbey wall below the old bell-chamber. Poultry, including geese, were kept in the grounds and were useful for keeping the grass cropped, possibly also to act as alarms to intruders. Vegetables were grown behind the refectory for firstly the Clapp family, Cleeva and her father, Cleeva with Frances, then while there on her own, making them virtually self-sufficient in their different ways and needs.

Cleeva Clapp bought one of the earliest cars and, having decided she didn't want to drive, arranged for various chauffeurs to take her wherever she wished to go. One of those drivers was Sidney Lovelace, another person who helped in the Abbey. In his turn, Sidney became an Abbey Guide and he was written about in *That Special Smile* (1951) by Monica Hutchings, who described him as 'happily doing the job he loved in the place of which he thought so much'. Like Cleeva in her latter years, he carried a stick with which he pointed out items he thought would be of particular interest to visitors. He was totally involved with the Abbey and used to sell sketches he made of the place, some of which were also produced as black and white postcards.

Steps to the Monks' Dormitory
(modern)

Sidney's wife Alice wrote that 'both of us spent a great deal of time helping our dear Cleeva in her endeavors to make the Abbey interesting to all visitors, and helping with her restoration efforts there.'

Where Sidney's talent lay in drawing, Cleeva's was for photography and many of her photographs of the Abbey and local areas were produced as postcards for visitors to buy. Sidney's black-and-white drawings, as well as being of specific areas such as the cloisters and the gatehouse, showed closer details of individual parts such as the corbels on the roof of the refectory or the window tracery. Cleeva's were of particular places like the gatehouse, the chapter house, the refectory and so on. Cleeva Clapp's cards were available singly or as collections in envelopes or small brown albums. A few postcards exist from even earlier, but those by Cleeva and

Chapter House and Steps to Monks' Dormitory c 1910

Sidney are of particular interest to fans of the Abbey books since they show the Abbey as it was in the early part of the twentieth century the time when Elsie Jeanette Oxenham began visiting the Abbey frequently, thus depicting it as it was when she first went there and as she used it for backgrounds to her Abbey books..

A Doctor Norris and his daughter Maud lived next door and Maud Norris and Frances Clapp became very friendly; they were both enthusiastic gardeners and worked together in the abbots' garden. By the time Maud and Frances were caring for it, there would only have been flowers grown there and possibly a few herbs, but they would also have tended the vegetable plot behind the refectory.

Maud joined Sidney and Cleeva in another direction: her talent lay in making water colour paintings of the Abbey which were offered for sale to visitors. Pictures of hers which still exist include the gatehouse and the abbots' lodge. During her years spent in the Abbey, Frances showed people around since, as Mrs Shirley was depicted by EJO in the Abbey books, once she was nearing middle age and using a stick, Cleeva Clapp didn't find it easy to climb the stairs.

Between them Cleeva and her niece provided teas for

visitors; Cleeva made scones, then Frances carried cream teas to customers who ate them in the abbots' garden on fine days. The notice advertising those teas is visible on some old postcards. An article about Cleeve Abbey written in 1923 included '... the caretaker, who provides most delicious Somersetshire teas.'

Dormitory c 1910

Frances was told that ' "Squire" Luttrell would not allow visitors to ramble about on their own after one of the tiles had been stolen and names had been written on the walls.' She informed me that 'Miss Oxenham would obviously have been one of the few allowed to go around on her own, thanks to her several visits over the years, but even regular visitors I rarely knew by name.' The Clapp family lived in the former Abbots' Kitchen where they had:

'A kitchen, larder and sitting room, both very big. The staircase went up from the kitchen to the bedrooms which used to be the lay brothers' dormitory. There was a long landing with three bedrooms leading from it; afterwards a bathroom was added. At the end of the passage was where the lay brothers handed the meals, the doorway had the remains of a place for the dish or tray to be passed through. There was a passage over the refectory

Inside the Refectory c 1890

steps into the 15th century refectory (built by the last Abbot Dovell).
We had a very large sitting room from this. At the other end of
that passage was a blocked-up door.' (Letter from Frances
Evered.)

A photograph of their living room downstairs taken at that
time shows a settle beside the fireplace; the wood from which
it was made came from a local tree. On one wall was a picture
of Queen Victoria, while pictures above the fireplace included
one of the Abbey gatehouse.

Elsie changed the caretaker's rooms in her books by making
them much smaller and putting them all on ground level.
Rather than write about the rooms the family inhabited during
the years she knew Cleeva Clapp, she implied that those in
her Abbey books were behind the cloisters on the site of the
lay brothers' dormitory. There, she described them as being
individual small cells. Joy's grand piano was put into the main
one, which seems slightly unlikely in view of the size of most
cells in the Abbey and their entrances. The well the Clapp
family used for drinking water was one used by the monks in
a cell just outside the Abbot's lodge, but there were others
within the Abbey grounds. Another, known as the Holy Well,
is in the garden of what is now a private house where it looks

Outside the Refectory c 1890

more like a small grotto, enclosed by and covered with ferns.

The author H. W. Kille (of *Rambles Round Minehead*, c.1910) was so impressed by Miss Clapp's abilities as a guide that in his booklet he wrote '... a guide whose description will be found so complete that no apology need be offered for omitting to enlarge here on the architectural or historic features of the place' then informed the reader that 'Guides to the Abbey may be obtained of Miss Clapp at the Abbey or of Cox, Sons and Co. Ltd., Minehead and Williton.' A curious point was made in his booklet where he advised people how best to reach the Abbey on foot. At the end of the walk, he wrote about descending the Cobblers' Steps at the side of the railway. Those steps, reached after walking across the field via the Monks' Path, or through the small village to the railway arch, have been known for decades as the Monks' Steps so it is interesting to ponder whether both names were used, if the name changed at any time, or who were the Cobblers after whom they were named in his version?

It wasn't only 'the girl with the pretty voice' who was put into the books. Many incidents which EJO would have learnt from Cleeva or Frances were used, such as the names written on

135

the walls by visitors then given by EJO to Dick Jessop in *Girls of the Abbey School*. The fact that an uncle and aunt of Cleeva's ran a ferry was a helpful idea for *Elsa Puts Things Right*. Artefacts having been found in the grounds gave the idea of abbey treasures for the first few titles of the *Abbey* run. The old man who loved the Abbey so much that he wanted to spend the rest of his life there came into *Schoolgirl Jen at the Abbey* and was probably based on Sidney Lovelace. The legend about the Felons' Oak may well have inspired her idea of a highwayman in that same story.

Until the onset of World War II, EJO tried to visit Cleeve at least once every year to wander alone and to sit in the rose window, dreaming plots and ideas for the next books. She had many photographs she had taken herself but a set of large sepia ones was done by a friend for her to use at any time she needed a quick reference while writing her books. It isn't always easy to work out the difference between fiction and reality if anyone tries to think about which rooms she took or invented for various usage, but maps have been drawn by readers of her books to indicate where some of the underground tunnels and treasures might have been sited

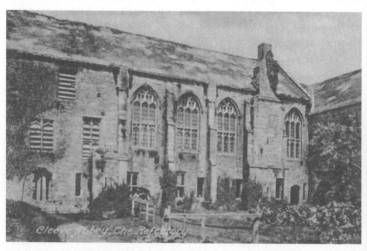

Outside the Refectory (the other side) c 1890

for the purpose of her plots. Another map has been made giving a possible lay-out of Mrs Shirley, Joan and Joy's fictional rooms.

The present custodians of Cleeve Abbey, two sisters, are members of English Heritage who now owns the site. They are keeping the tradition in the family, as their father Hubert

The Gatehouse and Stream (c 1920)

was the caretaker there for twelve years following a long period after the death of Sidney Lovelace, when, apart from someone from the village, few were there to take entrance fees. Maureen Freeguard has been there since 1978 and her sister, Dawn Berry, joined her in 1987.

Cleeva Clapp lived in the Abbey through different eras of the restoration work and many of those years coincided with the period when Elsie Oxenham was a frequent visitor. During the 1930s, Cleeva was able to see what was found in the monks' fish stream; earlier she had seen the remains unearthed in the cloisters which had once been the monks' burial ground. So EJO, as a known and regular visitor, would have been shown and told about all the latest finds on her next visits to the Abbey.

The Gatehouse (modern)

When one of the walnut trees in the grounds died and had to be cut down, Cleeva was allowed to have some of the wood from which to have a stool made for Frances' son, Cleeva's great-nephew Phillip, as a permanent memento. This was a real treasure; wood from a tree planted so long ago and still in use as a piece of furniture nearly five centuries later.

There had been at least two early walnut trees at Cleeve: one at a corner of the old church and another by the gatehouse where for centuries there was also a large sycamore. When the walnut tree at the end of the old church was removed, the base of a pillar was exposed and permission was given to excavate the west end of that area, thus making the outline of the whole site more clearly visible. As walnut trees were first grown in England from the early 1500s it is likely that those at Cleeve were introduced by Abbot Dovell.

Two booklets about Cleeve Abbey were written by Cleeva Clapp during the years she spent there. *Cleeve Abbey as I See It* took readers on a tour of the Abbey as seen through her eyes. In the first she gave a very brief account of the origins of Cleeve Abbey and a little about the history of the Cistercian Order. She also explained the work of the monks before the Dissolution, including the annual sheep markets which were held in the courtyard outside the Gatehouse.

'The monks would have been sheep farmers, used the fleeces for clothes and for floor coverings then, having cured and treated the skins, made vellum for their books. There is a room known as 'The Painted Chamber' upstairs and on the wall outside is a caricature of a monk; it has been suggested that some of the paintings there might have been done by the monks, practising, before being allowed to work on their actual books.'

Cleeva Clapp related how after Mr Luttrell took over the Dunster estate in 1875 and bought the Abbey, he began the work of restoring the ruins which for many years had been misused as has been shown, firstly as a great house, then as farm buildings. Her booklet then took the form of a guided tour round the site, explaining what would have been done by the monks in each part of the Abbey. Some items Cleeva mentioned are no longer there; for example, coffin lids dug out during the 1930s excavations were once kept in the sacristy but have now been removed. The floor tiles with the coats of arms of various benefactors and knights she described as being coloured, have now faded to a uniform grey and buff. She also wrote about the wall with the Crucifix which had been preserved for centuries by the ivy which had grown over it. Once the ivy was removed, the original plaster began to deteriorate to such an extent that the entire wall had to be re-plastered, thus the painting of the Crucifix and St John and St Mary have been lost for ever, other than as shown in old pictures and postcards. The income for one whole year from the wool gained from the monks' flock of sheep was given for the ransom of King Richard I.

Miss Clapp's other booklet, *The Voice*, described a vision she thought one of the abbots she suggested as being an Abbot Juan in 1484, might have had. In *The Voice* she named a few of the monks, saying what their work probably would have been. That second little book contains far less about the actual Abbey but gives more details of the surrounding countryside: the Brendon Hills, Watchet, the Church Paths, Bridgwater, Tintern and Forde Abbey, going as far afield as St Michael's Mount in Cornwall.

Elsie Oxenham owned copies of both booklets as well as one about the church of St Andrew in the village of Old Cleeve and a selection of the postcards produced in the first instance by Cleeva Clapp and Sidney Lovelace. She also had a copy of *Memorials of the Cistercian Abbey of S. Mary, Old Cleeve and the Benedictine Priory Church of S. George, Dunster,* to give it its full title, by Mackenzie E.C.Walcott B.D.F.S.A. who did the preliminary work at Cleeve Abbey for Mr Luttrell.

EJO obviously often referred to that last booklet as she marked several entries lightly in the margins. One of the most intriguing for collectors of the Abbey books is where Reverend Walcott cited names as examples of those used by the Cistercians when they were looking for relevant names to suit places where they settled. Elsie obviously debated using variations from those for her fictional Abbey of Grace Dieu, which was amongst those names she underlined in pencil as well as marking a few of them in the margin.

Cleeva's love of and for the Abbey comes through very strongly in both her booklets; and oddly, in view of EJO's Camp Fire associations, Cleeva gave Abbot Juan a possible creed, some words of which are very similar to the Law of the Camp Fire.

Abbot Juan's Creed:

The desire of Love	Joy
The desire of Life	Peace
The desire of the Soul	Heaven
The desire of God	A flame, white, secret for ever

The Law of the Camp Fire being:
Seek beauty
Give service
Pursue knowledge
Be trustworthy
Hold on to health
Glorify work
Be happy

The Abbots at Cleeve:

1198	Ralph
	[Waleran?]
	Alan?
	Hugh
	William
1248	John Godard
1297	Henry (Cleeve was then spelt Clyve).
1315	Richard le Bret
1321	Robert le Clyve
1338	Henry
1367-8	James
1407	John Mason
1416	Leonard
1419	William Seylake
1421	John Stone
1435	David Juynor (received a grant to cover the cost of re-building the Chapel of St Mary from Blue Anchor, at Cleeve.)
1487	Humphrey
14??	W. Donestere / William Dunster
1500	Henry
15??	John Paynter
1510	William Dovell (17 monks)

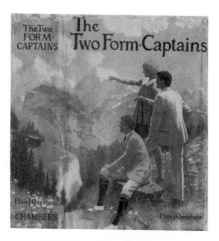

CHAPTER TWELVE

Some Places Abroad
or 'A Home in France' (*Damaris Dances*)

But on the south side the wall was most wonderful, for here were three great black mountains rising right out of the fields, and reaching up towards the clouds. Two ended at last in long ragged ridges, snow-capped, and with white in every rent of their rocky sides. The third had a magnificent snowy peak, thrusting boldly up, which easily crowned him king of the valley, and an immense rocky shoulder turned to the girls, as if to hold them off and bid them keep their distance. From this shoulder, the mountain fell in one sheer precipice to the valley, many thousand feet below, a straight wall of jagged black rock.
(*The Twins of Castle Charming*. 1920 p 161.)

In her biography of their father (*Scrapbook of JO*. 1946 p. 69), Erica wrote: 'J.O. was fortunate in being able to recall scenery which perhaps he had not seen for years and to describe it so that others could see it too.' That ability could equally have been applied to EJO, of whom Doris Acland confirmed that she:

'used every background that really struck her fancy and wove

Trummelbach Falls

stories against it. She didn't need be in a place long to seize its atmosphere and characteristics and she used all its details conscientiously.'

At the same time, EJO modified, combined or moved places to suit her story-line. Her sister Theo contributed that 'Elsie went to France once or twice with our father.' Elsie obviously remembered it well from the accounts in *Biddy's Secret* which were based on those holidays. But once Erica became J.O.'s secretary and travelling companion, Elsie made fewer subsequent trips with him, although judging by the dedications in her books, her journeys abroad continued for some years after that change and were still taken at times with either her parents or friends. Those later holidays were usually spent in Switzerland.

One memorable holiday, which meant spending a night in Paris, was when she and Margaret Bayne Todd went to Annecy with J.O. Somehow he and all their luggage went onto a train leaving Margaret and Elsie behind. Such an upset could well have given EJO the idea and experience of people missing trains and in consequence having to stay overnight, unplanned, as she portrayed Phyllida, Frances and Ven doing in *The Troubles of Tazy* (p. 24), thanks to Tazy having forgotten the time of the last train that day. 'But there's another - *my hat!* It isn't Thursday, is it?'

With the exception of *Expelled from School,* the Swiss books were all based around Mürren above Lauterbrunnen. Not many people care for *Expelled from School*, feeling it far too exaggerated in content, but one (anonymous) person enjoyed it so much that she inscribed her copy of the book with the following words:

'This is the best book I have ever read and is obviously a credit to its authoress. Adventure, comedy and tragedy are all three united in a perfect combination. Every girl of 14-21 should endeavour to gain and secure this book. Examples are set and misfortunes complied with in a general respect that makes every minute trifle a thrill to experience. The authoress is indeed in close communication with foreign boarding school [sic].

A satisfied reader - E.

The Blue Lake where Patience Joan Swam

Elsie's first trip to Switzerland was taken with her mother; but after the railway link was made, she went either with her mother, her father, both parents together, or with friends. An early visit with her mother was in July 1914 when they stayed at the Palace Hotel, Mürren. Elsie wrote to her sisters that 'Mürren is very wonderful, left one stunned and breathless.'

In Grindelwald Elsie stayed at the Schoenegg Hotel and although by 1994 there was a huge modern building there, the original old Chalet has been retained at the side, with the date of 1868 when it was built, inscribed under its eaves.

Of Trummelbach EJO wrote home, 'It is an awesome place! Wet and cold and torrents, and black walls - wonderful and quite unforgettable.' In that letter she informed her sisters she had been 'wet through and chilled to the bone.' The river where Billy had to leave Astrid with Jacques, and Tazy's underground puddle (*The Captain of the Fifth*) both have 'railings alongside the more dangerous stretches and there are bridges over some of the falls.'

144

from *Patience and Her Problems*

Expelled from School

More discoveries have been made since the time when Elsie was travelling to Switzerland for occasional holidays. There are seven glacier-waterfalls inside the mountain caves of the Lauterbrunnen valley; only the first and second waterfalls inside Trümmelbach were accessible by 1886 but all seven by 1911 when a lift and lighting were provided. This is what Elsie would have found when she first went there. Even a few years later and with more lighting inside, the caves are awe-inspiring, and must have been much more so when EJO saw them for the first time.

EJO's next story set in Switzerland after *Expelled from School* was *The Two Form Captains* which, as it was the first introduction of Karen and Tazy, has a remote connection with the Abbey Girls, through *The Abbey Girls Go Back to School* in which both groups of girls met through staying in the same house in Cheltenham and their mutual interest in dancing and the music.

The Blue Lake (Blaumsee) where Patience Joan swam in *Patience and Her Problems* has now, as well as tea rooms on its bank, a trout hatchery, and is a focal point for guided tours. The hotel in which EJO would have stayed looks much the

same from the outside as it was then. Brochures in a hotel in Wengen confirmed that anyone can still see the branches and tree trunks turned to stone, from a boat in the middle of the lake, as Svea and Doreen told Tazy in *The Two Form Captains*. As she felt with Nevin later, Elsie wouldn't have cared for the entire area once it had become more commercialised. The Blumenthal is included in an advertised walk which 'gives access to rich flora and fauna.'

The river in *The Captain of the Fifth* (1922) over which Astrid and Nils threw the tennis balls containing ideas for homework subjects at first, then Gulielma's messages in reply to the boys' notes, is narrow, very swift and deep, as it is described in the Swiss group of books. There is even a plank bridge across it although probably not in the same position as where EJO placed one for the boys and girls to cross when they went to the chalet to learn about woodwork, where Jacques and Jules the old Swiss carvers taught them in *The Captain of the Fifth* (Chap. XXI et seq.). The meadows across which Tazy walked to school in *The Two Form Captains* remain much as when Elsie first saw them, filled with the same types of flowers in which Tazy revelled on her first days going to and from her new school, but one side is now built up with chalets, a few shops, and more hotels.

A travel guide covering the area gave under a heading 'From Spiez to Brig railway' the information that '... this line known also as the Lötschbergbahn was opened in 1913 as a new short cut between France and Italy, and lessens the journey from the Bernese Oberland by three to five hours.' That must be the Lötschberg tunnel above the Blue Lake and Kandersteg, the tunnel which Elsie mentions so often, crossing the Rhone afterwards. She and her mother also once stayed at Spiez in the Hotel Erica, on the Thunnersee; the Kander valley leading to the Blue Lake is due south of that.

It is not known whether EJO had any contacts in Australia other than the collectors to whom she was sending books from the 1930s onwards, but she could have gleaned information from them if she needed any. All she wrote about Jandy Mac and Samoa was remembered from the Ealing days. When asked by collectors about any connection or knowledge of Samoa she replied with her standard reply of:

'The girls of the dedication in *Schoolgirls and Scouts* were the daughters of Samoan missionaries, who spent their school holidays with us - a great many years ago. 'Ma le alofa' is 'my love to them'.'

References to Kenya in Elsie's books would have been as a result of the years her brother Hugo spent there. He sent the family copies of the articles he wrote for his paper, many of which were about his life and what he saw around him all the time. As well as those, J. O. once visited Hugo and Prim for several months and wrote long letters home describing their experiences and all that the three of them discovered as they went on safari, or were simply about their daily living conditions. Details about J.O.'s trip and extracts from some of their father's letters are given in Erica's book *J. O.,* published in 1942.

EJO only wrote in depth about places where she had actually been herself so, as far as her books were concerned, although she had the information in her head, it was enough merely to say in the Abbey stories that Ken Marchwood had worked in Africa, and that Andrew and Joy went there for their honeymoon. There was also another brief statement when Jen and Ken went there on their tour after Ken's long illness. Ruth Devine, of course, must also not be forgotten, with the small reference in *The Abbey Girls in Town* to her father's poor health having 'taken him out to the Cape'.

In that same book The Writing Person had admitted to having 'cousins near Odzi' and being lax about writing to them and had then added 'I'm afraid my letters to Odzi are few and far between.' But there were relatives of the Dunkerley family living near Odzi in Southern Rhodesia (which later became Zimbabwe). The farm from which Ruth was said to come would have been very isolated back in the 1930s, with Salisbury (now Harare) being the nearest city.

CHAPTER THIRTEEN

Places in the North
or 'Reels and Strathspeys' (*Strangers at the Abbey*)

The loch was a smooth, unbroken stretch, gleaming silver in the sun, dark with reflections near the shore. On his right the hills rose steep and rugged. Across the water the lower slopes were clothed with dense woods of feathery torches and sombre firs, but the rounded crests above were bare. The shining water between stretched away to the mouth of the loch, where, instead of the sea, rose the fiery purple hills of a great island, with a tiny green islet at their feet. Above the heathery crags were two twin mountain peaks, palest blue against the sky.
(*A Princess in Tatters* 1908. p. 22.)

When necessary EJO modified, combined or moved places to suit her story-line. The most obvious example of this procedure is the Abbey being taken from Somerset and sited in Buckinghamshire/Oxfordshire, but she tended to do it with distances as well. Doris Acland always explained to correspondents that:

'Elsie has always been to the places she described; to the little seaside places in Wales and to the various bits of Switzerland

150

and France which come into her stories. But she was usually there for holidays; whenever she was drawn to a place, she liked her characters to be in it too.'

Goblin Island and the start of *Princess in Tatters* were based on the Cowal Peninsula, an area EJO knew well thanks to holidays spent with her mother's relations in Scotland. It is surprising she didn't use the little town of Inverkip itself as that is full of history which could have given her excellent background incidents to bring into her stories. The local big house, the Mansion of Ardgowan, belonged to a descendant of Robert III.

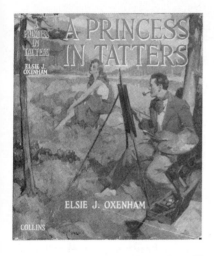

There is another slight connection there with Dorita Fairlie Bruce as Inverkip is only a short distance from Skelmorlie where Dorita Fairlie Bruce set several books. She used local historical facts in her stories, which Elsie would have known almost as well as those she used in her own.

Their books with Scottish settings read almost as mixtures of EJO and DFB as they both used parts of the Roseneath Peninsula, but opposite sides. The castle of Vairy is thought to have been modelled on Knockderry Castle which looks down over Loch Long. Transport when the Dunkerleys visited Scotland regularly would have been largely by means of steamers. Elsie was always a good walker, and once she had reached a hitherto unknown loch, would happily have explored the environs on foot then put combined details into subsequent stories. She is known to have visited Loch Fyne, so to add details of the Gare Loch, Lochs Long and Eck and amalgamate them for descriptions of walks would have been second nature

Knockderry Castle - the probable model for *The Secrets of Vairy*

to her. The writer Mabel Esther Allen thought that Elsie's Loch and Ben Avie were based on Loch and Ben Lomond.

The Lake District figured in books about Damaris and Rachel 'sitting on a rocky bluff gazing down at Rydal Water, where every leaf and rock were mirrored in the dark, gleaming surface of the lake.' Then in the fleeting visit from Jen and Maidlin in *Maidlin to the Rescue* (p.181):

'Huge rock walls, strewn with boulders, swept up on each side almost from the road; the Pass was a very real Pass and almost awe-inspiring. Streams came spouting down in numberless cascades, and tumbled along through heather and rocks; the still air was filled with the sound of splashing water. Then came another sound - the crying of sheep and lambs; and half the gray fallen rocks proved to be mountain mothers with their children.'

Buxton was a place she visited with Margaret Bayne Todd; a town which had a large cave in a hill with stalactites and stalagmites, many of which had been named and could, along with Cheddar, have given her some of the ideas incorporated in *Adventure for Two* when Elsa discovered the underground parts of the fictional Caer Ogo on the island off the Somerset coast.

The Edge where Rena and Nancy first met Lisabel in *A Go-Ahead Schoolgirl* was Froggatt Edge which, after passing along Curbar Edge, meets Curbar Gap. That whole area provided settings and ideas for books. Groups of rocks with local names such as Cakes o'Bread, The Ox Stones or The Salt Cellar would soon have given Elsie, with her quick visual imagination, The Hen and Chickens. But while she could easily have taken the Cow and Calf, a well-known formation of rocks near Ilkley and moved it for the sake of her story, it seems far more likely that she invented the name and combined several clusters of rocks to make one to fit her needs. There is a group known as The Rocking Stones which gave her the idea about some of those which Rena and Nancy discovered.

Elsie must have travelled extensively in Derbyshire and Yorkshire as rocks she mentioned are on Derwent Edge, but others are at Ilkley, Hathersage and Brimham Rocks in Nidderdale, yet described by her as if they were all close together in the same area. Lodge Moor Fever Hospital with the old smallpox unit next door provided the necessary isolation hospital for Priscilla, making another genuine place which EJO incorporated in *A School Camp Fire*. In that book (p.48) Dorothy Ann said, 'I want to see those two funny rocks we've looked at so often, standing up on the hill like pillars.'

When Priscilla took Dorothy Ann and Katharine to see them: 'to their vast amazement, they found the 'rocks' not rocks at all, but masonry, the ruined pillars of some ancient house or gateway, built of great squared blocks of stone, with the remains of arches springing

153

from their sides, and holes for cross-beams.'

It is strange that Elsie didn't go into more detail about Fountains Abbey, when Priscilla, Katharine and Dorothy Ann were taken there by Nurse Winifred. A long paragraph, pointing out how each of the girls reacted in the way the ruins affected them, doesn't seem enough from a person who was so interested in old buildings with monastic connections and usually described them vividly. The Abbey ruins weren't necessary for the plot, but it is an odd omission in a book which was much longer than average, and after the amount related about Southwark Cathedral in *The Tuck-Shop Girl* (p. 55 et seq.) the previous year. Perhaps EJO tucked Fountains Abbey away in her mind and had thoughts of using it in a later book if she ever set another in that district. Such a book could well have been planned, as it is thought that *A School Camp Fire* was originally intended to be three or four separate books. In which case, given time, she may have intended to write more about that group of schoolgirls.

The areas used for the books on the east coast of Yorkshire were factual and many of them still exist if anyone tracks

Goathland 1921 - the setting for *Rosaly's New School*

down those described in *Rosaly's New School* and *At School with the Roundheads*. The names have been disguised very loosely: Redburn and Castleford instead of Saltburn and Castleton. There was a school for boys from about 1893 to 1926, overlooking the Skelton Beck and sited quite close to the Zetland Hotel. In fact, from 1897 to 1906 one of the two houses was actually owned by the manager of the Zetland Hotel, and if EJO, with her talent for moving places to different sites, had chosen to move the *At School With the Roundheads* school to the present-day convalescent home, which is in the right position, it would have been in the correct spot for her story. That school for boys was originally two large semi-detached houses and held about seventy boys together with the Headmaster, at least four masters and a matron, as were shown fictionally by Elsie.

The tunnel in Saltburn through which Nancy ran to tell Susie that their tournament had to be postponed in *Finding Her Family* (p. 12) has been made into a shopping precinct, although until recently it was almost exactly as EJO would have known it. The Zetland Hotel where Brenda stabled her pony is now a block of flats. There is still a VR pillar-box which could have been used by Audrey in the book but also by EJO in real life. The Jewel and River streets are there too, although Amethyst Street is an invention placed amongst the genuine jewel names.

In *Finding Her Family* Elsie went into great detail about the Beach Missions. The idea for those came from work her brother Roderic did during his training to become a Congregational Minister. He lived for some time in Liverpool which, thanks to Elsie's impressions, provided the opening for *Biddy's Secret*.

The Pageant for *Finding Her Family* blended in well with the visitors, the Beach Mission, a charity collection for poor children, and the legend of St. Hilda. Staithes hasn't altered a great deal since *Finding Her Family* was published in 1916

Victorian Houses in Saltburn – possibly the Roundheads' School

and, even in the 1950s, some of the older women there were still wearing lace-trimmed bonnets and aprons.

Elsie once replied to a letter with: 'It is lovely country, all round Whitby, isn't it? I stayed in Goathland after a holiday at Saltburn, and we explored the moors in several directions.' Whitby was bound to appeal to her with the love she had for ruined abbeys and Whitby dates back much further than Cleeve Abbey: to 655 when King Oswy of Mercia promised he would found twelve monasteries, one of which was to be Whitby. The Abbess of Hartlepool was entrusted with the care of Oswy's own daughter Elfled in 657 when Abbess Hilda took charge of the early abbey at Whitby. Later Elfled became their Abbess and was buried there, as were King Oswy and his Queen Eanfled.

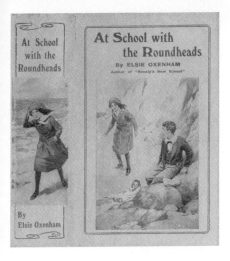

Whitby Abbey was for both men and women and perhaps its best known occupant other than St Hilda was the shepherd Caedmon. He is famous because, although said to be quiet and retiring, after having a vision during which he was charged to sing about the beginning of created things, he did so and his song was later transcribed by Bede.

The Peak District must have delighted EJO for Castleton, which she mentioned briefly in *Finding Her Family* (p. 79) with 'Isn't Castleton pretty from here, with all its red roofs straggling over the hill, and the big fir wood behind?', was famous for its morris dancers. Until the early 1920s they danced in procession around the outskirts with a Garland King, and the villagers grew the flowers used for decorations during the festival as Castleton is one of the places famous for its Welldressing ceremonies. Abbot's Bromley isn't too far away and, as Elsie saw the Abbot's Bromley Horn Dance performed at one of the E.F.D.S. displays, she would have made a point of seeing a live performance in its proper setting.

Jen's Tin Town came from the Peak District too. That was the name given to the village of Birchinlee when, between 1900 and 1912, temporary homes were built there for four hundred navvies and their families while the men worked on a new reservoir. Later, the small train used there for transporting materials was taken to France for use by the troops during the 1914—1918 war. Tin Town must have been as grim as EJO described it in *Jen of the Abbey School* (p. 19): 'The cottages were all in the same pattern, arranged in neat rows,

Lake Quellyn c 1900

all with roofs of corrugated iron, with at first glance no individuality to distinguish them.' No wonder Jen saw a need to provide something of beauty for the children in the area with dancing, then vivid knitted jumpers for the girls. However, it was a very well planned village, having shops, a hospital, school, post office and police station as well as several other facilities for the inhabitants.

Books have been written about the reservoirs in the district, explaining how whole villages had to be destroyed (as Miss Dean told the Rocklands juniors), to provide enough water to supply Sheffield and surrounding places in the area. One of the big houses to have been submerged is vaguely reminiscent of Joy's Hall and, indirectly, Cleeve Abbey. Derwent Hall (1672) had once been used as a common farmhouse and had a bridge, originally built by monks. But, when it was restored and rebuilt, it resembled most other manor houses of that era, with its oak panelling and great entrance hall. After being used as a Youth Hostel, the house was adapted to accommodate workmen working on the Ladybower Reservoir.

Elsie knew her birthplace of Southport and a lot about Liverpool, enabling her to use the area between Liverpool and Southport as the setting for *Damaris at Dorothy's* (p. 27). It is still possible to see the stretch of sands on which the girls used to play cricket or go for walks.

'To her left was a promenade and an ornamental garden, with paths and seats and flowers and grass; beyond, in the distance, was a mass of strange objects - derricks and cranes and masts, and fat yellow funnels, against a background of grey cloud. 'Those are the docks I showed you,' Patsy explained. "The funnels are big liners. The cloud at the back is Liverpool - smoke, you know.' To the right and in front were long, smooth stretches of sand, reaching to a distant tide; and beyond the sand was water; surely it was the sea? 'That's New Brighton and Wallasey, across the Mersey. Then there's the Dee and then Wales and Snowdon ...'

The Ruined Gatehouse of Madryn Castle

That was also the district given to Ruth Devine on p. 9 of *Biddy's Secret* where she went to debate whether she should hurry on to the Hall to avoid a proposal.

'To her left lay the forests of masts and derricks which were the docks, with an occasional yellow funnel where a mail-steamer was lying. As Ruth walked steadily out towards the river, the twin towers of the Liver Building at the pier-head came into view, dim in the smoke-haze.'

When using the Morven and Cowal Peninsulas, Elsie invented place names, yet she always used correct ones in her Welsh stories. A Welsh reader wrote, 'Unlike many writers, Miss Oxenham was always correct with her Welsh words and expressions.' Wales held happy memories for the Dunkerleys, who spent more than one holiday there. The three *Torment* stories were set around Lake Bala (Llyn Tegid) while Criccieth was the base for *The Conquest of Christina*. Plas Glyn-y-Weddw is where Christina took the children to see the ornamental gardens and all the walks, places and views described in *The Conquest of Christina* remain almost as when EJO first put them into that story. Lake Quellyn is roughly in the same district as the one in that book and it's clear that EJO, having used it originally for Robin, kept it in her mind, enabling her to include the name once she began her Abbey series.

Investigators have come up with the idea that Tygwyn, where Antonia and Marsaili lived, is the house now used as a centre for outdoor pursuits which once belonged to Sir Watkin Williams Wynne who entertained Queen Victoria to tea there in 1889. When the railway ran alongside the lake, he had a private halt made as described in the *Torment* stories. There is a small connection there with Sadie Sandell as there is still a boatyard in the area which could have been the original for the one supposedly belonging to Sadie's grandfather in *A Camp Fire Torment*.

The Girls of Gwynfa and *Sylvia of Sarn* are both set between Abersoch and Cilan Head. Another link between different groups is that Abersoch was where Blaise Morgan (*Mistress Nanciebel*) had a house while Madryn Castle appears to have been the setting for both *Mistress Nanciebel* and for Robertina Brent in *The Girl Who Wouldn't Make Friends*. It was referred to at the start of *Mistress Nanciebel* as follows:

NOTE

'To the best of my knowledge, the family of the Madryns of

160

Madryn has been extinct for about two hundred and fifty years. If any descendants should remain, I can only apologize for the liberties taken with their name, which of course exists to this day in mountain and estate. But the original owners were still in possession certainly within twenty-five years of the date of this story.'

When Sheila Ray and Stella Waring, two members of the British EJO Society, explored the district, they learnt:

'There was an old Madryn Castle which was the home of Colonel Thomas Madryn during the Civil War. This was higher up the hill than the one built in 1830 as a romantic baronial style hall by the Jones-Parry family and which, judging by photographs may well have inspired EJO's descriptions of Plas Quellyn. Madryn Castle was pulled down in the late 1960s; all that now remains are the ruined 17th century gatehouse and some traces of the castle which may have given EJO her idea for ruins in the gardens of Plas Quellyn. Today Madryn Castle is a caravan park.'
The Abbey Chronicle (No 8 p. 5)

After the first generation of the Seymour family (*Mistress Nanciebel*) were put ashore in their exile, they learnt that they were at the Land's End of Wales:

'Before them lay a lonely coast, with jagged, broken cliffs, and a long arm of fierce black rocks reaching out to welcome them. Above were hills, and later when these grew familiar, they remembered that they had noted with varying outlines, the two great peaks of one, which fell sheer into the sea, the round pimple on the crest of another.'

Cader Idris and Yr Eifl are both designated 'areas of outstanding interest' the latter being made up of three peaks. Although known to English visitors as 'The Rivals', the name EJO used whenever she mentioned them, the Welsh translation means The Fork. As with *Conquest of Christina*, walks in the district are still as in EJO's books while the villages haven't changed a great deal since the Dunkerleys first went there, with the exception of the approach to Nevin which was such a disappointment to Elsie and Hugo years later.

In 1930, when Elsie was touring with Hugo and his wife

Prim, they planned to return to Nevin. Their journey started at Carlisle where they met and began their sight-seeing with the Cathedral. Of course, she couldn't ignore any cats they met en route, and a letter from Elsie to the family informed them that there was one that first evening.

'We walked up a lane, accompanied by a nice black and white cat, who takes charge of us and shows us the way. The cat takes us home again; there are four pretty ginger kittens living in its house also.'

From there they drove up to Scotland taking in Carlyle's birthplace where they stopped to see his statue. At a morning tea halt were 'some pets of Cairn terriers looking over the wall' until they ended up with relations at Greenock where they

Cader Idris

spent a few days. They paid visits to more relatives, went over to Rothesay, Largs, Wemyss Bay, Dunoon and then to Edinburgh to visit Chambers, one of Elsie's publishers, before going down to the Lake District (Bassenthwaite Lake was mentioned here). There is no indication of whether this was a return visit for Elsie but it seems likely she must have been before as a quick drive through wouldn't have given her anything like the knowledge she showed when writing about

Maidlin's first home with her other aunt, and certainly not all the information included in her books about Rachel and Damaris, their rambles and their home. She was rather scathing about the lack of any decent cafés in the area which possibly gave her the idea for Miss Baldry and Hikers' Halt.

They made a brief stop in Chester, 'the beautiful Chapter-House with rare old books chained to the shelves and illuminated volumes covered by blue blinds to protect the colours; and the cloisters, with the central garden ...', and then to Llangollen from where they went by barge to 'Valle Crusis lies up a side valley, ten minutes walk away. Not very much remains; some big empty windows, some grave-stones in the cloisters, and some underneath parts, like the chapter-house.' They went on towards Caernarvon where:

'From a rise in the road we see the Rivals ahead, and rejoice in meeting them again after 20 years or so. The Rivals tower more and more, and the little one drops very straight into the sea, exactly as it used to do from Nevin. Just as we reach them and the country grows very wild, there comes a shock; a great white building and grey electric pylons, like ghostly skeletons; 'The *Rivals Electric Power Station*'. This is rather ghastly. We consult and decide not to go there. We'll keep Nevin and Morfa in our minds as they used to be.

(a letter to the family)

Instead they drove to Criccieth where 'the Castle looked just as it used to, and Llanystumdwy Bridge and Church are just the same'; on again and just beyond Dolgelly where '... there was a mother cat with a little striped Quentin', and then to Tintern which brought forth:

'It is annoying to arrive too late but we prowl round and see a great deal from outside, as the wall is low and the big shell of the Abbey towers above it. It is strange to see the real place, after knowing it so well in pictures all one's life.'

A quick run now with '... views of the Berkshire Downs with little Chanctonburys here and there ... and so to Farncombe Road.'

CHAPTER FOURTEEN

Places in the South
or 'Over the Hills and Far Away' (*Selma at the Abbey*)

All the breezes reached it also, and from whatever quarter they blew they came laden with the scent of thyme and turf, grasses and flowers, for from every quarter they blew from the hills. The south wind was heavy with salt as well, and often came tearing over the southern down with all the force of the Channel at its back. On those days the roaring of the breakers on the shingle could be heard at high tide even in Woody Dean; but other winds brought only the murmur of the trees, the hum of village life, or the ripple and splash of the stream.
(*The School of Ups and Downs*. 1918. p. 32.)

It has been noted that Elsie Oxenham modified, combined or altered places to suit her story-lines. Letters written by her in reply to queries explained the reason for moving the Abbey of Cleeve/Grace Dieu from Somerset to Buckinghamshire:

1936 ... 'The Abbey is a real one, but it is not near Wycombe. I described fairly exactly the ruin of Old Cleeve at Washford, near Minehead. It was not Wycombe Abbey School they went to; it

Whiteleaf Cross 1991

was a big day-school.'

1936 ... 'I suppose you have discovered the Abbey? It must be very close to you at Williton. So far as the ruins in *The Abbey Girls* are concerned, I was describing the Abbey of Old Cleeve at Washford Cross though I put it into Buckinghamshire - or rather just into Oxfordshire - to link up with the Hamlet Club people. But the underground discoveries of *Girls of the Abbey School* and afterwards, and the Hall and the Manor and village are made up, of course.'

1949 ... 'I am sending you a photograph of the Abbey I took some years ago. But you won't find the Abbey where I put it! You can see the Cross and the hills, but the Abbey as I have described it is in Somerset, near Watchet. It is the Abbey of Old Cleeve at Washford, near Watchet.'

1974 ... 'EJO told me about her first discovery of the Abbey, near Minehead. She showed me photographs, taken by a friend; really wonderful pictures, cabinet size, in sepia. Of course, as she pointed out 'The Abbey of Grace Dieu' ended up being far bigger than its prototype.'

Thanks to the hamlets mentioned and described so clearly

in *Girls of the Hamlet Club*, everyone accepts that, although EJO admitted Joy's Hall was based on one seen in Oxfordshire, both the Hall and the Abbey were set as if in Buckinghamshire, close to the county border. Yet in *Rosamund's Victory* (p. 31) Rena commented on Rosamund's pictures with, 'I see they're original paintings. How topping! Here's a lovely garden!' to which Rosamund responded, 'That was the view from my bedroom window for six years ... In Oxfordshire, on the edge of the Chiltern Hills.' Then after further discussion about the ruined Abbey ... 'That painting is the abbot's garden; I used to keep it in order.' This puts the Hall with the Abbey in its grounds very firmly, if rather surprisingly, into Oxfordshire. That is the only book in which such an obvious distinction is made and in view of the Buckinghamshire hamlets and villages supposedly all around the Abbey, it can only be surmised which county EJO intended as her setting for each story, or perhaps that she visualised the Hall and Abbey roughly as straddling the county border.

Elsie Oxenham visited Cleeve Abbey every year for as long

Whiteleaf Cross 1991

as she could, and she used to wander around dreaming up fresh stories. Muchelney Abbey, near Langport, isn't as well known as other abbey ruins in the west country, but was used as a farm as Cleeve was; in fact, there is still a working farm there within a matter of yards from the Abbot's Lodge. But Muchelney has been excavated to the extent that the lay-out of almost the entire site may be seen, from what is left of the original walls. There was a church there (probably dating from 688) with a

later one (950) built over it. There are also suggestions of a Saxon church dated about 933 or 939, then a Norman church said to be from 1100. When the Norman church was built over the Saxon one, the older building was used as a crypt or cellar below the new church. There isn't much clearance in height and certainly nothing like enough for anyone to have walked below the second church, far less build tunnels underground, but it is a fascinating concept that Elsie would also have been to Muchelney and had that idea as a result, which she put into *The Girls of the Abbey School* when Dick and Della discovered the first of the unknown underneath parts of Grace Dieu Abbey.

EJO was very fond of Buckinghamshire and its connections with John Hampden. When she wrote *Mistress Nancibel* and *Girls of Gwynfa* she: 'deliberately stressed the Puritan and Quaker side because everyone else writes about the more romantic Cavaliers.' She knew all the places in Buckinghamshire and the tales associated with her hero, the village churches described so lovingly in *Girls of the Hamlet Club* and the big houses in the district. She used the story of John Hampden and the Ship Money whenever she needed to illustrate the way in which people, if given a choice, must make the right decision.

Cecily's Cottage in Whiteleaf Village

It has been suggested that the May Queen scenes in her books were based on the May Day Festivals at Whitelands Training College. Those began as a result of correspondence between John Ruskin and the then Head of Whitelands. The first Queen [Queen Ellen] was crowned there in 1881. EJO would have known all about the ceremonies if only through reading about them, as the Whitelands coronation rituals were frequently the subject of articles in annuals which she and her sisters owned. It is quite likely that she could have watched their May Day crownings or merely the subsequent processions and festivities.

However, it is far more conceivable that the coronations she described in her books were a combination of the May Queen ceremonies she had seen herself in other parts of the country. Dancing round a maypole was done at Shoreham, only a few miles from Worthing. Near Sheffield where she went for short holidays more than once, crownings of the May Queen were held with spectacular processions and morris dancing, while morris dancers at Bampton (Oxfordshire) were 'accompanied by strange characters as they danced'. One known as the Sword Bearer carried a cake impaled on the point of his sword, and 'offered slices to the watching people ...' That was done by Maggie Puddephat at Miriam's crowning in *Girls of the Hamlet Club* (p. 281), the first time Elsie described a May Queen ceremony in her books.

The pub in Whiteleaf Village

Bringing in the may has been a tradition all over the world since ancient times. In the chapter on Maypoles and Maypole Dances in *Peeps at English Folk Dances* (1923) Violet Alford quoted Greek women five centuries BC, peasants in France c. 1400, *Corinna's Going a-Maying* by Robert Herrick (1591—1674); and other incidents related to May Days from 1490

Chanctonbury Ring and Dewpond

onwards.

Elsie was always interested in churches, other places where she would have gleaned information of local ceremonies from pictures and old accounts. Think what she would have learnt of traditions, once she became involved with the E.F.D.S. too. Those came into *The Abbey Girls Go Back to School* more than into her other books, but she certainly knew all about the tree worship of olden days and how that was described as a spring ritual alongside May Day. It is far more likely that her descriptions were based on scenes she had watched, than what she might have read as a girl about the ceremonies held at Whitelands, especially as she was still pretty meticulous with actual descriptions even if she moved places, changed names and juggled distances. So to be as adamant as some readers are that the May Queen ceremonies in the Abbey books must be based on those held at Whitelands and nothing else, is a little too arbitrary.

When EJO spent holidays in Buckinghamshire most villages there were still very feudal. Until the 1930s the cottages and farms had neither electricity nor mains water; the latter didn't reach the village of Whiteleaf until 1926. The cottage women were expected to curtsey outside their doors whenever the local squire passed by. The main street in Whiteleaf has hardly altered, although some of the cottages have lost their 'creepers, vines or climbing roses' (*Girls of the Hamlet Club*) as well as their thatch. The lane 'barely two feet wide, overhung by branches of honeysuckle' is still visible, but the one-time village store known as Barn Cottage, is no longer a shop as it was when the Dunkerley family first went there. Whiteleaf Cross where Cicely met her father is overgrown and, thanks to houses which have been added outside the village, is difficult to see from any distance, although it remains a landmark.

Clematis Cottage – the model for the Rose and Squirrel

There are several ideas about the origins of the name, ranging through Whiteleaf, Whyteleaf, White Cliff, Whitgils or Wiglaf, that last having been either the father of Hengist and Horsa or an early king of Mercia. There are many theories about how and why the Cross came to be made. Tradition has it that the Cross and the one at Bledlow four miles away are monuments of Alfred's victories over the Danes; in the churchyard at Prince's Risborough is a mound, supposed to

171

be the remains of a Danish camp. Bledlow derives from Bledelau: 'a bloody field' and is related to a battle between the Danes and Saxons. Some authorities date the Cross as far back as 325 A.D., saying it could have been cut in commemoration of a battle between Cymbeline and an unnamed Roman general. Other ideas include the theory that the Cross was cut as a mark of pagan worship as a plain upright, but that the arms of the Cross were added many centuries later to indicate conversion to a Christian symbol. Another surmise is that it was cut by soldiers during the Civil War, but local legend has it that the Cross at Whiteleaf merely marks the place where an ancient track road crossed the Chiltern Hills.

For years there was a field known as French School Meadow at Penn where Edmund Burke had provided a school for French children who had lost their parents, something EJO modified slightly in *Girls of the Hamlet Club* on page 232 when Marguerite told of her part-French ancestry. Ewelme, where Maidlin and Jock went to give thanks after their engagement, is reputedly one of the prettiest villages in England. The church, school and almshouses date from 1437 and were given to the village by the then Duchess of Suffolk.

Elsie went to Sussex with Maida, Roderic and Theo when she was barely into her teens, for a holiday in Littlehampton. Her Ven and Gard books were all based on the area between Bognor Regis and Selsey; the lagoon was part of Pagham harbour. A few converted railway bungalows along parts of that coast, some inhabited while others are used merely for holidays, may still be seen although the majority have disappeared in the last fifty or so years. Rottingdean was the scene for *Patience Joan, Outsider* while the Camp Keema books and *Dorothy's Dilemma* were both set around Worthing and the Downs.

The third book which EJO wrote about Deb Lely was rejected originally but published privately in 1993 by her niece. Surprisingly, considering how much description normally went into her earlier books, *Deb Leads the Dormitory* contains very little scenic detail, although it is extremely accurate. Most of

ARUNDEL CASTLE.

Arundel Castle

173

the action takes place within the school itself and there are far fewer outings or walks on the Downs than in the previous two *Deb*s.

From her home in The Glen where she moved towards the end of the second World War, Elsie took visitors for short walks uphill then informed them that they were standing on the chalk of The Downs. Nowadays that area is covered by houses, small shopping precincts and new roads. The chalet bungalow into which she and her sister Maida moved was named Inverkip after the small town near Glasgow where Mrs Dunkerley had relations. Aunt Dora Anne's little house Dunoon in *Daring Doranne* was based on Inverkip. The arrangement and colouring of the rooms were the same as when *Daring Doranne* was written, even down to the pictures on the walls.

For years the bungalow supposedly bought for Maidlin by Jock was thought to be one Elsie and Maida had liked but felt wasn't big enough for them. But 'Step Down' could well be similar to the bungalow to which Theo and Erica moved; 'Conifers', as they called it, had a similar step down inside the front gate. Elsie once told Doris Acland

'As Roy came after Maid and me we divide naturally into pairs and we decided to live that way. Theo and Erica live on The Hill.'

The room in which Elsie did her writing 'long-hand in notebooks at first, always bent double' was a combination of the rooms discussed by Mary-Dorothy, Biddy and Ruth in *The Abbey Girls in Town*, and the ones eventually given to Mary-Dorothy at the Hall, and chosen by Barbara in *The Junior Captain*. Gold and brown cushions were there as people often gave Elsie cushions as presents because her back was troublesome, and many of the Farnham pots.

The room was brown, a colour Elsie liked as shown in *A School Camp Fire:*

'The same warm shade, the colour of the rolling moors for the greater part of the year, soft and rich as velvet ... that deep warm brown which Priscilla wore herself and loved almost as much as the royal glow of autumn.'

174

Then in *The Junior Captain*:

'... its colouring was that of her [Barbara's] Camp Fire gown with the soft yellow walls, brown wood, curtains of brown and green and fawn, pictures in brown wood frames, some in water-colour but more in brown tints, carpet of deep leaf-brown, ornaments in brown Dorset ware, or little wooden curios from Switzerland - bears and chalets and carved photo-frames.'

Later in *The Abbey Girls in Town* EJO wrote about the gentle shades of brown chosen by Jen for her May Queen train.

'... think of your brown and gold pots! Think of the woods in autumn! Think of our moors in winter! - the most glorious soft brown velvet.'

There was a school for gardeners at Clapham, just five miles from Worthing, run by a woman Swanley-trained who, with a friend, taught girls handicrafts as well as country lore. Those girls wore the uniform EJO described as being worn by Rena in *A Go-Ahead Schoolgirl* when she worked for Sheila Thorburn in the gardens at Rocklands, that is, breeches, long boots and brown hats. Some of this uniform was given to the Wood End girls, although they wore smocks rather than shirts or jackets.

An ex-pupil of the Clapham School who went there in 1919 described their work with all its different aspects referring to the animals, the two dedicated teachers, exams., outings to various nurseries in the vicinity and their clothes.

'We had brown Liberty linen smocks with white collars pinned in. Some of the girls wore land army type coats but I always preferred my smock. The breeches came from a tailor in Arundel and the smocks were made by a cottage woman somewhere between Clapham and Arundel. We made our own butter and also kept bees.'

Elsie and Maida had a lady gardener and it was largely thanks to her that Elsie was able to describe Rena pruning Rosamund's roses at the Rose and Squirrel as accurately as she did. There were keen gardeners among her sisters, too. She gardened herself as well and wrote to Doris Acland:

'If the weather allows I shall weed and clip hedges for a few days, as a change to more peaceful occupations.'

The Clock at Abinger Hammer

Tea rooms (Clematis Cottage) in Washington, now an antique shop, were the original models for The Rose and Squirrel. The little wall between the two cottages is still there and visitors can imagine how they looked on Rosamund's memorable visit when she realised there was an empty cottage next door to The Squirrel Tea House into which she might be able to move. She intended to use it as a shop for selling the craft work she was envisaging made by people who couldn't sell what they made in the normal manner and who would appreciate having found an outlet. There is even a large house nearby which would have been the model for Wood End School, the one where Rena and Lisabel were sent by Sheila Thorburn, in *Rosamund's Victory*, to tidy the grounds and where Gail was to set up 'a gem of a tuck shop' for the schoolgirls once Wood End School was established.

Elsie was very friendly with the housekeeper at Arundel, her model for Kentisbury Castle, which meant she was able to spend time there to absorb the atmosphere and background for her books about the Kane family and Rosamund in particular. Members of the E.F.D.S.S. did dance at Arundel, but for the sake of the story were turned into schoolgirls in *A Fiddler for the Abbey*. Arundel Castle has an oratory which may have given her the idea to provide something similar in *Guardians of the Abbey*.

Another interesting fact about Arundel Castle comes in a

176

description of the family tombs which relates that some effigies were shown wearing the Collar of the SS, a secret sign used by those who supported John of Gaunt. The Kentisbury collars were first mentioned in *The Secrets of Vairy* but reappeared whenever one of the Kane girls was shown as attending a special function. When a girl of the family married she was expected to wear a '**Kentisbury dog collar**', as the younger members of the Kane family lightly referred to those bands, each of which was set with matching jewels of diamonds, rubies, garnets, emeralds or pearls. These were much the same stones as those of the jewel streets EJO used in *Finding Her Family*.

Sandy's Silent Pool

The Secrets of Vairy has a complicated background, almost implying illegitimacy amongst Kane ancestors. EJO obviously spent a lot of time and thought on that angle as she made complex family trees showing how a spurious marriage could have taken place in the past, thus giving her the opportunity to produce remote cousins who in turn might have been possible heirs to the title. In the case of Cousin Jeffrey, he was convinced that there had been a miscarriage of justice;

he was wrong but tried to discover the proof in a criminal manner. That book is another which must have been in EJO's thoughts for a long time before it was written because she mentioned a Kane connection as early as *Schooldays at the Abbey*, nine years before *The Secrets of Vairy* was published.

Kentisbury was moved by Elsie in the books, to be within easy reach of the Hall and, later, the Pallant, which name she could have found in Chichester (Pallant House, 1712), while there is a Kentisbury in North Devon, just over the border from Somerset and quite near Cleeve Abbey, which might have been another inspiration for the name given to 'her' castle.

A revelation experienced by Elsie came while she was at the vacation school at Cheltenham and she immediately thought she must bring 'Joy, Joan and Cicely to Cheltenham. Somehow the dancing revelation experienced at Cheltenham, then getting it into proportion and perceiving how delightful it all was, but without being exaggerated.'

Other experiences she looked on in this way were her first sights of places described briefly in *The Abbey Girls Go Back to School* (p. 183) as '...the beauty of Gloucester and the wonder of Tewkesbury" then 'Joy led them through the Abbey gateway, so that they came unexpectedly on the great west window in all its splendour ...'

That west window has been described by one authority as of 'spectacular Norman artistry' with the cloisters at Gloucester being 'artistically satisfying.'

Doris Acland said that wanting to put these experiences into her stories were why EJO: '... jumped three years in the lives of her book characters at that point. Twenty years later she filled up the time-gap with the inset books but by Collins' own request told them in the way then appreciated by the ten-year-olds for whom they were catering; nothing discursive, no analysations, only action and conversation were to be included.'

CHAPTER FIFTEEN

Publishing and Publishers
or 'The Editor Decides' (*Dorothy's Dilemma*)

'That Writing Person in London, told me to type my first few chapters and send them, with a synopsis of the rest, to a publisher, because it's getting so late for this year. And this is to say he likes the beginning and the idea of the story very much, and if the rest comes up to the opening chapters, he'll be pleased to publish it this year ...'
(*The Abbey Girls in Town* p. 310)

Elsie Oxenham's books were published by a number of different firms. Collins produced the majority of her Abbey titles, but weren't prepared to take all of them. In 1948 she wrote to her friend Doris Acland,

'Collins won't even look at *Guardians*; are devoting themselves to reprints and expect to take nothing for 2-3 years.'

Yet four years later she followed that with:

'They [Collins] have always been annoyed that anyone else should have Abbey books.'

Collins published her first book, *Goblin Island* in 1907, then three more of that run (*Princess in Tatters* 1908, *A*

Holiday Queen 1910, and *Schoolgirls and Scouts* 1914). They did *The Conquest of Christina* (1909) before the Abbey series which began officially as that series in 1920, and all but four of her Abbey books with 'Abbey' in the title, until her final *Two Queens at the Abbey* in 1959. Strangely Collins also published her scarce *The Camp Mystery* in 1932 although it's unlikely anyone at the firm realised its faint connection with the main sequence.

In a letter EJO wrote to Doris Acland that she had:

' ... offered it [*Guardians*] to Muller, but if he takes it he isn't likely to be able to use it - I mean bring it out - till 1950 at earliest. Muller hasn't yet got *Fiddler* to the stage of proofs, and after that there is all the printing and binding. *Vairy* is printed, but not yet bound, just like *Margery*. I expect both this year, but can't say when. I hope for *Fiddler* next year, but it's only a hope; and *Guardians*, if taken, will follow that. A second *Damaris* story would probably have to wait till 1951. I may do something else first.'

In fact, of those titles discussed by post in January 1948, *Fiddler* was published in that year after all, *Guardians* not until 1950 while *Vairy* and *Margery* were both dated 1947. This implies that, when EJO wrote that they were printed but not bound, the expected date was added even if the books weren't completed and available for sale until the following year. After EJO's death enquirers were told by Doris Acland that:

'*Maid, Champion* and *Two Joans* were written in their correct order, but published out of sequence and separated by insets. But the insets were planned roughly as a whole. The facts of Jandy Mac and of Rykie were in Elsie's head years before.'

Another of her books to suffer excessive delays was *New Girls at Wood End*. Originally it had been accepted as two short books for girls by a new publisher, but after two years both were returned because the firm which had accepted the pair was unable to publish them after all. EJO reported to Doris: 'Evidently she [the publisher] had too big ideas and times have been too hard. I would rather buy them back from her than have them given to some cheap place.' Four more years passed before Elsie found another firm to accept the two manuscripts

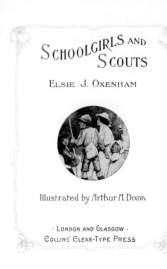

SCHOOLGIRLS AND SCOUTS

ELSIE J. OXENHAM

Illustrated by Arthur A. Dixon

· LONDON AND GLASGOW ·
COLLINS' CLEAR-TYPE PRESS

which she then had to amalgamate to make one normal-length book.

EJO frequently had to face dispiriting delays over publication as in 1936, when she replied to an enquiry from a reader with:

'I am afraid there won't be another book in the Abbey series this year. I have written one, *Rosamund's Tuck-Shop*, but Chambers did not care for it and so far I have not been able to find any other publisher who would show any interest in it. It's getting late for this year now. I am very much disappointed, of course.'

Luckily, six months later she was able to report that *Rosamund's Tuck-Shop* would be available early the following year after all.

EJO couldn't always choose her own titles either. *Two Queens at the Abbey* was meant to be called *The Abbey Twins at School* because she thought the suggestion of *Two Queens* would give away too much of the actual plot. But her wishes were over-ruled. She was often concerned about treatment by different firms, too, and frequently had to point out errors to readers. As when she wrote to any who complained to her directly :

'There are bad mistakes after I had corrected the proofs. It was Merrilie, not merrile. It is full of mistakes; they have edited it since it left my hands. All right in the proofs but messed up in the final printing. It's not my fault! There may be others; I have not had time to read it through yet. I am quite helpless.'

One example of poor proof-reading is in *The Song of the Abbey* (p. 15) where two lines were misplaced on one page but corrected in the reprints. Probably as a result of EJO's 'I am sorry and very angry' when she pointed out the faults to Collins.

Another time she wrote to Doris Acland:

'I am ignoring a lot of his reader's suggestions; but am hoping for the best. I believe his people criticise just to show their own efficiency (?) and to keep me in my place.'

Frederick Muller published eight of her books; four with Abbey titles and four which connected slightly with the series.

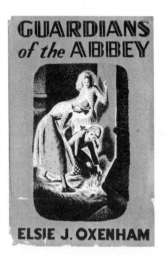

Other firms which published her books over the years as well as W.& R. Chambers and William Collins and Sons, were Frederick Warne and Co., Hodder and Stoughton, S.P.C.K. (Society for Promoting Christian Knowledge), Swarthmore Press, Cassell and Company Limited, Partridge Brothers, Lutterworth Press, Harrap, Newnes, and O.U.P. (Oxford University Press). In addition to their imprint of R.T.S. (Religious Tract Society), Lutterworth Press were also responsible for books under the Girls Own Paper (G.O.P) imprint. It has not been possible to ascertain full details, as in more than one case records were lost during World War II. Some of the firms have disappeared over the years or been amalgamated with other companies. One of the latter reported quite casually that during the take-over period:

'archive material went missing so information about the printing and publishing history of Elsie Oxenham's books is no longer available.'

A Dancer from the Abbey had to be completely re-written because when she had the idea of using a different kind of dancing, EJO knew little about ballet. Later she watched several and she also checked with friends who could advise her. New chapters from that story were read to her father during his last illness and much enjoyed as, unlike Mary-Dorothy's unsympathetic father, once Elsie was established

182

as a writer, he and his wife encouraged her in her work.

Prior to that it is felt that perhaps he wasn't always as sympathetic as he could have been towards her aspirations. Maybe he thought her early writings were too immature to justify trying to have them published and was simply being kind in trying to avoid disappointment for her. Although since her previous attempts had gained praise, it seems odd he didn't accept that once started she was going to be as capable of writing as he had proved to be himself.

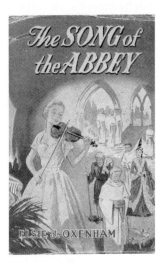

In *Goblin Island*, Elsie, as the fictional aspiring writer Jean in the book, obviously didn't want her father to see her work. She wrote in there (p. 227), 'I felt too shy to show it to father and ask his opinion', then further on in that same book on p. 253:

'... he would be sure to insist on seeing it, and at the thought, I became suddenly conscious of its imperfections and shortcomings. I had always hated being laughed at, and I felt that I could not bear to have my story made fun of.'

This is another case of something she had may have experienced when her early work was shown to anyone, even if not to her father.

Whether J.O. was helpful or not in her early days, Elsie

obviously always thought she and her siblings owed everything to their parents for their help, ideals and encouragement. That is clearly shown in the dedications of her books, with half being to her parents, singly or together. Not all her books had dedications, but of those which did, more than half were to her parents.

Things were different when she first started but, once she was an established author with many books behind her, she could or should have done far better for herself financially. It can be accepted that the Dunkerley/Oxenham writers weren't producing their books with a view to making vast amounts out of them, and John Oxenham paid for at least one of his books of verses (*Bees in Amber*) to be printed at his own expense during World War I. This proves yet again that some books printed privately can sell in such vast numbers that they soon become best-sellers even when no known publisher had been prepared initially to risk producing them.

With so many writers in the family, it is sad that no one appears to have investigated the possibilities of perhaps finding an agent, or ensuring some form of royalties to be paid for each of their books. Elsie sold most of her early books outright for fairly small sums of around £30 to £40 each. This was then quite reasonable for a new writer in the beginning but not once she was producing up to four books almost every year, a regular series with a new book annually, and several smaller series as well as working with a dozen different publishers. She had had more than sixty books published before she doubled those sums when the amount for buying the copyright of her books increased to £80 in the mid-1940s.

At one stage of her writing career, EJO had to suffer the 'there is no longer any interest in stories for girls' attitude which was growing amongst nearly all publishers at the same time. No one pretends that her books were masterpieces, although the author Mabel Esther Allan maintained that *Girls of the Hamlet Club* should have become a classic. Trivial faults may be found in a very few of the books but in view of their popularity when they were written and again today — along with other school and family type stories for girls from the first half of the last century — it is a pity publishers were so adrift in their judgement. There may have been a fraction less appeal when various firms made that decision, but interest in books for girls has never really died completely; school and family stories have always lasted in popularity and been much more collectable than any about ponies, Guiding, ballet, hospitals, film or television stars and other specific topics, all of which have been favoured for short spells. The attraction and interest in more general themes has remained acceptable and long-lasting while older books have become more sought after.

Doris Acland told enquirers that:

'Elsie never looked up to see if she'd got things right, and she made only a few mistakes. She made minor ones by listening to early readers who used to want her to make characters do things over and over again; for example Jen had to utter loud shrieks and Joy had to jump down people's throats. Many of her books were written alongside each other and a few of them long before. She wrote numbers of books together. Years later she could be asked for sequels and often the latter were coloured by problems of the moment - such as 'popularising Girl Guides' and so on. Sometimes she would add a longer story to an already completed short serial if she felt the latter too good to waste. She had heaps of material ready, and used it according to circumstances.'

Elsie was made to cut down on what she admitted herself as being wordiness and answered a query from one of her regular correspondents to whom she gave a typed copy of one of her manuscripts, with a letter saying:

'They [books] used to be much longer, but with the present shortage of paper it seems better to make them shorter too. I feel those early books are rather wordy and spun-out. There is probably just as much story in the modern ones but it is told 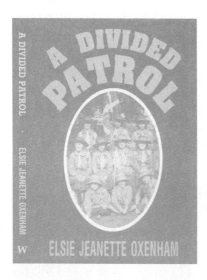 much more tersely and neatly. I used to put in whole pages of what people thought. Now I let you discover it from the things they do. Even now I've been pulled up for letting them think aloud. So I cut as much of that sort of thing as I can. By the way, these books are full length though they are so slim. I do assure you of that. They are war babies but inside they are just as long and big as the earlier books. I like them myself; they take up so little room and are light and easy to pack and carry.'

Elsie Jeanette Oxenham was a prolific writer. During 1920 to 1930, no fewer than thirty of her books were published. Had she been able to carry on at that rate and to write as she wished it is likely that her subsequent books would have been equal to her best ones. And there would definitely have been many more.

Fortunately Elsie's niece, Elspeth Dunkerley, discovered some unpublished manuscripts of her aunt's in 1993. They included *A Divided Patrol*, the fourth story about Jinty Cameron from *The Tuck-Shop Girl* sequence and another story about Deb. Elsie had written *Deb at School* as a serial which appeared in a run of schoolgirl papers in 1928. The first issue of *Schooldays* was headed as: *No. 1 of a NEW PAPER for SCHOOLGIRLS!* and dated 'Week ending November 3rd 1928.

No.1. Vol. 1'. Inside was the first instalment of *St Margaret's* by Elsie Jeanette Oxenham.

The actual book, retitled *Deb At School*, didn't appear until August 1929, when it was published by Chambers with illustrations and dustwrapper by Nina K. Brisley. That was followed by *Deb of Sea House* in 1931. But when Elsie offered her third story about Deb, *Deb Leads the Dormitory*, to that publisher she was told, firmly, that 'there is no longer any interest in stories for girls.' Collectors of her books, many of whom had known that a third *Deb* story existed, were understandably pleased when it was discovered and produced at last. Not many people were aware there was a fourth *Jinty* story, so the finding and subsequent printing of that early manuscript was another bonus. The third unpublished manuscript is thought to have been written even earlier than Elsie's first published book *Goblin Island* which came out in 1907. It is a historical novel set in the time of Elizabeth I, but hasn't yet been published.

It is a pity that some of Elsie Oxenham's publishers didn't accept her normal writing style during her life-time. While they were trying to make her change her methods and instructing her to write for younger children (which she found

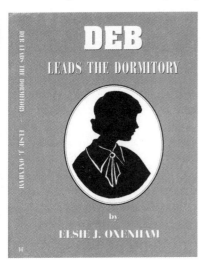

difficult), her books were still wanted by slightly older readers in the way she had always written.

The entire story-line of the main series had been considered almost from the very beginning. In 1946, Elsie wrote to Doris 'I can tell you one thing that happens when the twins go to school. It's been planned a long time.' She then gave a complete account of Margaret-Twin's episode when she wasn't chosen as first violinist in the school orchestra, ending with:

'In spite of care on Joy's part, Margaret has inevitably felt herself the leader in the family trio; as violinist and standing where the others sat, she could hardly help feeling the most important. But at school she finds herself merely 'Oh, just another fiddle!' in the school orchestra, and though she does in time emerge as soloist, for some time she has to [sink] herself in the general music. While Elizabeth, as a 'cellist, is hailed with joy, as really a treasure, and is soon used for solo work and to lead the one or two 'cellos they already have. It's a terrific shock to Margaret and does her all the good in the world. She doesn't allow herself to be jealous of 'Twin' and she is all the better for the struggle.'

Yet *Two Queens at the Abbey*, the story in which that event about Margaret and Elizabeth and the school orchestra appeared, wasn't written until thirteen years after that statement had been made, during which time the twins had only just reached nearly fifteen. No one knows how long the idea had been in Elsie's mind even before she related it in 1946 when the twins were only nine and when she first admitted to Doris Acland the episode was there, just waiting to be used.

CHAPTER SIXTEEN

Illustrations in the Books
Or 'Robin Buys Pictures' (*Robins in the Abbey*)

The Writing Person and the artist friend sat apart from the rest that second day, and talked business, discussing the possible illustrations to a new book.
(*The Abbey Girls in Town*. 1925. p. 141.)

In view of wartime shortages and a lack of paper available for books, it is understandable that EJO wasn't excited by a picture of a red rose and a note being introduced in the middle of a page while she was limited to how many words she put into each story. After the first few Muller Abbey titles and *Damaris Dances* had been illustrated by Margaret Horder, Elsie asked for her to illustrate more of her titles. Despite having some slight reservations about some aspects of this artist's work, she liked it enough to dedicate *The Secrets of Vairy* (1947) to her.

An Australian, Margaret Horder was well known for her work, and was doing illustrations for quite a lot of different publishers while living in England from approximately 1935

— 1950. She had a unique style in that, as well as her full page pictures, she liked to insert small ones on the pages of the books, breaking up the script. Sometimes she added small vignettes to chapter headings.

Elsie wasn't always enthusiastic about those small inclusions, particularly in books which were governed by word-length. Once she wrote to Doris Acland that 'the pictures will look much better in the finished book, clear and sharp, so don't be worried by their smudginess. I like two and possibly three or four others, but several seem to me completely wasted labour.' She agreed with the slightly adverse comment made in reply by Doris about pictures drawn by Margaret Horder, responding to that with:

Margaret Horder illustration (from *The Secrets of Vairy*)

'I'd felt exactly like that myself. Margaret Horder was really trying to show lovely gardens as well as houses in a very small space, but I think she attempted too much, and neither houses nor gardens are as nice as she meant them to be.'

After the death of Margaret Horder in 1978, an article in *Reading Time* (1979) reported that:

'She made friends of the authors whose books she illustrated, such close friends that they discussed their work with her ... no wonder as she never contradicted the author as to action, atmosphere or character.'

Other people asked to illustrate Elsie Oxenham's books

Elsie Anna Wood illustration (from
The New Abbey Girls)

varied. Once she became a member of the E.F.D.S. and was onto her third Abbey title, she took the artist Elsie Anna Woods to classes in London, so that she could 'sketch figures and positions' for drawings of folk dancers.

'That one's doing capers. And those are circles. I can't say I recognise any of us!' The artist laughed and reclaimed her note-book. 'You aren't meant to.'
(*The Abbey Girls in Town*) (p. 140)

Not all the poses drawn in that instance by the artist Elsie Anna Woods were used in the resultant books, but some appeared in the early editions. It was rather casual of some editors who, having found an illustrator capable of providing adequate pictures and knowing something about the contents and characters, did not then ask that same person to do other books for the author.

On illustrations Doris Acland always told enquirers that:

'They [the old illustrations] had so much feeling and imagination in them. They really were an attempt on the artist's part to illustrate the story. There are some quite horrid pictures in later books; one edition in which Joan and Joy were given shingled hair! Elsie protested at the time (formerly illustrations were submitted to her first) but they told her that long hair would have seemed out-of-date to the readers! Considering that there are full descriptions in the text, it would seem pointless to try and bring the pictures up to date and in any case only really silly readers would suppose that the stories are meant to be contemporary. They would realise that fashions have changed over the years, but that the problems of human nature are never old-fashioned or out-of-date.'

The first edition of *Goblin Island* is desirable in any condition as the illustrator was T. Heath Robinson, and the book contained sixteen black and white illustrations. Even early reprints are charming, with up to four coloured pictures, a pictorial cover, often decorated end papers, and swirly goblins on the illustrated and coloured title page.

Nina Kennard Brisley was an early EJO illustrator. She worked for Chambers and did nine of Elsie's books during the 1920s, mainly those set in Sussex. Of dustwrappers (or dust jackets as they are also called) and internal drawings showing girls in Camp Fire clothes, hers were accurate even down to showing the bullrushes on Barbara's gown. Other gowns drawn by diverse artists were merely shown with geometrical figures and plain headbands, except those on the dustwrapper provided by Enid Browne for *The Camp Fire Torment*. She portrayed moon and stars for one gown along with the cedar trees on Antonia's. The most ornate headbands were those drawn by P.B. Hickling for *The Testing of the Torment*.

The first appearance of *The Girls of the Abbey School* was as a serial in *Little Folks* (1921) where it was given the title *Secret of the Abbey*. The colouring and styles of the girls' hair in there were wrong; Jen was shown with cropped black hair and Jacky-boy with Jen's fair plaits. Inexcusable, of course, had the illustrator read the story, but often in those days the editor merely issued instructions about scenes to be portrayed and in many cases the artist didn't

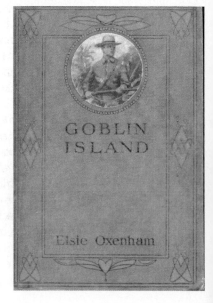

know what he/she was expected to do when it came down to the finer details. Elsie received innumerable letters from readers complaining and asking what had gone wrong. She had to alter all her descriptions to match the pictures in the annual version, then change them back when the book was published.

One illustration Elsie appreciated, and praised for its fidelity to her vision, was of Joy, Joan and Jen drawn by Frank

Varty for the short annual story *Adventure in the Abbey*. She also liked the pictures in the *Joy* and *Maidlin* books drawn by Rene Cloke, but, even so, complained to Doris Acland about 'the little dolly faces in some of them.' Those were before Rene Cloke became better known and began working largely for publishers such as Dean, Warne and Blackie, illustrating their books for the young, so perhaps childish faces came to her more easily. Rene Cloke wrote to me that:

'Instructions to an artist vary. Sometimes the publisher will mark a passage as he knows just whereabouts an illustration should fall in the make-up of the book. I much prefer to choose the incidents myself and as far as I remember I was allowed to select the incidents which most appealed to me in Elsie J. Oxenham's books. I had a letter from her discussing the appearance of the characters in one of her books.'

Elsie didn't always agree with the choice of dustwrappers and told Doris Acland, slightly crossly, of the one chosen for *Guardians of the Abbey*:

'The scrapped jacket was just two lovely arches, with Damaris kneeling in one and lilies behind her, and Rachel standing in the other, wearing her gown and holding a plant in a pot with the two kittens playing at her feet. But it seemed to me a strong simple design and clearer than the repeat of the frontispiece, which has too many figures in it, I feel.'

She had her own way with *The Song of the Abbey*. The original suggestion made by the publisher had been for the spine of the dustwrapper to show a male pianist playing the accompaniment when Nanta Rose made her first public solo. In a letter to Doris EJO wrote:

'I have made suggestions ... put in the Abbey twins, holding daffodils to present to the soloist.'

She complained bitterly to her in another letter about *The Song of the Abbey*:

'The frontispiece? Just that they ought to be in wedding garments. Derek most certainly is not. They were coming back from the wedding dance in the barn. He does not look dressed to be the best man!'

She also wrote to Doris about that same book:

'There is one terrible mix-up - a real typical Collins effort. All right in the proofs but messed up in the final printing.'

An even worse mistake was made with a late reprint of *The Conquest of Christina*.

Grace Beuzville Foyster was still credited as the artist in the reprint although her delightful pictures for the first edition had been up-dated by someone who was not named and who had completely failed to reproduce the charm of the old-fashioned ones drawn for the 1909 publication. Those, as period pieces, had been correct and ideal, showing the Jackanories in their matching sailor suits and big hats, and Christina with her long skirt to go riding.

Occasionally, illustrators were asked to provide dustwrappers but not the internal illustrations, so there is as little uniformity amongst those as in the appearances of the books themselves. Some are delightful, particularly the dustwrapper of *The Girls of Gwynfa* by Nina K. Brisley, depicting a group of young people dressed in Puritan costumes. Unfortunately she wasn't asked to do the wrapper for the reprint. Other pleasing and accurate ones include the dustwrapper for *Damaris at Dorothy's* and the up-dated version for the 'Fat Orange' *The Abbey Girls at Home*, showing Rosamund, Maidlin and the hen huddled together in the road after the car taking Betty McLean home after her visit to Jen had an accident while avoiding the girls.

from *The Conquest of Christina*

A few of the early Abbey dustwrappers were quite acceptable, but some later ones definitely were not, while frequently the scenes shown bore no relation to the action within the stories. Sport was popular for several years which meant it was decreed by someone who didn't know the stories and characters that Maidlin, who rarely played games if she could avoid doing so, was to be shown on the cover of *The New Abbey Girls* holding an unlikely tennis racquet. A girl holding a hockey stick was used for the cover picture on *A Go-Ahead Schoolgirl* while no hockey came into the story. Anyone fortunate enough to own an original or early copy of *Queen of the Abbey Girls* will be amused by the illustration of Mrs Shirley, looking twice her estimated age of between forty and fifty, wearing a floor-length dress, with glasses and a lace cap more suited to a nonagenarian of almost a century earlier than a widow during the late 1920s.

Illustrations for stories by EJO in some annuals or on reprint dustwrappers were often totally wrong: a girl polishing a silver cup when none appeared in the text; girls on a paper chase, something which didn't take place in any of the stories; three girls leaning over a gate labelled 'three friends' and supposed to depict Joan, Margia and Carry (of all people, Carry was the last person to be friendly with the other two girls). The frontispiece in *The Girls of Squirrel House*, where swimming was never mentioned, shows girls bathing at the edge of a lake behind Elspeth and Audrey, while Elspeth was given the wrong colour hair. Showing girls with the wrong hair styles, uncharacteristic clothes, carrying games equipment not mentioned in the story and similar errors were far too common. The general opinion is that stocks of pictures were used indiscriminately in annuals, then taken for reprinted stories when and wherever an illustration was needed, without ensuring the chosen one had any relevance to the book concerned. This was far too casual. Even more careless was taking an illustration from an annual where it had been used to illustrate a story by another writer, without checking its authenticity, then assuming it would do for an EJO story being reprinted, and using it for a new Oxenham

G.S.H.   Frontispiece
Audrey and Elspeth.

from *The Girls of Squirrel House*

dustwrapper.

A few early dustwrappers showed the same picture as that on the cover of the book in question, but not always. Others were accurate in relation to their contents, mostly those published by Chambers, Muller, Lutterworth, and some firms which only did a few of her books. That was due to the fact that their illustrators in those cases, particularly Nina K. Brisley, Rene Cloke and Margaret Horder, took the trouble either to read the books first, or to check with Elsie herself for their pictures. As already mentioned, Elsie Anna Woods was taken by Elsie to dancing classes to see the figures and positions she was to draw. If Cleeve Abbey appeared in the background, that could have been taken from pictures of the Abbey easily enough, but there is no way now to learn whether any of the artists who incorporated the site took the trouble to go there to make sure that their images of the ruins were accurate.

During her life-time EJO had the big early illustrations of the first dustwrappers from the *Abbey* books framed to hang in her bedroom. Doris Acland admired them and told people 'They looked lovely, especially the one of the girls dancing by moonlight.' (*The Girls of the Abbey School*.) Copies of Elsie's own books were kept there in her latter years, and in her will, written three years before her death, she requested:

'I should like my own books from my bedroom to be kept intact.'

CHAPTER SEVENTEEN

Elsie Oxenham Editions
or 'That Book' (*The Camp Mystery*)

On Sunday afternoon Rena came to Rocklands, but not to work in the garden. She came, wearing a pretty summer frock and a shady hat, to have tea with Mrs Thorburn.
(*The Girls of Rocklands School.* c. 1928 p. 72)

Unfortunately, there is no simple and clear-cut way by which to identify first editions of Elsie Oxenham's books, about which there is a lot of curiosity. However, this chapter will give a few general ideas as a rough guide for collectors for whom the details might be considered important.

In descriptions of the books, covers, cloth or boards refer to the outside of hardback books (HBs). So if a book is described as having a pictorial cover, it will have just that and the picture on a first edition will probably be in colour. Sometimes a book will have a pictorial onlay; in that case a small coloured illustration (usually a copy of part of an internal one) will be stuck on the front cover and another one on the spine of the book. Some elderly books are decorated by indented patterns.

First edition should mean just that and in most instances these days every book has the date of its first appearance given inside. Impressions are normally marked as: 'This impression 1900' (or whatever the year was) or merely 'The 2nd, 11th, 29th impression' depending on the number of times that title was reprinted. Impressions are taken from the original type settings with no alterations unless a glaring fault has been discovered which has to be changed. When reprints were made of popular titles they should be dated but rarely are. They may be taken from the original but could be printed on different paper or be in a different format. Badly cut or abridged books should be marked 'revised' but too often nothing is said to explain that they are cut. Laminated and pictorial covers have been given to the 1970s abridged copies of books by Oxenham.

Most of EJO's books were not reprinted in many editions so there are few problems in identifying first editions but others, mainly the Abbey titles from Collins, were reprinted too often. Books in the main sequence were reprinted virtually every year from 1921 to 1961, and the Children's Press editions were printed up until the 1970s. I shall thus consider the Collins' titles first.

The first few Abbey titles were dark blue with a picture in shades of blue with white, and were followed by an identical

Blazer Girls

edition, varying by no more than a minimal difference in size. During the 1920s came those known as the 'Fat Navy'; a darker blue with the head of a girl on the front cover. At roughly the same time, some titles were produced in small, pocket-size books, still blue, with pictorial end papers and a frontispiece. Another group of reprints, the 'Blazer Girls', was also brought out during the 1920s; those usually show a group of one to three girls' heads with bobbed or shingled hair on the cover, and a girl on the spine wearing a red/white striped blazer. There have been arguments as to which of these groups came first during that decade, since the 'Blazer Girls' were even larger than the first reprints at a time when big books were still the norm. Another version had a plain lighter blue cover with horizontal gold stripes on the spine while another in the early 1930s was normally in red with black lettering.

There were five abridged books which were printed without Elsie's permission during the early 1930s; these are usually referred to as the *Rocklands Group* (see Appendix 5) although only two have that word in their titles. Their covers

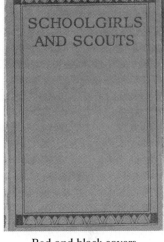

Small blue covers   Red and black covers

are orange, light brown, yellow or blue and they only comprise
a few chapters taken from the books *Jen of the Abbey School,
Queen of the Abbey Girls* and *The Abbey Girls on Trial.*

The quotation at the head of this chapter appeared in *The
Girls of Rocklands School,* which was a cheap reprint from
part of the book *Jen of the Abbey School.* There was an extra
chapter about Rena in *The Girls of Rocklands School* which
didn't appear in the original. It is assumed that the chapter
was removed because *Jen of the Abbey School* was too long as
a book and the removed chapter was kept by the publishers,
who may have planned to use it as a short story in an annual
but added it to the *Rocklands* version instead. Another theory
is that *Jen* was originally written as three separate short
stories, then made into a single book, in which case the chapter
might have been left out.

The 1930s saw the first Abbey titles issued by Collins under
the Children's Press imprint; these were similar in appearance
and size to their later Seagull reprints. The Seagull reprints
are perfectly acceptable with their plain light blue bindings
as they are nothing like the drastically abridged 1960s and
1970s Children's Press reprints which have laminated pictorial

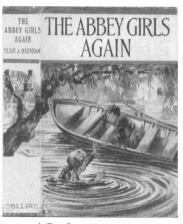

A Fat Orange wrapper

covers and have lost nearly two thirds of their contents. Over the years there have been a few single books with different covers. An edition of *Secrets of the Abbey* in pale yellow with primroses scattered all over its cover is an example. Another is *Two Joans at the Abbey* in light brown with the head of a girl, reprinted as part of Collins Schoolgirl Library no. 12. Occasionally a copy might be found with the head of a knight at the top of the front cover. Also in the 1930s came the 'red and black' editions; these are reasonably thick, and should not be confused with the later 'Red Abbey' editions.

The Abbey School (1928), an omnibus containing *The Abbey Girls, The Girls of the Abbey School* and *The Abbey Girls Go Back to School* is blue with gilt lettering and because it has all the original illustrations and no changes in their texts, is considered collectable. The *Elsie J. Oxenham Omnibus* containing *The Abbey Girls Win Through, The Abbey Girls*

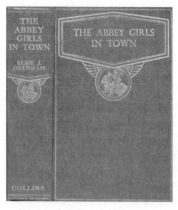

Blue and Silver edition

Seagull logo

Seagull spine

Play Up and *The Abbey Girls at Home* is a large orange book but isn't much wanted, since those titles are fairly easy to find as single books.

In the late 1930s came a major alteration; the 'Fat Oranges' which were produced regularly, gradually becoming thinner as paper became more difficult thanks to wartime scarcity. About a dozen titles of the main run were produced regularly from 1938 onwards, but not every title was re-done automatically at the same time. One reprint run could be made of perhaps half a dozen titles; the next would duplicate three or four of those, omit the rest but include fresh titles. Since the first Abbey titles were never all included in any of the runs of reprints, some titles are less easy to track down than others.

After the first few runs, the 'Fat Oranges' came out with different coloured covers; maroon, blue, brick-red, black and an anaemic yellow being the main alternatives. So amongst collectors they are usually referred to as 'Fat Orange' but with the actual colour added in parenthesis. Those were large books but not as thick as the first Abbey editions had been. The most noticeable other change was that they were given dustwrappers by fresh artists who pictured the girls with more modern clothes and hair styles than the originals. The dustwrappers were sensible and quite pleasing with their front cover illustrations duplicating the frontispieces, showing the girls in recognisable gym tunics and standard

Red Abbey logo

Red Abbey
spine

blouses or summer dresses and, with the exception of Jen and Rosamund with their fair plaits, nearly all with bobbed hair. All other illustrations were removed.

Seven Abbey titles made their first appearances in dark green boards with silver lettering on the covers and spines; they each had three or four illustrations. The second impression of this group was identical but thinner, (*Maid of the Abbey* in that run was thin, even as a green/silver first edition) after which they were added to the other Abbey titles brought out as Seagull reprints. Those reprints weren't consistent; the paper quality varied so differing versions can be found marked with the same date, indicating both were from the same print run but with different grades of paper. A few non-Abbey titles were also brought out as rather poor reprints while paper supplies were still difficult during the 1940s and subsequent years of shortages. The quality of those is not good at all. *The Camp Mystery*, *Expelled from School*, *Goblin Island* and *The Conquest of Christina* come into that category. They all appeared with blue or green covers and silver lettering. There had been an interim version of *The Camp Mystery* in 1940, retaining an original illustration as its frontispiece, also the small line drawings at the heads of the chapters, making it much better than the later poor reprint. However, that is a scarce title, so the discrepancies are less important than in the case of some others. The first edition of *The Camp Mystery* is very firmly dated and has the same gilt head of a girl on the cover as appeared on some of the early Abbey books. Another way of dating editions is by the list, if one is included in the end papers and if their dates are known of which other books the author had written previously.

Almost all the basic Abbey titles, were published with blue covers on which there was a seagull. These are known as Seagulls. They had attractive dustwrappers which were updated for their time.

Following the Seagulls came the version known as the 'Red Abbey' series with the words 'The Abbey School Series' printed inside each one. *Two Queens at the Abbey,* Elsie's final book, was published in that format as a first edition, then again as a reprint with a few of the later inset Abbey books, including *Tomboys* and *Schooldays at the Abbey.* The very last reprints which began just before Elsie's death and continued until the early 1970s were the laminated Children's Press books mentioned above, the texts of which were cut to approximately one third, although the main themes were retained in each book.

Children's Press edition

The different editions of the Oxenham books are quite interesting but complex. The date inside a book is no guarantee that that is when it was published or even that it is a genuine first edition. In any case dates weren't given in many, certainly not all those published by Collins. A few of the romances published by Chambers were definitely marked as 'Original edition' followed by the date, but once the gilt used for the title and author on each cover had been finished and the lettering became black instead, the books still contained that same 'Original edition'. Quite accurately, but copies with black lettering are scorned by purists as being printed after those with gold letters.

However, few of the scarce, older books went to more than two to four editions, most of which retained their pictorial covers, so they cause no particular problems by being dated or not while being still virtually identical. Sometimes fewer colours were used on the covers in reprints, while the internal pictures might be black/white instead of in colour. Often the only difference between a true first edition and a first reprint is simply a lack of a date in the second print run, otherwise the books appear identical to the first edition. Unusually, *Rosaly's New School* had one reprint clearly marked 1922 although there were fewer colours on the cover and the original came out in 1913. It is strange that *Girls of the Hamlet Club* is fairly scarce as it is known to have been reprinted at least six times. It was well publicised when it first appeared as it was reviewed in *The Bookman* in 1914 as '... will fascinate girls of all ages ...' which may have made it more popular than if it had merely appeared in book-shops. The first edition

had a blue cover and was dated 1914. Reprints to have been traced have blue or green covers, lettering in gold, black or white and anything from one to four plates. Later dustwrappers for this title include duplicates of those also used for *The School of Ups and Downs, The Tuck Shop Girl* and *Dorothy's Dilemma.*

A small peculiarity is the fact that sometimes the same cover picture was used on more than one title. *The School Torment,*

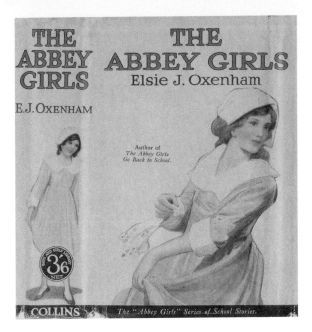

although marked and dated as a first, shares the same cover picture as *At School with the Roundheads* which had been published five years earlier. The first edition of *The School Torment* appeared in light brown or dark blue boards although both contain the same 'printed 1920'. The same applies to some dustwrappers, with that of *A School Camp Fire* being identical to *The School of Ups and Downs*, apart from their different titles. The cover picture and spine of *Girls of the Hamlet Club* appears on books by at least two other writers of the same era also published by Chambers; *Golden Square High School* by May Baldwin and *The Record Term* by Raymond Jacberns. The illustration used for the dustwrapper for *A Go-Ahead Schoolgirl* (illustrated in Chapter 19) later appeared on *The Bolted Door* by Mrs Molesworth. (This edition of *The Bolted Door* interestingly shared the same spine illustration as on the first of Elinor Brent-Dyer's *Gerry Goes To School*.) There are several other instances of cover and dustwrapper illustrations being reused for totally different books.

Dustwrappers are less easy to find and describe as so few have survived from the early books or their reprints and since ownership of complete collections of works by Elsie Oxenham is fairly rare. There were small differences there too: the first dustwrapper of *Two Form Captains* showed Tazy and the Thistletons half-way through their walk to the Sanatorium but a later wrapper was plain, thick rust-coloured paper with the title in letters of a darker shade of the same colour.

Many of the earliest books had pictorial covers automatically, particularly those published by Chambers; this group covers the majority of the Swiss and Sussex stories as well as most of the Oxenham Camp Fire tales. Others had a lined pattern on the cover or a small picture onlay which usually duplicated part of an internal illustration. As with the gilt or black print on some covers, those on-laid pictures vary on what can appear to be identical copies of the same titles. *Finding Her Family* is an example where there are different pictures on the covers of first editions; the reprint is thinner but otherwise identical to the first edition. The

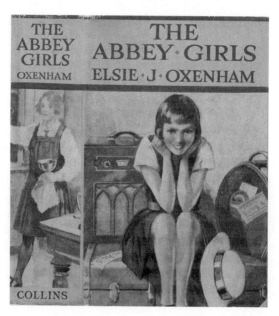

publishers printed extra copies of the internal plates and used any one of these on the front cover (also known as front boards). Both *Debs, Dorothy's Dilemma* and *The Reformation of Jinty* were all plain red with gilt lettering, later that became black. The cover illustrations on both *At School with the Roundheads* and *Rosaly's New School* depicted scenes from the stories.

Internally, other than the very much shortened 1960s 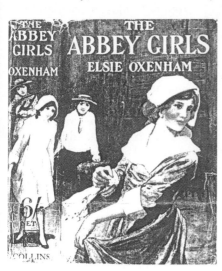 Children's Press versions, there is rarely anything concrete by which to judge. Reprints of *The Abbey Girls Again* and *The Abbey Girls Go Back to School* with their changed references to the war have been noted elsewhere. The fact that one of Jen's brothers had been 'killed in the war' was changed in the 'Fat Orange' edition to 'one was killed in a car smash.' In that same book, instead of Miss Newcastle teaching dancing to the girls who made munitions during war-time, she was teaching those who were unemployed. The use of a carriage or pony trap was sometimes up-dated to a car, which seems unnecessary since even after that had been done in a few places, a pony trap was still likely to appear elsewhere in the text where a reference had been missed.

The first reprint of *Damaris Dances* was identical but thinner; later reprints by Spring Books which were given new illustrations, left out or altered a few words; nothing to which anyone could object. The illustrations in the Spring Books version are pleasant and it is a reprint where there is no desperate need to feel it is vital to own a first edition to ensure

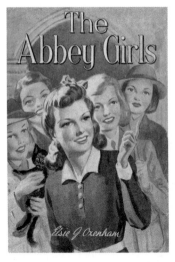

having a copy with no important alterations or omissions.

Goblin Island is attractive in early reprints with decorated title pages but fewer of the original illustrations. The same applies to most of the pre-1920 titles since they were normally much the same as the first editions other than for the order in which the illustrations were inserted. However, some early reprints of *A Holiday Queen* and *Schoolgirls and Scouts* were given a design of geometrical flowers on different coloured backgrounds for their covers, normally blue, red or green; others had a small pictorial onlay.

Titles first serialised in annuals were usually very well illustrated, with far more pictures than the book editions contained when they came out afterwards. *The Testing of the Torment, The Silence of Dorothy Cheney, Tickles* and others all demonstrate that difference very well. *Peggy and the Brotherhood* has only a frontispiece in the actual book, but every episode in the annual serial had at least one large illustration.

A few collectors try to add variations and editions to their collections, which isn't easy when many titles are hard to find in any age or condition. This can be an absorbing exercise but is perhaps a little hard on those who may not own rare titles at all. Obviously there is a vast difference between an original dustwrapper of the 1920s, an updated one ten to fifteen years later, then a more modern idea of clothes and hair styles thirty years later again, but they all add to the general interest. The collecting of annuals which contain serialised versions of Elsie Oxenham's stories, complete with many pictures (a number of which were usually by artists other than those who did them for the eventual book versions) is also of interest.

It is easy to be disparaging about the dreadful cutting which took place in the four Children's Press Abbey titles of the 1960s. The saving grace for them is the attractive pictures on their laminated covers. These were mainly quite engaging and, for readers discovering the books for the first time, the pictures portray the characters and settings well. *The New Abbey Girls* and *The Abbey Girls Again* which were produced in that version are slightly less easy to trace in either their original forms or early reprints so are better than nothing until a good and uncut copy turns up. And all four give the gist of each story for anyone not fortunate enough to own the complete versions.

Over the years dealers became understandably annoyed when pestered by collectors about finding first editions of Oxenham books.

'We cannot keep up with the demand as it is and it's ridiculous of people to expect immaculate first editions of books which are already hard to trace. They have no real value anyway, except to those who collect works by Miss Oxenham.'

(Letter of 1963 from a then dealer.)

That situation has worsened steadily since the early 1980s. Dealers realised they could ask almost any sum they liked for some of the rarer EJO titles. The interest in collecting juvenile literature has increased enormously in recent years and today a dealer can advertise a scarce EJO work with the word 'Offers?' and know that someone may push the bidding up to such an extent that the next copy of that particular title will start at its newly inflated price.

Genuine collectors have been — and generally still are —

211

satisfied with the contents of their books, regardless of their condition, edition or age. They are only interested in learning what happened to the Abbey Girls through to the next generation or in working out the intriguing links between them and the other small groups of stories. They enjoy reading about romantic ruins, joyful dancers, colourful costumes and attractive ceremonies. They find pleasure in reading slightly old-fashioned books with unusual themes, then satisfaction when they identify where each has been set. Worrying about whether staff or servants were in the background doesn't affect their pleasure in reading the stories any more than they care a great deal whether their copies have three pictures or none at all; or, if after being constantly re-read, the books look well-loved, tired, worn-out, battered and shabby, but cherished.

Elsie would not like the greed shown by those who are over-pricing her books, nor that of some who are prepared to pay the prices being asked, in some cases merely to add another title and then be able to gloat about owning another scarce book, flattering to her memory though it might be that people are so anxious to own all she wrote. It must be stressed that those cases are relatively few as most collectors searching for the books are genuinely interested in the stories and completing their collections to read, rather than boasting about their acquisitions or caring about the condition of their editions.

By the early 1990s a few specialists in Juvenile Fiction were trying to out-do each other by advertising they would 'pay more than anyone else for x' which of course put the prices up still further. Very sad and not at all what Elsie would have looked upon as being 'Camp Firey'. It is only fair to add that dealers can't sell books for nothing or they couldn't afford to continue their trade, but there should be a reasonable limit.

Yet at the same time other collectors might be lucky enough to find copies of those same scarce titles for coppers, making a complete nonsense of the present price range. In the 1960s that range was anything from 1/6 (about 7½d) to £2 for the majority of Elsie Oxenham's books. By the 1970s that had become more like £25 for a greater number of uncommon titles but twenty years later again, some people were so busy outbidding each other for rare books — not only by Elsie Oxenham — that the maximum prices had become quite ludicrous. In one year alone the price for *Joy's New Adventure* increased from £200 to £750. But copies occasionally turn up for very much less.

If a book has been badly abridged in a reprint it is important to try to find a copy with the full and original text, even though there is no need to crave an expensive first edition. But to seek a replacement simply because the one already owned is minus a scrap of gilt lettering or has no dustwrapper, seems a little unnecessary.

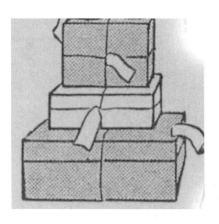

CHAPTER EIGHTEEN

Writing, Lending, Buying and Selling the Books
or 'The Missing Papers ' (*The Secrets of Vairy*)

I was anxious, if possible, to finish the story before Sunday. So I sat at
it all morning and afternoon, and by five o'clock had done five thousand
words since breakfast and felt I had earned a rest. I was very tired of it,
and for a time, felt as if I never wanted to see a typewriter again. But
the story was finished, and if I spent the evening in correcting it I
might give it to father by supper-time.
(*Goblin Island*. 1907. p. 76.)

During her lifetime, Elsie's first edition books lived in
special bookcases at Inverkip, one each side of a fire-place
where visitors reported 'they looked so nice, all with their original
jackets.' Authors who visited Elsie and gave her copies of their
own books were very proud to see them displayed with those
written by other writer friends in another bookcase in the
same room.

One aspect of being an author came when Elsie Oxenham
was continually asked if she could supply readers with copies
of her older and out-of-print books. Whenever she found

duplicate copies she either gave them to schoolgirl collectors, or resold them to adults. She always told anyone who asked, that when people told her they had gaps in their series she liked to help them, but didn't often get the chance.

She had constant letters to answer from people anxiously searching for her early books, hoping she had a stock from which to supply collectors. That stock was something she constantly tried to build up once she realised how scarce her first few had become and how much they were wanted. She also had to reply to queries about what happened to her characters in those stories people were unable to trace, when she couldn't help with a spare copy.

From the 1940s she found herself running almost a postal lending library. It wasn't at all easy to fit that and looking for second-hand copies of her books into her busy life but, being 'Camp Firey' she deemed it a service she must try to provide. Reaching the local post office was no problem to a person who, even by the time she was in her sixties and seventies still liked a daily walk, but over the years keeping lists, writing notes to enclose, packing parcels then checking the condition of the books on their return, became quite a chore. 'Both my publishers want books from me and I can't do both books and letters' she wrote to Doris Acland. The cost must have been considerable too as proved by: 'It was kind of you to add the postage; many people don't think of it.' That was a comment made in a letter to the late Regina Glick who, with a cousin during the 1930s, was borrowing lending copies from Elsie.

Regina eventually managed to acquire a collection of all of the Oxenham titles.

Once she realised how many people wanted her books but were unable to find them, Elsie retained a copy for lending purposes of every new one she wrote. The new duplicates were all prepared in the same way. Under the words 'Lending copy' on the inside cover Elsie added her name and address. If she had a second spare copy complete with a dustwrapper, the spine from that was pasted next to her name and the front cover stuck opposite. Whenever she found a second-hand out-of-print title, she kept it for lending in turn to all the collectors waiting, rather than re-selling it to just one person as she had done previously. Those lending copies weren't treated at all well and often by the time they'd  been out and back several times, she had to spend her precious time repairing loosening pictures, or even to re-sticking complete pages. She didn't always get her more wanted books back either; her lending copy of the scarce *The Twins of Castle Charming* was one of those which was never returned.

Demand always outweighed supplies of the rarer titles, mainly those which due to lack of paper during and after the 1939—1945 war and other difficulties, weren't reprinted as frequently as the main Abbey titles had always been. So typed or hand-written copies of the scarcest ones were made by the keenest readers. Not strictly legal, perhaps, but it went a long way towards satisfying collectors who were unable to trace

216

copies of the actual books. Elsie herself wouldn't have minded; she gave away her own proof copies to genuine collectors or those she had met and knew well, with the proviso of:

'In the meantime would you care to have these typescript and proof copies? They are quite clear and easy to read and they will give you the story for the time being and if they are reprinted you can get real copies then. I only ask one thing! When you have finished with these MSs will you either burn them or tear them up into small fragments and put for salvage? That is best, of course. I don't want them put for salvage as a whole and complete book when anybody could get hold of them. That would hardly be fair to the publishers. I don't want them any more, I was thinking of tearing them up. The proofs may be better than nothing.'
(Letter to May Hill 1948.)

She had given manuscripts away previously, also out of kindness, in an effort to help keen collectors. Her final draft of *Rosaly's New School*, complete with coloured pictures from the book, was passed to a friend with the message 'With love and all best wishes from Elsie Jeanette Oxenham. October 1913.' At that time it was entitled *Schoolgirls and an Heiress* but typed below were alternative suggestions of *'Managing Malvie, Malvie and the Moor School, Vina Victrix,* 80,000 words.' Another

original manuscript she gave to a collector was her own typed copy of *Finding Her Family.*

Nowadays it is possible for members of the Abbey Societies to borrow the rarer titles (not the actual books but typed or photocopied bound versions) as each branch has a librarian who deals with requests.

When she signed books for people, Elsie used variations of the wording in the message above, but very occasionally and if to her dancing friends, signed herself as Jean, with her full name in brackets. If she didn't know the person well, she normally wrote 'Yours sincerely' followed by her name.

No record appears to exist of the books EJO gave or resold to collectors other than a brief mention in one of her letters that she had eighteen books being borrowed, all out at the same time. After her death, the duplicates of her books, the lending copies she had managed to amass, and the few typed copies, were given to her great friend Doris Acland. At the same time, Doris was asked to deal with all the correspondence relating to Elsie and her books and to take on any future lending and selling.

When Roderic or Theo Dunkerley were asked to supply a list of Elsie Oxenham titles, they only provided details of the books they knew were still easily available and, if asked for any further information, advised people to write to Doris Acland. They both felt there was no point in giving details of titles the enquirer was unlikely to find, so those lists, although supplying titles of the Abbeys, romances and close connectors, contained no information about any of the other books and

stories Elsie had written. As far as answering queries about the actual contents of any books was concerned, it's unlikely they could have done so as 'they [members of the entire family] were all always so busy reading and writing they could never have read everything Elsie wrote' (letter from Theo Dunkerley). Is this a sad indication of the way her books were regarded by members of the family as not being particularly important?

During the next decade (excluding the main Abbey titles and what at that time were considered easy titles hardly worth keeping a note of as there were so many around then, such as

Damaris Dances and Adventure for Two, plus the less wanted non-connecting books like *Goblin Island* and *Expelled from School*), Doris Acland bought and sold no fewer than two hundred of the scarcer titles. She contacted book dealers in her efforts to help collectors and spent a lot of time on that angle, whereas Elsie would not have been able to do that as her writing was of far greater importance and was already taking most of her time. Consequently Doris gradually built up a stock of Oxenham books with which to help people.

Including those she had been given which EJO had found and the books bought and passed on or kept to provide a fresh

supply of lending copies between 1960 and 1970 of the main Abbey and connected titles, the total dealt with by Doris Acland included approximately over three dozen of the Swiss and Sussex stories, a dozen *Torment* titles, three dozen of the romances, a few *Girls of the Hamlet Club* and a selection of some fifty copies of the various Muller titles. There were also a few of the non-connecting books to be distributed amongst fans.

At the same time, there were regular requests coming along for the basic Abbeys and the more readily available related stories, all of which accounted for the many parcels constantly being packed and posted. Posting wasn't easy for Doris; for many years her husband took those parcels to the post office, but after his death it was done by anyone who called at the house. Gradually, dealing with all the lending copies and any new correspondents was taken over by me as by then I was already doing a lot of the parcel packing and posting.

During that 1960—1970 decade the prices ranged from 1/- to £2 (5p to £2) with *Maidlin to the Rescue* and *Rosamund's Castle* each averaging anything up to £2.00. *Joy's New*

Adventure and some of the Swiss stories at that time could be nearer £5. A number of the books were sent to collectors in Australia and New Zealand as well as to the many fans in Great Britain. Since it was one of the two books dedicated to her, a copy of *Pernel Wins*, of which Doris had a large supply, was given to every new collector she was trying to help. A copy of *Pernel Wins* was one of her own titles EJO had asked to have taken in for her to re-read in the nursing home.

Unknown to each other, a similar buying-to-pass-on service was being operated by collectors all over the country to help each other, and during the period from the 1950s to the 1970s many of the books were being discovered, bought and re-sold at reasonable prices, ranging from mere coppers to not more than a couple of pounds.

Some twenty years after EJO's death, a new element crept into the collecting of her books. Readers who had only been interested in the stories started to look for earlier and better copies of their books; first editions, if possible, complete with the original illustrations and hopefully also their dustwrappers. The desire to own books with the full texts and early pictures is understandable since they portrayed more accurately the era in which each had been written. That craving to own older editions played havoc with prices, though, and resulted in the slightly rare books becoming collectors' items, almost before the time of Elsie's death.

She would have been quite horrified, as she had thought some of the books were far too expensive when first printed. 'How very kind of you to buy *Rachel* — at that price!' (8/6 old money; less than 50p today) she wrote to a collector who contacted her excitedly when she had managed to find a copy of that title. Both *Rachel in the Abbey* and *Guardians of the Abbey* were reduced in price at one time from their original 8/6 and 7/6 respectively to 3/6 (42½p and 32½p, down to 17½p) and Elsie advised correspondents to buy them at the reduced price, should they see copies in any book shops. *Rachel in the Abbey* some thirty years or so later had risen to £25 and by the 1990s had soared to a ludicrous £100 at least via certain sources — although copies could still be found for as little as a few pence if a really dedicated searcher happened to be lucky enough to find that or any other similar scarce books by EJO. Ten years later again the cost of *Rachel in the Abbey* and most of the others of the group published by Muller had trebled.

Some unfortunate buyers, not knowing the length, scarcity and value of individual titles, have bought expensive books

which should have been priced more sensibly: *Tickles,* for instance, which was once purchased by a new collector for a silly sum. Yet *Tickles* is a short book of only 160 pages and not one of the most difficult to find, so it was wrong to price it as much as a longer book of nearer four hundred pages which is much harder to find. While sellers who think that as long as they have a book by EJO but know nothing about the general situation have been known to ask for well over £50 each for easy titles such as *Robins, Maid, Stowaways* and *Schoolgirl Jen*, which were reprinted so often that many people own them and similar titles in duplicate and even give copies away.

What Elsie would think about the prices being asked for some of her books nowadays hardly bears thinking about. It is to be hoped she would be flattered by the anxiety of individuals to find, read and own as many of them as possible, but she would consider such high prices quite ridiculous, particularly in comparison with what she had been paid for the copyright of each book, which was never a great deal. It has been learnt that some of her publishers paid no more than £30 for the copyright of most books they produced during the early 1900s. As far as EJO's Abbey books are concerned, with their constant reprints, it's unfortunate that she usually sold the full copyright and doesn't appear to have negotiated for some form of royalties or found a different publisher.

Elsie Jeanette Oxenham

Once it was known that a 'new' high price had been offered and accepted for any second-hand book, subsequent copies usually fetched at least that same amount but probably a lot more. Since records no longer exist via many firms, exact figures aren't available but one publisher who was buying manuscripts regularly from Brent-Dyer (who produced books for teenage girls over a period of nearly fifty years), paid the same amount for each successive one, unless they were of vastly different lengths, outside her main Chalet series, or completely dissimilar in content

Admittedly £25 to £35, the sums paid for the average book written before the 1920s, was fairly generous at a time when the wage for a working man was probably something between £2 and £5 a week. So during the years when EJO sold more than one book she was doing fairly well in comparison with the average wage, but not when one considers the amounts paid by a few firms — including one which accepted a lot of her early books — to other authors. Yet at the same time some firms were paying as much as £200 to their authors of longer standing.

Although once the details were clear in EJO's mind and while she wrote her books quite quickly, she doesn't seem to have benefited financially for the amount of work involved. Writing each manuscript in long-hand, then typing it out complete with carbon copies, must have taken weeks if not months of hard work. Neither does the remuneration seem adequate in view of the fact that most of her first books ran to well over three hundred pages.

From her middle age and in order to save her eyes, she had to pay someone else to do the typing of copies to be sent out. There were constant letters too; the problems of finding a publisher who wanted her work, then worrying about delays in publication and often having to wait years in many cases for whoever was responsible for the Oxenham manuscripts to have time to deal with them and to cope with any possible queries.

Once each manuscript was accepted, there was still the proof-reading to be done which she found such a strain and which did neither her eyesight nor her back any good. So, looking at the amount of time involved overall and the number of books being written, she should have been in a position to have negotiated for a much better price for each one.

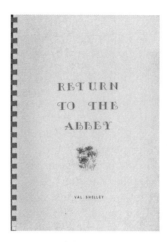

RETURN
TO THE
ABBEY

VAL SHELLEY

CHAPTER NINETEEN

All the Sequels
or 'Afterwards' (*Mistress Nancibel*)

The Abbey is home to all of us; this house and the Abbey - it's all the same!
(*Two Queens at the Abbey* 1959. p. 256.)

Elsie Oxenham appears to have discussed her books, plans and ideas with no one except her sister Maida until, from the early 1930s, she extended that to include her great friend Doris Acland. After EJO's death, and with much persuasion from other collectors, Doris agreed to write a sequel to the Abbey series. It should perhaps be pointed out that she was the only person who knew something of EJO's thoughts and plans for the continuation of the series. So any other ideas may have nothing to do with EJO's intentions.

The original idea was merely to write something to continue the story-line for a chosen few people to read. As EJO had done when asked to include certain points, Doris also incorporated details requested by those collectors who knew of the project. For instance, the item describing Lindy's

wedding was written for the sake of a very young collector who thought it important. All the people who knew of the scheme were told: 'I've tried to invent as little as possible but to expand ideas Elsie had herself. But obviously various points and thoughts EJO had wanted to use needed to be woven together in her own way.' So the result became an amalgamation of collectors' wishes, ideas EJO had mentioned to her friend or discussed in detail over the years, together with the writer's own favourite subject of drama — she had taught Junior Stage Technique to Silver Medal Standard.

Those requests from the handful of waiting readers which Doris tried to incorporate included:

'You should bring in something about Camp Fire.'

'What happened to Sandy who faded out too quickly?'

'Make Karen re-appear in person as Tazy has done, instead of just having people say what she is doing which is all that appears in the later stories.'

'Can people from the Swiss and Sussex groups meet the Abbey Girls somehow as when they first met Karen and Tazy in *The Abbey Girls Go Back to School*?'

'Did Elspeth marry?'

'Could Phyllida and Joy meet at some musical event?'

'What happened to Berry and Gard?'

'Would Tormentilla be likely to meet the Abbey Girls at a dance party?'

'What about bringing Joan back again?'

Doris did her best to bring all the pleas in but not every person, place or incident could be combined and brought in successfully. She was more anxious to write about the basic Abbey sequence than to bring in too many characters from the remotely connected books, feeling that since not everyone collected those, they wouldn't mean enough to the greater number of likely readers.

One of the ideas Elsie wanted to include in future stories was for the return of Sandy Alexander. Doris Acland wrote: 'Of Sandy, I had to expand ideas Elsie had had herself, as we had discussed her future in letters.' Then she expanded that by explaining:

'She was one of the most obvious members of the musical circle to mention when Joy wanted to reassure Jen about the dependability of a musician's ways. The wayward Angus became entirely dependable after he started his career, so music had a good, not a bad effect on him. When Elsie mentioned special things in her books, such as music, it would have been prompted by and based on what she had heard over the wireless of which she was

extremely fond, or sometimes it was the good concerts which were given at Worthing.'

Eventually there were four sequels written by Doris Acland which were originally only to be read by those few people she considered were the truest devotees. Under no circumstances were they to be published and they were never to be read by anyone else without her permission. Since the death of Doris in 1980, half the interested parties have said they don't object to the sequels being read by members of the Oxenham Societies, but a few owners of the original copies feel morally unable to share theirs even this long afterwards. Even knowing there are now lending copies available through the Societies, they had that instruction so deeply instilled into them at the time when those sequels were written that they feel it is wrong to lend them indiscriminately.

The first sequel was completed in March 1961 and contained three main themes. Whether they incorporated EJO's ideas or not, for the benefit of those unable to read the actual sequels, here are summaries of all four.

The Abbey Twins Take Charge

Wycombe School became the main setting and showed how Elizabeth and Margaret behaved in their rôles of being the elected twin May Queens. A new mistress joined the staff bringing her daughter as a senior pupil. Once the daughter Deborah realised this was a permanent post for her mother so that she could allow herself to join the Hamlet Club and other school activities without the fear of having to change schools, as she had had to do too frequently before, she became a useful member of the school and its new Dramatic Society.

Biddy Devine reappeared, bringing a gift for the Abbey. An uncle of her second husband had discovered a silver chalice which had been taken to France by Ambrose before the Dissolution with a message that, one day, it was to be returned to its real home in the Abbey of Grace Dieu. The third sub-plot was the development of the various Abbey children and their friends. Sir Ivor was impressed by Andrew Marchwood's musical ability and encouraged the twins, Andrew and his friend Jeremy, plus Jennifer, who had once led the school orchestra, to form a small quintette.

That story wasn't enough for the eager readers, so a second sequel *Friendships in the Abbey* was written by Doris. Again set mainly in the school instead of The Hall and this time showing the development of shy Rosemary Marchwood as a budding actress, the progress of Rosamund's Double Two when they went to Wycombe and Cliff End schools (and giving the reasons why they were sent to different schools) and how Rosamund, after a timely reminder that she was taking life too seriously as a Countess, became more like the person she had once been. The other theme in the second story was about Joy writing an opera. Her librettist, a connection through Jennifer Meadows, fell in love with her.

Number three sequel, *Grandchildren for the Abbey*, was set in the Hall where Joy was boarding those children of the clan who were attending Wycombe School; that entire

sequel was mainly about the much younger children of the families but also about some of the original Abbey Girls. Thanks to the production of Joy's opera, Joan had returned to the Hall to attend its first performance. That story brought back more of the older characters as they were invited to attend either Joy's opera production or the special Hamlet Club coronation when Cicely's daughter (Cis) was crowned as the new Queen. Being the 25th time the

ceremony had been performed, an extra effort was made to have a complete procession of queens and their maids. In those instances where the maids had become queens themselves, their children (if any were old enough) carried their trains.*Grandchildren for the Abbey* ended on Andrew Marchwood's twenty-first birthday at which the announcements were made of Joy's twins' engagements. There were other engagements, a couple of weddings and one surprising new baby in the story. There was also the promise of a children's opera/ballet to be written for the younger children choreographed by Madelon-Marie, with the dancers to be trained by Mary Damayris on her return to ballet.

The final much shorter story, *The For-Always Abbey Girls*, concentrated on the slightly unlikely prospect of Maidie-Rose and Joan's Jill, destined like Mary-Dorothy then Rachel, never to marry, spending their lives as the next generation of Abbey Guardians.

It was explained to the various correspondents how the sequels were planned with the inclusion of ideas gleaned from Elsie over the years. Most of which add a lot to EJO as a writer as well as a person. Doris always said that 'Elsie's characters were "real" to her. She "discovered" them - she didn't invent them.'

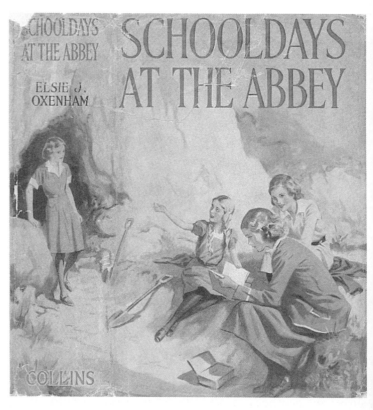

May Queens in Doris Acland's sequels.

1941	Cicely-Ann	Ruby on gold
1942	Angela	Moonstone/?
1943	Diana Edwards	Turquoise/?
1944	Rosemary Marchwood	Opal/anemones
1945	Jennifer Raymond	Amethyst/

Well over twenty years after Doris Acland wrote hers, more sequels have been written. The most feasible relates accurately to the Abbey books. Although the writer had not read any of the other sequels when she wrote hers, she actually used an idea already portrayed therein by concentrating a lot of the action around a big May Day coronation. But where the next Queen of the English sequels was to be Cis, (Cicely Hobart's daughter), that sequel written in Australia had Jen's Barbara Rose as Queen and is set many years later. It was sensible to make it later since by doing so, it seemed to follow logically in EJO's world.

The story opened with plans to bring back nearly everyone who had ever been in contact with any of the Abbey Girls and to have the fiftieth coronation procession complete right down to the maids. Several distant characters were brought back to the story which ended with a grand procession of fifty Queens and their attendants.

Two other Australian writers wrote sequels using World

War II as an integral part, thus rendering their concepts impractical as being too unlike anything EJO would have put into her stories with their slightly idealistic backgrounds. As it was clearly obvious that EJO herself would never have had her idyllic settings implicated in such a way, sequels using the war to such an extent made them unbelievable for some readers, however good the stories were.

In themselves all these other sequels are written extremely well, but those incorporating the last war just don't ring true however thoroughly and accurately the research about conditions has been done. Apart from that angle, it is interesting to read what some people thought might have happened in the future to the personalities invented initially by EJO and to discover how these modern writers envisaged the possible after-lives of her imaginary characters. It is also intriguing to come across characters who had extremely minor parts in the original stories and to learn what some people thought might have happened to them, as well as to the better-known characters.

Although seven books by EJO were published between 1914 and 1918 and she actually wrote several more during those years, she didn't use the war as such to influence the plots in any of them a great deal except in *A Go-Ahead Schoolgirl*. The death of Rena's father in that book was necessary for the drastic change in Rena's circumstances and for the expansion of her character. *The School of Ups and Downs* needed Jock to have been wounded and therefore to be at home on leave. In *The School Torment,* Dorothy Grant had to take the place of a schoolmaster who had joined up in World War I. Those were relevant factors and just enough, without being made a vital part of the action of each story, to make the readers aware that a war was going on at the same time. But none of those references affected the individual stories other than to help towards a little reasoning in some aspects of their plots.

World War II formed no part of the action in the later books at all although again EJO was writing a number of her second generation and other stories during those years. Admittedly, her later books were all written as if still set during the late 1920s on to the 1930s and Doris stated:

'Elsie deliberately introduced airmen into two stories, realising that flying was going to become more normal in the future'.

Of *Pernel Wins* (1942) Doris told me:

'She [Elsie] knew that Civil Flying grounds would be useless if a war came.' However, EJO's ideas served their purposes, her intention, as she told Doris, being that 'the story could be read in any period of time but that if read during the war, contemporary readers would not write to say she was at fault.'

The last book of the series, *Two Queens at the Abbey*, was set by Elsie as if during the time of the late 1930s.

Most of the ideas in these other sequels were sensible in themselves. Had the authors kept their stories to show the late 1930s or leapt forward about twenty years and then continued the earlier type about an idealised world of schoolgirls, adults, dancing, large families and a ruined abbey, the results would have been far more likely, more pleasing and perfectly acceptable to readers. And very much more convincing.

CHAPTER TWENTY

Criticisms
or 'Questions ' (*A Princess in Tatters*)

'I think we'd better chum. My friend left last term. ... You can chum with me, if you like.'
'Don't you think we'd better try it for a week? Like being engaged before getting married, you know? I don't like changing once I've made friends.'
(*The Girls of the Abbey School*. 1921. p. 10/13.)

For years critics have tended to pick out certain incidents in books by Elsie Jeanette Oxenham, then quoted them as hinting at latent sexuality or lesbianism. Perhaps it may be as well to look at some particular criticisms in more detail.

The incidents given are invariably:

1) The example quoted above. When Jacky-boy (Jacqueline Wilmot) in *The Girls of the Abbey School* suggests that she and Jen Robins, a new girl, should be 'chums', Jen responds with the sensible suggestion of seeing how they get on first. Later in that same book they inform the Headmistress that as they're a 'married couple', they should adopt the child, Della

233

who has to stay at the Hall for a while and has been given a bed in their room. They hope that by doing so they will be able to teach her that her way of life isn't the best.

2) At the start of *The Abbey Girls Win Through* one reads that Norah and Connie were 'different. They were a recognised couple. Con, who sold gloves in a big West-End establishment, was the wife and home-maker; Norah, the typist, was the husband, who planned little pleasure trips and kept the accounts and took Con to the pictures.'

3) *Queen of the Abbey Girls* when, purely to comfort Maidlin who was unduly upset at the prospect of Joy's marriage, the night before the wedding Joy took the child to bed with her to talk about the fact that nothing should change their mother/

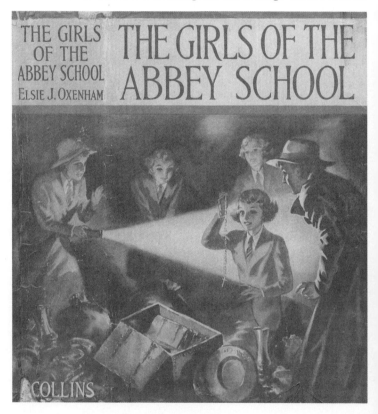

THE GIRLS
OF THE
ABBEY SCHOOL
ELSIE J. OXENHAM

THE GIRLS OF THE
ABBEY SCHOOL

COLLINS

THE ABBEY GIRLS WIN THROUGH

ELSIE J. OXENHAM

daughter relationship.

The critics never quote from *A Go-Ahead Schoolgirl* which has Rena saying to Nancy:

'I'm the man of the party. I go first to choose the path and keep the cows away! ... You're the Squaw, following behind with the food. The woman always trots along in the rear, meekly carrying the grub, doesn't she?'

Critics never comment either how, in *Finding Her Family*, Audrey automatically takes care of Hazel who has obviously led a more sheltered life and has never had to look after herself before.

All the examples above were perfectly innocent and harmless at the time the books were written, yet thanks to the modern trend of looking for hidden meanings in books written years ago, some misguided people pick on small points and provide their own interpretations of anything which they think could have sexual implications. They ignore the fact that many other writers of school stories had girls 'sleeping together' at school or at Guide Camps in the first half of the last century.

Can anyone forget the time when Anne and Diana in *Anne of Green Gables* by L. M. Montgomery were to spend the night together in the spare room at Diana's home and leapt onto the bed — and onto poor unsuspecting Great-aunt Josephine — not knowing she had been given that bedroom in which to spend the night? Then later that the two girls 'slept together' in Great-aunt Josephine's spare room for a whole week? Not to mention various other stories of that era written by countless writers in which girls were depicted going through variations of 'I'm coming into your bed to tell you about it' or 'Move up old thing, I'm coming into bed. It's cold out here', usually when sharing harmless secrets or while comforting someone homesick or upset. Again, perfectly reasonable and harmless, bearing in mind the time when such books were written. Not forgetting that girls then were far younger in their ways and knowledge than in the present day.

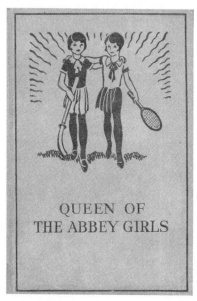

QUEEN OF
THE ABBEY GIRLS

Elsie Oxenham, as the Guardian of a group of Camp Fire Girls, took her girls away for short holidays when they had to share beds in small or confined places. However, she was usually given a room to herself, even if once it was only a kitchen. It seems highly unlikely that any thoughts of lesbianism would have entered her head and in any case those girls would have been far too tired, after their strenuous days spent in walking ten miles towards a total of forty miles which would entitle them to claim another Honour Bead, to think about a great deal else while doing their own cooking and cleaning, again towards claiming Honours. Most of those evenings ended with a sing-song or games around the camp fire and the girls also frequently indulged in apple-pie beds followed by a second supper before settling to sleep.

Does anyone really think that in the early part of the last century, an unmarried woman living in a very Christian home, surrounded by unmarried sisters, would have known what lesbianism was or meant? Even if she learnt about it once *The Well of Loneliness* appeared in 1928, it is quite unthinkable that EJO would have written anything into any of her stories which could possibly be misinterpreted by the girls and young women for whom they were intended.

Thanks to the charity work done by Mrs Dunkerley and her daughters, Elsie knew all about poor children living in slum conditions where single beds, far less single bedrooms, were unheard of. So to her the fact of sleeping together was a normal situation, whether in the slums, at camp, taking friends home for the occasional nights, at boarding school if one of the girls was unhappy or had any problems, even her own experiences of sharing rooms during Vacation Schools.

In *Rosaly's New School* (p. 101) she had Rosaly sleep with her little sister Rona when the younger girl, on her first-ever night away from home, was expected to sleep alone in a big empty dormitory. Then Rosaly comforted home-sick Freda the first night of the term: she 'crouched on the bed beside her.' Were either of those instances implied lesbianism? Or any more liable to lead to criticism than Joey saving Elisaveta in *The Princess of the Chalet School* (1927) by Elinor Brent-Dyer and the pair of them having to sleep together on the mountains all night? In fact, Elinor Brent-Dyer's books were full of instances of girls being caught on the mountains by snow storms or accidents and having to spend nights in shepherds' huts, or in coaches, huddled in close proximity on beds of hay or with seats arranged to make double beds for extra warmth. But no one pulls Elinor Brent-Dyer's books to pieces by saying they were full of implied lesbianism.

What about books written later which had Girl Guides sleeping together in shared camp tents? Were they open to equal censure as a result? The books written by Angela Brazil, slightly earlier than Oxenham and Brent-Dyer, had girls 'adoring' each other, or developing 'pashes' on their prefects and school mistresses, as well as kissing and cuddling each other and walking with their arms round the waists of their best friends.

Critics forget that Elsie wrote many of her books during the years of World War I and shortly afterwards, when it was perfectly normal for women to live together as she portrayed Norah and Con doing in *The Abbey Girls Win Through*. Often in that situation there was one woman with a strong character living with and taking care of a smaller, more delicate or domestically-inclined one. After World War II, it became sensible for single women to share their homes for safety, companionship and economy.

Whether they were shown as living together or not, one of EJO's chief skills lay in her ability through her books to show friendships between women in the nicest and best possible way. She was extremely good always at portraying friendships between opposing temperaments too. Joan and Joy were complete opposites in being thoughtful and 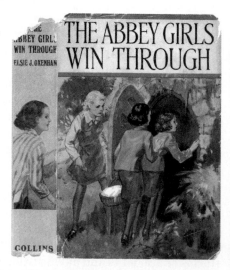 thoughtless. Others of EJO's contrasts covered the sisters Rachel and Damaris Ellerton and Elsa and Daphne Dale: good friends, both pairs, though they had completely opposing aims and ideals. Tormentilla and Antonia in the *Torments;* the one healthy and sports-mad, the other pretty and gentle. Polly/ Olwen and Jenny/Gwenver in *At School With the Roundheads;*

238

the first very clever but careless, while Jenny was slow with her school work, domesticated and appallingly self-conscious. Littlejan and Nanta Rose; Rosamund and Maidlin and also Maidlin and Biddy; Audrey and Hazel; Katharine and Dorothy-Ann; Rena and Nancy then later Rena and Elisabel: the list of fictional pairs is almost endless.

Yet in nearly every case of a deep, genuine and fond affection of females for others, they frequently just happened to be a couple in which one character had a stronger personality and was more capable than the other. At the same time Elsie showed that the seemingly boyish person of her couples often had a more private and gentle side. Rosamund choosing delicate lilac colours for her bedroom when it was decorated is perhaps the best-known instance, but Tormentilla revelling in the beauty and ceremonial of Camp Fire clothes and rituals, and Jinty going into raptures about Southwark Cathedral are others.

A lot more harm than looking for instances of sexuality can be done in a completely different direction when people have the effrontery to up-date books by altering original work. All they do in most cases is make themselves laughing stocks with their attempts to delete references to past historical events, alter words and phrases, update slang expressions, modernise references to pocket money and end by doing no more than making a mockery of those angles, whilst spoiling the originals for those who re-read the new versions remembering them as when they were first written. Early illustrations are often modernised too, often losing the charm of the originals and resulting in an important chapter of historical reference being lost for present and future generations.

Another recurrent criticism is that Elsie was 'unbelievably coy' if she wanted to say one of her characters was pregnant. True, but was that her fault? Publishers disliked all mention of pregnancy or birth in stories for girls before the 1950s and usually requested any such details to be removed. As her stories were written for older girls and included young married women as well as schoolgirls, what was she supposed to do? Perhaps, with those restrictions, the only solution was to do exactly as she did and show any young pregnant women as being 'wrapped in a loose coat', needing to 'buy a new dress', or not thinking it wise to join in any dancing, as the safest ways to imply, delicately, that a baby might be on the way.

Surprise has been expressed that when Joy was expecting twins ('wearing a loosely-falling wrap of pale green and white,') Maidlin didn't notice. Why should she have done? It was always stressed that Maidlin was young for her age so she probably genuinely thought Joy had put on weight during the months of her honeymoon abroad. Particularly when it is remembered that *The Abbey Girls Win Through*, in which Joy's twins were born, was published in 1928 when most young girls were innocent and extremely naive. The same thing happened when Jen was pregnant for the first time. Meeting Rosamund on her return from Switzerland after the death of her mother there, Maidlin, obviously referring to the arrival of the new baby which she had been warned not to mention, said of that secret, 'Oh, but we didn't know. I didn't!'

By *Biddy's Secret* (p. 96) only four years later, when Maidlin had no idea what she would find when hurrying to Biddy, while wondering just what was wrong and considering a possible baby, there was no thought of an illegitimate child; such things didn't happen to nice girls in those days. However much Biddy had always put herself first, she had been brought up to believe that marriage came before sex, so Maidlin had no fears in that direction.

Even the most devoted of her fans dislike the number of children given to EJO's main characters far too quickly. The pattern was to have a wedding, promptly followed by one of the above hints, then a comment about how much the person concerned would like to have boy or girl twins, and, nearly always, getting her expressed desire down to the wanted sex and even the planned names.

Since the *Abbey* series continued well into the second generation, Elsie Oxenham constantly needed to introduce new, younger characters to continue the series. Consequently her large families were a sensible way by which she ensured that there would always be several young girls coming along within the Abbey Clan to take on important rôles if she didn't succeed in bringing in anyone completely new or introducing someone from a previously written story.

She re-introduced girls from her much earlier books in many cases, such as Rena and Lisabel, Karen and Tazy, Robin and Gwynneth, Rachel and Damaris, Elsa and Daphne. Then, very importantly, came the return of Jandy Mac which paved the way for the introduction of a new character in the form of Janice's daughter Littlejan, thus starting the entire next generation of Abbey books.

Critics tend to be scathing about EJO's books, using expressions like 'cloud cuckoo land', 'maudlin passages' or 'impossible plots'. It must be remembered that her books were written for older readers than is generally assumed, and for more than one generation. As her original Abbey Girls matured and reached their early twenties and were thinking of marrying, yet another generation was coming along to prolong the entire story-line. Some of her older characters were bound to produce babies enabling her to provide another batch to follow them of the younger girls Elsie needed for future tales.

Critics also appear to forget that Elsie Oxenham was born well over one hundred years ago when standards were vastly different and when the girls for whom she was writing only wanted to read about others similar to themselves, but with a little something extra in their lives. Again it must be remembered that 'girls' to EJO indicated anyone up to the age of around twenty. For instance 'A tall girl, of twenty-one or thereabouts...' (*Girls of the Hamlet Club* p. 44) would be more likely to be described today as a young woman than as a girl. It was a time when girls who didn't have to leave school to go out to work stayed there if there was enough money for them to do so, until they were eighteen or nineteen. By which time they had put their hair up and lengthened their skirts although they were still looked upon and treated in many ways as schoolgirls.

Most of the girls with whom Elsie was in fairly close contact, such as those of her Camp Fire or in her Sunday Classes, were aged from fourteen to their early twenties and she was far better equipped to write for them than for the younger group about which people are so caustic when they dismiss her books as being 'only for children'. When she was asked to write for a younger age group, the sad result was her inset books being less good in comparison with those written the way she wanted and which came more naturally to her.

A legitimate criticism is that there were far too many twins within the families and that they almost always came to order. Another complaint is the way EJO gave her characters attractive, unusual, family or Biblical names, then promptly turned them into less pleasant nicknames. Dammy or Damson for Damaris, Patty-John for Patience Joan, Santa for Claudia, Pearly for Pernel, Turkey for Torkel, Dot and Blot for Dorothy and Blodwen are a few of the unfortunate examples. There are also combinations such as Raimey-Rose and Maddy-Rose, or shortened forms as when Rosanna and Rosilda were cut down to Zanna and Zilda. It was a pity she didn't keep the full names she had chosen in the first instances.

Ideas she had for names ten years before writing the books where they were needed included:

'We might call Jen's last boy Francis Patrick ... Chris could be Christopher George - I hate George but it would never be used; and Bernard could be Bernard David then she'd have all the 'Knights of the British Isles.'

It is interesting to note the 'we' at the start of that sentence, implying correctly, that she was in consultation with someone else on that point. In that case, the above statement was made in a letter to Doris Acland but the names were listed in *A Fiddler for the Abbey* (p. 26).

Another accusation by modern critics is of snobbery. With Arundel Castle so close to her own home, it was possibly no more than a desire to use the castle and at the same time bring in yet more 'extra' by showing girls that anything is possible in life. Using the castle gave EJO the chance to produce more plots with Roddy and his future with such an inheritance by birth, then the further additions when she wrote about more Kane cousins, thus again extending the new characters she needed to develop that connection.

Doris Acland told the keener enquirers:

'There was a certain amount of inverted snobbery attached to the houses of the various characters with little mention of servants of any kind and with the ex-May Queens usually chosen to take over as nursery nurses to the children in the homes of the more affluent members of the Clan. Joy with her 'never call me Miss Joy' yet having surprise expressed because she wouldn't leave one of her staff to be in hospital alone in America. Mrs Watson's speech slipping into dialect at times; Anne Bellanne taking over the kitchen at the Hall but expected to act as 'one of the family' as soon as she had finished her domestic duties, and many more instances. But as the series progressed it was clear that most of the girls, whether they had inherited fortunes or not, were living where they couldn't have managed their very busy lives without assistance of some kind for domestic chores. And EJO always made a point of expressing the opposite side of the question with making her main characters do a lot of voluntary and charity work, which would not have been possible had they been unable to afford help to leave them free to open garden parties, spend days taking poor children into the country, teach dancing or run Guide and Ranger Companies.

'Yet when the majority of the books were written, even middle class people normally managed to have a certain amount of help with housework, so really there was little wrong with the attitudes shown in the books bearing in mind when the majority were written and where some of the characters had to be shown to live. And at the same time although there were references to cooks and chauffeurs EJO was careful not to keep writing about gardeners, maids, cleaners and the other staff members there would probably have been in the backgrounds of nearly all the bigger houses given to the Abbey Girls.'

EJO was born when Queen Victoria was on the throne and large families were normal even if they didn't all have the numbers of twins she was so anxious to provide for her fictitious mothers, so it is rather pointless to make disparaging remarks about the number of children Joan, Joy, Jen etc. produced. So apparently easily too, with the exception of Joy when she had the twins, then when David was born in America. The only fault EJO committed about the constant births was in having the mothers lead ordinary lives with no worries about having to cope with the everyday problems which large families could bring, whether there was help in the house and nursery or not. Nothing as crude as morning sickness was ever mentioned, neither were any complications met nor described in her fictional families.

Another complaint has been the lack of anything in the books dealing with wars. It has been shown how in some

reprints of her Abbey books, references to World War I were removed. Elsie certainly wrote about the situation with troop trains, rations, helping in hospitals, relations being killed and, in her letters to Ribby, described events she experienced herself during air raids. All she wrote about Madam and the Pixie having taught dancing to the soldiers during World War I, was allowed to remain in the books, so it was rather pointless to delete sentences which mentioned any other war-time situations which had fitted naturally into her texts, even if only a casual reference in her backgrounds.

It would be sensible if critics of works by Elsie Jeanette Oxenham remembered that she was born some thirty years before women were allowed to vote and when hardly any young women of the (then) middle class went out to work as a matter of course. Unless it was essential to add to the family income, they stayed at home or did voluntary work.

CHAPTER TWENTY-ONE

The World-Wide Elsie Jeanette Oxenham Societies
or 'The School Societies' (*Girls of the Hamlet Club*)

'The Outcast Brotherhood is for people who can't join other things,'
Freda explained. She had drawn Peggy into a corner for a chat before
the school dinner was ready.
(*Peggy and the Brotherhood.* 1936. p. 102.)

In 1955, Elsie Jeanette Oxenham, via her main publisher,
received a request from four young readers collecting her books
in Australia who had formed themselves into a group of
'pretend' Abbey Girls, calling themselves Joan, Joy, Jen and
Jack. They were so fond of the books that they acted scenes
from them and had written to ask if she could provide any
fresh ideas they could portray as new playlets.

Elsie replied with two suggestions which the girls wrote
out as short plays they could act during their future meetings.
One was said to have been typed by Elsie and was headed
'written exclusively for my friends in 'The Abbey Club', with best
wishes, E.J.O.' Oddly, there was no part in either idea for
Jacky-boy.

The first plot for those schoolgirls was a variation of *Strangers at the Abbey*; about a girl from the village who had become an actress, instead of a hitherto unknown relation of Joy's who wanted to become one. The second idea was supposedly set soon after the time of Jen's accident and the discovery of Abbey treasures, which became Jen falling into an unknown tunnel and finding Ambrose's Bible.

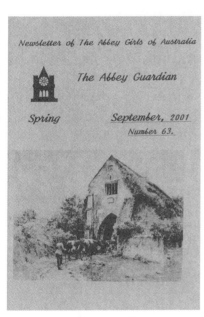

Newsletter of The Abbey Girls of Australia

The Abbey Guardian

Spring

September, 2001

Number 63.

Australian newsletter

Thirty years later one of those four Australian girls became a founder member of the Elsie Oxenham Society in Australia. That society, The Abbey Girls of Australia, with its newsletter *The Abbey Guardian*, was formed in 1985 by Kath Filmer, Kerry Griffiths and Val Shelley but within a couple of months there were more than fifty members. By the early 1990s there were over three hundred members, a number still rising, for whom their editor Val Shelley produced four newsletters a year, as she still does.

It wasn't until a meeting in 1988 that a similar Society was suggested in New Zealand, with a preliminary outline which was to have as editor Carol Grey, as well as a typist and a treasurer. Their first newsletter, *The Abbey Gatehouse*, was sent out in May 1989, coinciding with the first issue of *The Abbey Chronicle* in Great Britain. The British society was fortunate to have several typed copies of the scarcest books to pass on to the voluntary librarian Barbara Harris, due to the fact that after the death of Doris Acland, I (the first editor of *The Abbey Chronicle*) had been asked to take over all the lending. We also had a researcher; Olga Lock-Kendell, who suggested the name of *The Abbey Chronicle*. By the year 2002 membership in Britain had reached over five hundred. The position of editor was handed over to Ruth Allen in 1995. She has now retired and Fiona Dyer, formery her assistant, is the new editor.

The South African Society (*The Abbey Chapter*) was started in 1992 with an editor Polly Whibley plus a treasurer and librarian but sadly ceased when, soon after Polly had left South Africa, its second editor, Valerie Thomson, realised that due to pressure of work she could no longer continue.

The regular newsletters, journals or even fanzines as some people call them, and their members and gatherings vary greatly. The Australians, thanks to their climate, are able to organise outdoor functions for entire families with few problems regarding the provision of alternative venues should the weather be too cold or wet. As a result their newsletters usually contain details of outside activities and photographs of group meetings. An interesting fact is that the Australian members are generally younger than those

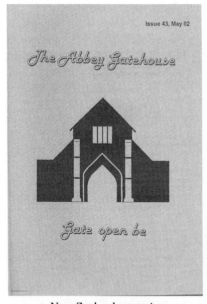

New Zealand magazine

elsewhere although, as in all the societies, their oldest are in their eighties. Being scattered over such a vast area, they hold regular local group meetings with voluntary secretaries to send reports of those, and any outings, for inclusion in *The Abbey Guardian.*

The Australians have copied Elsie's idea of holding coronations, members being crowned in ceremonies based on those described in the Abbey books. Their editor was invited to crown the first new queens but, with small groups in each state, every new person is now crowned by its previous queen. Ten years after the inception of *The Abbey Guardian,* Val Shelley was presented with a silver medal, matching those given to the May Queens of the Abbey books. At the same time she was made their President-for-life as Cicely Hobart had been in the Abbey books.

At each of their coronations there is a procession of as many previous chosen queens as possible from each area to welcome the new one. Queen Elaine had for her maid-of-honour Rita Lacy, the friend with whom she had been at school in England some forty years before, who had travelled there for that purpose. On a later visit Rita was made a queen herself, as have other members from Great Britain when they have visited Australia. If any queen is unable to attend, her flowers are carried on a cushion by someone to represent the missing person, as was shown to happen in the Abbey books.

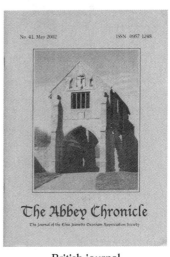

British journal

With voluntary help from members from different states in turn, bi-annual week-end camps in Australia are held with entertainments ranging from a Camp Fire meeting for onlookers to see their ceremonial rituals: a coronation; singing and plays; morris, sword and country dancing. There are book sales, workshops for members to learn the dancing, beadwork and other crafts described in the books, and always an

Australian queens

interdenominational service on the Sunday.

The New Zealanders also hold regular meetings, usually at the home of a member or at Ewelme Cottage because of its faint EJO associations. They include folk dancing whenever possible and invite speakers on subjects which link with the books. If any members from either country has been able to visit Cleeve Abbey in England, a talk about the site with photographs is often given and those visits will also be written about for their newsletters; a couple of enterprising members have taken video recordings back to New Zealand to show others. When their editor, Carol Grey, moved to Australia, Jane Webster took over as their second editor. She was succeeded by Barbara Robertson at the beginning of 2003.

In 1992 the first official weekend visit to Cleeve Abbey was organised for the society in Britain and people attended from all over the country with members from as far afield as Wales, Cumbria, London and Australia. Those have become bi-annual events and always start with lunch followed by dancing in the Abbey on the Saturday afternoons, then, later a typically Devon or Somerset cream tea. A book sale is held that Saturday evening before a dance party in a nearby village hall. Music and calling for the dancing are provided by members who also belong to the E.F.D.S.S. Sundays there are spent going to church, exploring the local area or revisiting the Abbey, wandering around trying to relate the different parts to the books.

During 1996, a coach trip was arranged for members from Australia to visit Great Britain and over a dozen of them plus one member from New Zealand and a few husbands (honorary Abbey Girls?) visited England to tour the Oxenham sites used in the books. Again the Abbey and Camp Fire spirits came to the fore as they were met at Heathrow by a London member and for their first weekend it was arranged for them to go to Whitelands to watch the crowning of the 1996 May King, then on to an Abbey dancing party that evening. In Sussex, as well as being taken for a walk on the Downs they were shown over Arundel Castle (Kentisbury) and invited to an Abbey/EJO meeting in a member's home. After going to Somerset the next day, where they met as many local people from *The Abbey*

Ewelme Cottage

Chronicle as could attend, they spent a morning in Cleeve Abbey. They then had lunch with those there from Devon, Somerset, Dorset and Hampshire before moving on to their next stop to explore Cheddar Gorge, for its faint relationship with *Adventure for Two*.

In Great Britain members have organised trips to various sites used in the books, including France and Switzerland, then written up their discoveries for issues of *The Abbey Chronicle*. Their earliest meetings were held at book fairs in different counties when members who lived locally were able to meet each other. The first group meeting, held in Brighton — rather special, in view of its nearness to Elsie's home in Worthing and the fact that she must have known the area - was attended by their editor, researcher and librarian as well as by a dozen of their original members.

In 1987 an extra weekend meeting was held at Cleeve Abbey, to present a seat with a plaque on it about Elsie Jeanette Oxenham's involvement, through her books, with the Abbey. Nearly eighty people attended that function.

A flourishing group in Sussex has always held weekly meetings and they are the main hostesses for any overseas visitors, being a convenient base for those making pilgrimages to where Elsie lived and worked during the second half of her life. It is also the district in which she set many of her early books; notably *The School of Ups and Downs* group, the *Debs* and the Ven and Gards so is a useful area to explore for backgrounds of those books. The Sussex members, largely as so many of the Oxenham places are local for them, tend to do their researching in groups, usually joined by others from London and anywhere else nearby. They then write up their findings for *The Abbey Chronicle*. Every editor has to rely on her members to fill the newsletters, most of whom do a wonderful job in supplying articles or providing photographs to compare places from old postcards as Elsie knew them, with how they appear today.

Some people belong to all the Societies, take all the newsletters and, if they travel abroad, attend any functions available in other countries. It is quite normal to contact the editor of whichever country a person is visiting, knowing she will then lay on meetings for as many to attend as possible, to include the overseas visitor or in some cases arranging accommodation with a member, thus making for more of world-wide friendships.

Society members poised for a group photograph 1995

Several members have traced genuine people, or their remaining relatives whom Elsie knew and put with disguised names into her stories. Then, with permission, they have passed on information about background details, dates and any other snippets of information. Madam's son Roger for instance, was able to supply details about the time his mother lived in Africa. Margaret Simey (née Bayne Todd) was visited by Rita Lacy, thanks to both of whom Elsie's Camp Fire Minute Books were retrieved after Margaret had cared for them for many years, and given back to Elsie's niece. Information was gleaned by Ros Bayley about an early school for gardeners in Sussex and the clothes they wore for their work, to connect with *New Girls at Wood End*. She also makes the bead badges and bookmarks used by members.

When Elsie's niece, Elspeth Dunkerley, found the three unpublished manuscripts her aunt had written (as described in chapter 15), the Sussex group helped with a lot of the work involved, to ensure the books would be printed. One member re-typed the original manuscripts and did illustrations for the first book to be published posthumously. They all helped with publishing details, proof-reading and general arrangements. Then with Elsie's nephew, Desmond, who, like his sister, is another writer in the Dunkerley family, the group assisted

The British Team – Ruth Allen, Monica Godfrey, Stella Bateman (Librarian) and Fiona Dyer

with helping to pack and post the eagerly awaited books.

Literary Societies have long been popular and are now available for authors such as Elinor Brent-Dyer, Lewis Carroll, Dorita Fairlie Bruce, Charlotte M. Yonge, Enid Blyton, Rudyard Kipling, Violet Needham, Arthur Ransome, Richmal

Crompton (*William*), W E Johns (*Biggles*) and Beatrix Potter. There are more generalised ones as well, such as *The Allied Literature Society* and *The Children's History Society* while *Folly* (*Fans of Light Literature for the Young*) began in 1990 to cover all books written in (loosely) the first seventy years or so of the twentieth century by authors old and new whose books are now collected seriously.

The collecting of what is mistakenly in many cases referred to as juvenile stories has become wide-spread in recent years with book fairs, antique fairs and dealers' lists making the interest more widely known. Many collectors belong to all the societies for the 'Big Three', as Oxenham, Brent-Dyer and Fairlie Bruce are known, and this makes for an extremely friendly world-wide kinship with so many people taking several newsletters, collecting books by similar writers and knowing each other well thanks to various meetings and their shared interests.

The individual EJO societies aren't only for receiving and reading each newsletter as it comes out and being content to leave just one person to do most of the work as happened in the beginning. The keenest members are those who do the most; not only helping with the production of hitherto unknown manuscripts and acting as hostesses to members from other parts of the country and those from overseas. They spread the word to publicise the fact that there are hundreds of people who still read EJO's and other writers' books and are doing their utmost to learn more about the places and people used in all of them, then taking time to write about what they have learnt for other interested persons to read in the various newsletters. There is also a small social side to each society with their meetings and outings. Members of them all go out of their way to find out-of-print books they can pass on to those still building up their collections.

Elsie herself was always enthusiastic about friendships as is clearly shown by her portrayals of them in her stories. The friendships being made between people nowadays who 'thought I was the only person who knew about her and her books', which is a standard comment when anyone learns about the

Societies, amount to an incredible number. Another version produces: 'I shall be forever grateful to you for rescuing me from the 'orphaned' feeling I had when I heard of Elsie's death and I was left assuming I was the only person on the planet remotely interested in the Abbey series.'

A member who is over eighty found her first book when she was ten. She reported that:

'Finding another soon afterwards about the same people meant that I was hooked at once and I've collected and re-read them ever since.'

The sight of an identifiable badge, or meeting anyone known to belong to one of the societies is an immediate indication that one is talking to the equivalent of an old friend rather than a stranger previously completely unknown. The talk is about mutual friends, of course, albeit starting with the fictional ones made and known through books.

POSTSCRIPT

What Happened Afterwards
or 'Sanctuary' (*Two Queens at the Abbey*)

'So you've come to say good-bye, Jenny-Wren.' 'We're all facing up to it; I'm so glad of that. It would be awful if they couldn't bear to think of it, and we all knew and let it haunt us in the background, but no one dared to speak of it!'
(*Queen of the Abbey Girls*. 1926 p. 276.)

With the death of her sister, Maida, on December the 2nd, 1953, Elsie lost her closest companion. They had been together from childhood, then as a pair for nearly the last twenty-five years and Maida was the person who helped her the most by looking after their home and with her proof-reading. Erica and Theo took over that latter task during Elsie's time in Marlposts Nursing Home while she was trying to complete *Two Queens at the Abbey*, which was to be her final book. *Two Queens at the Abbey* was dedicated to the staff there, where EJO spent the last two years of her life. She died in the Nursing Home on January 9th, 1960 not knowing that Erica had died in the same Nursing Home just a few days

The International Team – Jane Webster (New Zealand), Val Shelley
(Australia), Monica Godfrey (Britain), Ruth Allen (Britain)

earlier, on December 28th 1959.

The house in which Elsie and Maida had lived was left to
their remaining brother Roderic; it then passed to his wife
and afterwards to their daughter, Elsie's niece, Elspeth
Dunkerley. In her will Elsie wrote that after Roderic's death:

'I should like if possible for the house to be kept in the family
rather than sold to strangers ...'

The books Elsie had written were bequeathed to Erica but
as Erica predeceased Elsie by a few days, it was decided they
should be retained within Elsie's house together with the
original dustwrapper illustrations, rather than be moved to
be kept by her (then) remaining sister, Theo, at Conifers. After
the deaths of her three sisters, it must have been a long and
lonely time for Theo on her own; she died on her ninety-fifth
birthday, the 21st December 1981.

At the time when Maida died, Elsie wasn't too well herself
and was becoming increasingly tired. She wrote to Doris

Acland: 'I am a bit exhausted. It is the close reading that gets me down. Now having finished I have to try to relax from the nervous tension it [proof-reading] always causes in me.' She was also concerned every winter about bad weather conditions and another time wrote to Doris, 'I am taking no risks on icy roads, having had several bad falls.' Luckily, after Maida's final illness Elsie managed to find two morning helpers and an afternoon gardener.

The plaque on the seat presented to Cleeve Abbey in 1995

Following Elsie's death people were told by Doris Acland: 'Quite often Elsie knew in her head a mass of details about our Abbey friends, which were in her manuscripts but which never came into the printed books. She was tied down to a special length by publishers and was also prevented from including certain things. There is an inverted snobbery with one set of publishing people which objected to the mention of anybody's having a staff. (If *Girls of the Hamlet Club* was ever reprinted, all mention of servants was to be cut out!) This, I think, caused Elsie to make so many of her Hamlet Club Queens rush to be nurses to Rosamund and Joy - so it would look more as if friends were backing them up and they weren't employing a lot of nurses, maids and nannies. So silly, because however drearily a modern child may be taught, she must know that a huge castle and a big country manor couldn't be run by mother alone or a 'daily' once a week.'

As mentioned in the previous chapter, the appreciation of those belonging to the EJO Societies for her and her books became more tangible in 1995 when members of the Australian, New Zealand and Great Britain Societies contributed towards the buying and siting of a seat at Cleeve Abbey, complete with a plaque in memory of Elsie Jeanette Oxenham and her books. Nearly eighty members, Elsie's niece and nephew, a married couple from New Zealand, the Abbey caretakers, Cleeva Clapp's great-nephew and various friends and relatives, gathered there to watch the seat being presented to a representative from English Heritage who now owns the site. Many society members unable to attend sent cards and good wishes; one even made a telephone call from New Zealand that morning asking for her goodwill message to be passed on to those attending the ceremony. Unfortunately, Rhoda Collins, who did all the work towards choosing the seat and organising the plaque, was unable to be there on the day.

Speeches were made by the Patron of the English Society (Desmond Dunkerley, Elsie's nephew) and myself as the first editor of *The Abbey Chronicle*, as well as by Alan Henshaw from English Heritage, who accepted the seat on their and Cleeve Abbey's behalf.

Desmond's speech included the comment that if he'd known as a boy he'd have to make this speech in 1995, he 'would have taken notes', which caused much amusement. He ended with messages of good wishes and regrets because it was too far for them all to be there as well, sent by both the Australian and New Zealand Abbey groups; even a short piece in Maori. When he wrote his account for an extra issue of *The Abbey Chronicle* about the affair, he ended it with: 'Wouldn't Aunt Elsie have been amazed!'

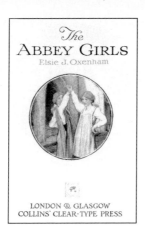

The
ABBEY GIRLS
Elsie J. Oxenham

LONDON & GLASGOW
COLLINS' CLEAR-TYPE PRESS

ENVOI

Elsie once wrote:

'I'm afraid the Abbey girls are only real in our minds. But I think they are ideals of mine - that is what I think girls ought to be like: so it is quite safe for you to try to be like them. I often feel that I should meet them if I went back to the Abbey; they seem very real to me.'

APPENDIX 1

THE ABBEY MAY QUEENS

Page numbers have been taken from first editions with the exception of *Girls of the Hamlet Club,* an early reprint. As will be seen, incidents in several of the books overlap. Page numbers cover those books in which each queen was either first suggested, discussed, chosen, crowned or appeared in her new role for the first time.

Date	Name	Colour/Flower	Book
1913	Miriam Honor	White/forget-me-not	*Girls of the Hamlet Club* (p. 288) *The Abbey Girls* (p. 48)
1914	Cicely Hobart	Gold/autumn leaves	*The Girls of the Abbey School* (p. 49/148) *Strangers at the Abbey* (p. 32)
1914	Marguerite Verity	Pink/marguerites	*The Girls of the Abbey School* (p. 102)

1915	Joy Shirley	Green/traveller's joy	*The Abbey Girls* (p. 70/196/276)
1916	Joan Shirley	Violet/violet	*The Girls of the Abbey School* (p. 8) *The Abbey Girls* (p. 314)
1917	Muriel Bayne	Blue/speedwell	*Strangers at the Abbey* (p. 29) *Robins in the Abbey* (p. 181)
1918	Nesta Green	Silver/honesty	*Strangers at the Abbey* (p. 18)
1919	Beatrice Randall (Bee)	Stripes/tulip	*Selma at the Abbey* (p. 243) *Tomboys at the Abbey* (p. 6)
1920	Barbara Honor (Babs)	Cream/wild rose	*The Abbey Girls Go Back to School* (p. 296) *The New Abbey Girls* (p. 152)
1921	Rosamund Kane	Crimson/rose	*The New Abbey Girls* (p. 304)
1922	Jen Robins	Brown/dancing yellow flowers	*The Abbey Girls in Town* (p. 276) *Queen of the Abbey Girls* (p. 108)
1923	Madalena di Ravarati (Maidlin)	Primrose/primrose	*The Abbey Girls Win Through* (p. 115/226)
1924		Dark green/ivy	*Robins in the Abbey* (p. 181)
1925	Anne	Dull pink/clover	*Tomboys at the Abbey* (p. 38)
1926		Blue/bluebell	*Robins in the Abbey* (p. 181)

| 1927 | | Scarlet/poppy | *Robins in the Abbey* (p.181) |

There is a small discrepancy with the order of the last, unnamed queens. The above is the way they are listed in *Robins in the Abbey* but in *A Fiddler for the Abbey* the flowers are quoted as being clover, bluebell, ivy and poppy, before Molly and Mirry. In *An Abbey Champion* the flower colours are given as clover-pink, dark ivy green, purple, lilac, bluebell, scarlet, before moving on to grey with garden flowers, then hyacinth in pink, blue and white.

Year	Name	Colour/flower	Source
1928	Grace Gray	Grey/a garden	*Robins in the Abbey* (p. 181) *A Fiddler for the Abbey* (p. 171)
1929	Molly	Blue/pink/hyacinth	*Robins in the Abbey* (p. 181)
1930	May	Lilac/lilac	*Robins in the Abbey* (p. 75)
1931		Purple/heather	*Robins in the Abbey* (p. 75)
1932	Miriam (Mirry)	Blue/forget-me-not	*Maid of the Abbey* (p. 191) *Robins in the Abbey* (p. 181)
1933	Joan Fraser (Littlejan)	Orange/marigold	*An Abbey Champion* (p.97/138/180/189) *Rachel in the Abbey* (p. 16)
1934	Jean Guthrie	Blue/green/rosemary	*Robins in the Abbey* (p. 75/166/183) *Guardians of the Abbey* (p. 72) *An Abbey Champion* (p. 199/201)
1935	Janice Raymond (Jansy)	Dark blue/lobelia	*Two Joans at the Abbey* (p. 221) *Robins in the Abbey* (p. 75)

			A Fiddler for the Abbey (p. 181/196)
			Guardians of the Abbey (p. 170)
			Rachel in the Abbey (p. 16)
1936	Rosalind Kane	Lavender/lavender/	*Rachel in the Abbey* (p. 184)
	(Nanta Rose)	grey	*Rachel in the Abbey* (p. 51/133/147/182/184)
			A Dancer from the Abbey (p. 98)
1937	Tessa	Yellow/lupin *Abbey*	*A Dancer from the Abbey* (p. 201/223)
			The Song of the Abbey (p. 148/210)
1938	Phyllida	Chestnut/wallflower	*Two Queens at the Abbey* (p. 8)
1939	Elizabeth Marchwood	Gold/buttercup)	*Biddy's Secret* (p. 53)
	Margaret Marchwood	White/daisy)	*Two Joans at the Abbey* (p. 221)
			The Song of the Abbey (p. 30)
			Two Queens at the Abbey (p. 186/248)

May Queen possibilities for Doris Acland's sequels

EJO suggested that one day Rosemary and Hermione might be queens. (*The Song of the Abbey* p.30)

1940	Elizabeth/Margaret for a 2nd year		*The Abbey Twins Take Charge*
1941	Cicely-Ann	Ruby on gold	
1942	Angela	Moonstone/?	

1943	Diana Edwards	Turquoise/?	
1944	Rosemary Marchwood	Opal/anemones	*Grandchildren of the Abbey*
1945	Jennifer Raymond	Amethyst/	

Possible names and flowers for future stories had the main series been continued. A mixture of Doris Acland and Elsie Oxenham's ideas.

Diana	Columbine
Cis Everett	Dahlia
(those two were to return as cookery students)	
Cis Honour	Aster
Rosemary Marchwood	Laburnum
Myonie	Fuchsia
Jennifer Raymond	Peach blossom
Katharine Marchwood	Camellia
Jillian Raymond	Delphinium
Maidie-Rose Quellyn	Pansy
Jantyjoy Fraser	Jasmine
Barbara-Rose	Cornflower

XVI. TAH-HOO-TAH-NA-KE

APPENDIX 2

ADDITIONAL CAMP FIRE NAMES AS IN CHAPTERS 5 AND 6

Camp Fire Names in the Oxenham Stories

Amahya	To plant a field
Amalaya	To plant a field
Amasika	To wake up
Ansudi	Cedar tree: protection, strength.
Apukwa	Bulrush
Ayashe	Chipmunk
Camp Keema	The camp to face the wind
Camp Tatapochon	The camp that cannot be pulled apart
Camp Watéwin	The camp of those who conquer
Catalina	Lighthouse: light
Cheemaun	Canoe: glides gracefully
Chekesu	The North-West wind
Chelan	Pure water: clear, untroubled thoughts
Dahinda	Frog
Disyadi	Moon-child

Estrella	Star: light and thought
Gitala	Straightforward
Hakanaki	The Sunrise
Heather	Covering ugliness: thinking of others
Iris	Rainbow: radiance and light
Ivy	Fidelity
Kataga	Stormy Waves
Kayoshk	Sea-gull: riding the storm
Keewaydin	North-West Wind
Keya	Tortoise
Killoleet	Song sparrow: make music
Kiloqua	Lake of the Great Star
Kimana	The butterfly
Kitigan	A garden: to plant seeds and rear beautiful flowers
Kiyugan	To Open Doors: doors of understanding
Kokokoho	The Owl: lover of books and wisdom
Koon	Snow: the beautifier of people's lives
Kootima	Moonlight Brook
Kudeska	Bird
Lexso	The Clover leaf: leaves are Work/Health/Love
Mavis	Thrush: joy
Minnehaha	Cheerfulness
Mnanka	Spider
Mutoma	Canoe
Nanistina	I make it
Nawadaha	The singer: mother of sweet music
Noonatomen	Rejoicing
Notaway	The Thinker
Nyoda	The Rainbow: the sun will shine after rain
Odatoka	Friendship
Ohitaya	To be brave
Olive	Peace

268

Omeme	Pigeon: tenderness, gentleness
Opechee	Robin: cheerful on dark and dreary days
Oyaka	To tell a story
Pamela	Harp: tuneful
Renee	Queen: leads people in the right path
Rosemary	Remembrance
Ruth	Friendliness
Senhahlonee	The builder: she is still building
Shingbesis	Diver: plunges to the bottom of things
Shuhshuhga	Heron
Shutanka	To meet in Council together
Sinajo	Grey squirrel
Sinago	Grey squirrel
Sisoka	The Robin
Tampa	Silver Birch Tree
Tamwokna	The Beaver: busy life
Taté	Wind: freshen things up all around
Tawasi	The Camp that gives service
Tawatenya	Willing for anything
Tchuka	To swim upstream
Tiamalia	Little Eagle: let your thoughts reach to the clouds and dwell in the high mountains
Tinega	Sunset
Toandoah	The Inventor
Tude	Poplar
Tumaga	The Bee: look for the sweetness in life and pass it on to others
Uda	Firefly: doing sudden and unexpected kindnesses for people
Udeska	The bird
Watowa	To be observing
Wawa	Wild Goose:
Wabasso	Rabbit: runner
Wabun	East Wind: piercing, going to the heart of things

Wacinpiyokipi	Contented
Wahwahtaysee	Firefly
Wanaka	Sun-halo
Wanakiwin	Tranquillity
Watanopa	Adventurous one: new experiences and opening new ways in life
Watowa	To be observing
Wenonah	Thoughtful
Winnakee	The birch wood
Wiwanga	To ask questions
Wowasake	Strength
Witawentin	Learn to live together: to show unselfishness with others around
Witonohi	She who withholds nothing: gives all of herself
Wopida	Gratitude: always to show her gratitude
Yalaila	Clear Water
Yallani	The Mountain: stick to what is right
Yemis	Wild rose
Yoki	Rain Cloud
Yulalonan	To move to and fro

Some other Camp Fire names and meanings

Most of these were among EJO's notes; not all used in her books or by her own Camp Fire Girls.

Ahneah	Rose Flower
Aju	
Amahya	To plant a field
Amasika	To wake up: wake oneself and people to new thoughts and ideas
Ataensie	
Hahnahwen	Butterfly: warmth in the sun
Iwa	Among the hills
Kanxi	Honey bee: sweetness
Keego	The fish
Marenpo	Pollen dreamer
Minnetoska	Happy Laughter

Minobi	Of the glad heart
Minowe	Magic voice: bird song.
Mutoma	The canoe
Naditalia	Adventurous, brave
Nakanabi	Sunrise
Nanistina	I make it
Neechee	Needed and cheerful
Nodoneyo	The hill of the winds
Odakonya	Friendly
Odakola	Friendship
Okiciyapi	Helping each other
Owasaka	To accomplish and to be strong
Oyaka	To tell stories
Pakwa	The frog: skill in diving
Ruth	Friendliness
Sesoka	Red breasted robin
Shada	Pelican
Shawandasee	South Wind
Shingebis	Swimmer
Shivixi	To become stronger
Takima	To form a circle
Tawatenya	Willing for anything
Tehuka	The one who swims up-stream
Temskwahtawah	Hospitality: open door
Tinega	Sunset
Udeska	The bird
Wacinpiyokipi	Contented
Walohi	Thrill of dawn
Watowa	To be observing
Wawa	Wild Goose
Winnakee	The birch wood
Wowasake	Strength
Yaka	
Yobenish	Barberry

These names have appeared in American Camp Fire stories, other books and in various Camp Fire Handbooks published over the years:

Aicicya	Try hard
Agogo	Hush thee child
Agokay	
Akaga	Creator
Akiyuhapi	Carry together
Apadenska	Butterfly
Ataya	Go direct
Awakiya	Band together
Camp Chattahoochee	
Camp Keewayadin	
Camp Manasquan	
Camp Winnebago	
Cantewasteya	Generous
Cheskchamay	Friends
Ehawee	Happiness
Exetu	Right
Hachee	
Hahhnahwen	Butterfly
Hinopa	
Iyopta	Making progress
Kinunka	Growth
Konza	Influence
Migwan	
Miniheca	Industrious
Minoway	
Naswawkee	Feathered arrow
Nyoda	
Odako	Friendship
Ohanpi	Generous
Oicitinza	Command self
Okiciapi	Helping others
Okihi	Can accomplish
Oawwensa	Flower of the sun
OhPshaw	

Owa	Painter
Pisipika	Leader
Phumalua	To write
Saquasipi	River of mystery
Sawah	
Snahnah	Merriness
Soangetaka	Strong heart
Stella	Star
Tanda	Respect
Tawanka	Willingness
Tayiito	Counsellor
Waasniyan	Healer
Wacankiya	Loving
Wacinton	Understanding
Waditaka	Brave
Wahanka	Achieve
Wakmusuda	Little Buttercup
Wanaka	
Wapikiya	
Waspanikiya	Baker
Wendat	People of one speech
Wawbansee	Mirror water
Wicaka	Faithfulness
Wohdekeca	

APPENDIX 3

DESCRIPTIONS OF FIRST EDITIONS

These are described from my own collection with help from other collectors on some angles. (N.B. Colours of boards were often changed during print runs and black lettering replaced gilt. The same illustrations were not always used for the covers, even within the same print run.)

Each book is given with:
1. Date of the first edition plus actual month if known, names of illustrator and publisher.
2. Description of colour and front cover.
2a. Description of spine.
3. Description of the front dustwrapper if known.
3a. Description of the spine of the dustwrapper if known
4 Dedication if there was one.

GOBLIN ISLAND

1. 1907 T. H. Robinson. Collins. 2. Red. Gilt lettering. Picture in a strip down right side of girl walking through wood, reading. Goblins in the trees. 2a. Goblins in trees. 3. An island with large goblins. (The end papers, frontispiece and title page

are on glossy paper, highly decorated with swirling goblins.)
A PRINCESS IN TATTERS
    1. 1908 F. Adams Collins. 2. Red. Title in gilt frame. Picture in rectangular onlay of Mollie Raby thinking. 3. Artist in square onlay, watched by Eilidh. 3a. Title/author. 4. *To my mother.* (Frontispiece and title page on glossy paper.)
THE CONQUEST OF CHRISTINA
    1. 1909 Grace B. Foyster. Collins. 2. Dark green. Title in a gilt square. Three people on horses in an onlaid square. 2a. Christina against the wind. 4. *To my Father.*
THE GIRL WHO WOULDN'T MAKE FRIENDS
    1. 1909 P. B. Hickling. Nelson. 2. Green. Robin, Cuthbert and Dicky clambering over ruins. 2a. Girl standing. 4. *To Hugo.*
MISTRESS NANCIEBEL
    1. 1910 James Durden. Frowde/Hodder. 2. Blue. Nanciebel and her father standing on the shore. 2a. Nanciebel tending her flowers. 4. *To my dear father and mother with love.*
A HOLIDAY QUEEN
    1. 1910 E. Overnell. Collins. 2. Dark green. Gilt lettering. Picture in square onlay of Miss Sparrow and Alexa seated at table aboard a ship. 2a. Girl with long hair. 4. *To the members of Queen Lexa's Chinese meeting. (*Frontispiece and title page on glossy paper.)
ROSALY'S NEW SCHOOL
    1. 1913 T. J. Overnell. Chambers. 2. Bluey green. Gilt lettering. Rosaly in green, holding her beret on, with a stick to throw for Rough. 2a. Both their heads in a circle. 3. Hubert sitting on a rock, talking to the three elder children. 3a. Part of the Chinese tea party. (Both taken from internal illustrations.) 4. *To my dear mother and father with best love.*
SCHOOLGIRLS AND SCOUTS
    1. 1914 A. Dixon. Collins. 2. Red. Gilt lettering. 2a. Title/author. 4. *To Mildred Elizabeth Hills and Gladys Mary Hills my friends from Samoa - 'Ma le Alofa'.*
    (Frontispiece and title page on glossy paper.)

GIRLS OF THE HAMLET CLUB

1. 1914 Oct. Harold Earnshaw. Chambers. 2. Dark blue. Cicely and Miriam with school books. 2a. Cicely. 3. Three girls walking in woods, followed by two others. 3a. Cicely sitting on a fence. 4. *To all who share my love for the hamlets, hills and beechwoods of Bucks. This story of the Hampden country is dedicated in remembrance.*

from *Expelled from School*

AT SCHOOL WITH THE ROUNDHEADS

1. 1915 Oct. H. Earnshaw. Chambers. 2. Dark blue. Polly/ Olwen explaining their presence to the boys. 2a. Polly and Pinky walking. 3. Nesta leaving Desdemona with Oliver. 3a. Polly walking against the wind. 4. *To Roderic Dunkerley a lover of girls and boys this book is affectionately dedicated.*

THE TUCK-SHOP GIRL

1. 1916. H. Earnshaw. Chambers. 2. Green. A Girl Guide holding a staff. A fire burning behind her. 2a. Jinty. 3. As

276

internal illustration. Four Guides; Theo attending to their fire. 3a. Jinty climbing down the ivy. 4. *To my dear mother and father I dedicate this book with all best love.*

FINDING HER FAMILY

1. 1916 W. Stacey. S.P.C.K. 2. Pale blue. Audrey and Mr Dunster sitting in the sand dunes. 2a. Floral swathes. 3. One of the internal illustrations duplicated. 3a. Plain. 4. *To all friends of the S.H.S..* (Frontispiece tissue-guarded.)

A SCHOOL CAMP-FIRE

1. 1917 Percy Tarrant. Chambers. 2. Yellowy/fawn. A Camp Fire Girl. holding a candle. 2a. Girl on a swing. 3. Two Camp Fire girls and a Girl Guide sitting at a fire. Schoolgirl standing looking at them. 3a. Schoolgirl standing on cliff top. (n.b. dustwrapper by Elizabeth Earnshaw). 4. *To the girls who sit with me around the Camp Fire this book is dedicated with love and all best wishes by their guardian.*

THE SCHOOL OF UPS AND DOWNS.

1. 1918 Nov. H. Earnshaw. Chambers. 2. Pale green. A Camp Fire Girl in her 'middy'. 2a. Schoolgirl in outdoor jacket. 3. Camp Fire Girls sitting around a fire, with Libby standing. 3a. Schoolgirl standing on cliff top. (N.B. dustwrapper by Elizabeth Earnshaw). 4. *Dedicated with love and best wishes to my little "Bestest friend", "Ribby" (Reginald Willis Wilson)*

EXPELLED FROM SCHOOL

1. 1919 Victor Prout. Collins. 2. Blue. Retta in black skirt, blue top and beret, waving. Mountains behind. 2a. Schoolgirl. 3. Two girls, in red and blue, one with a stick, walking up a mountain. 3a. Retta and Malcolm talking. 4. *Dedicated to my dear mother and father with best love in memory and anticipation of happy days in Switzerland.*

A GO-AHEAD SCHOOLGIRL

1. 1919 Nov. H. Earnshaw. Chambers. 2. Rusty-red. Girl in red jersey, beret and black skirt holding hockey stick. 2a. Rena and Nancy rock-climbing. 3. Rena and Nancy on moors, watched by 3a. Rex and Rufus on spine. 4. *Dedicated with much love and all best wishes to Reginald W. Wilson (Ribby) and Violet A. Ellis (Bear) the 'Wriggles' and 'Eddy' of this story.*

THE SCHOOL TORMENT

1. 1920 June. H. Earnshaw. Chambers. 2. Fawn. Plain.
2a. Floral hanging under title. 3. Tormentil on a bicycle, riding
ahead of two boys. 3a. Boy on a bicycle. 4. *To my father with
love and many thanks for many things.*

THE TWINS OF CASTLE CHARMING.

1. 1920 Swarthmore Press. 2. Red. 2a. Plain. 3. Melany
and Zanne looking towards the castle. 3a. Carried round to
the spine. 4. *To my travelling companion in Switzerland, my
mother, this story is dedicated with much love and many happy
thoughts.*

from *Girls of the Hamlet Club*

THE ABBEY GIRLS

1. 1920 Arthur Dixon. Collins. 2. Blue. Joy with stick over
her shoulder, walking. 2a. Joan working. 3. Joy in Quaker
costume dancing. 3a. Watched by other schoolgirls. 4. *To the
Camp Fire Girls who have joined with me in folk dance
evenings this story is affectionately dedicated.*

278

TWO FORM CAPTAINS

1. 1921 July. P. Tarrant. Chambers. 2. Dark blue. The title in a large oval, background pale green floral with vertical lines. 2a. Title in oval. 3. Tazy, Bill and the Spud on the mountains, admiring the view. 3a. Continues onto spine. 4. *To my dear mother and father this my twenty-fifth book is dedicated with deepest gratitude and best love.*

THE GIRLS OF THE ABBEY SCHOOL

1. 1921 Elsie Anna Woods. Collins. 2. Blue. Dick and Della examining an old door. 2a. Two schoolgirls with a torch. 3. Two girls dancing on the abbey garth. 3a. Two others. 4. *To those members of the English Folk Dance Society from whom I have received so much helpful enjoyment this story is dedicated in grateful acknowledgement of all their kindness.*

THE ABBEY GIRLS GO BACK TO SCHOOL

1. 1922 Elsie Anna Woods. Collins. 2. Blue. Green panel with Joy and Jen, both with short black (?) hair, in gym. tunics in a motor bike/sidecar. 2a. Joy on motor bike, head-on view. 3. Jen with fair plaits in blue dance dress. 3a. Girl dancing, face-on . 4. *To Helen Kennedy North and D.C. Daking with thanks for all they have given to me.*

THE CAPTAIN OF THE FIFTH.

1. 1922 April P. Tarrant. Chambers. 2. Fawn. Thora in school uniform. 2a. Head of same girl. 3. Four schoolgirls greeting another who is running towards them. 3a. Watched by another schoolgirl. 4. *This story is dedicated with much love to my dear mother and father.*

PATIENCE JOAN, OUTSIDER

1. 1922 Cassell. 2. Purple. Oval onlay of two schoolgirls and Patience Joan carrying her coat. 2a. Gilt outline of schoolgirl. 3. Camp Fire girl tending a fire. 3a. Schoolgirl running. 4. *Dedicated to the Camp Fire Girls of the British Isles and Their Guardians by a Camp Fire Guardian.*

THE JUNIOR CAPTAIN

1. 1923 Oct. Percy Tarrant. Chambers. 2 Fawn. Camp Fire girl holding a candle (the same as *A School Camp Fire*). 2a. Also the same as *A School Camp Fire*. 3. Barbara in her gown making the sign of fire to Ven and Gard seated on the

ground. A cushion and tray before them. 3a. Not known. 4. *With best love I dedicate this book to my dear father and mother.*

THE NEW ABBEY GIRLS

1. 1923 Elsie Anna Woods. Collins. 2. Blue. Maidlin with black plaits in green outfit and tennis racquet. 2a. Schoolgirl with green blazer and black skirt. 3. As cover but now wearing pink. 3a. Jen dancing. 4. *To Cecil J. Sharp and his Folk Dancers who have brought so much colour into our everyday life.*

THE SCHOOL WITHOUT A NAME

1. 1924 Oct. Nina K. Brisley. Chambers. 2. Fawn. Audrey as a Camp Fire Guardian handing her torch to Marjory. 2a. Berry admiring her new girdle. 3. Elizabeth and Gard sitting/leaning on a wall, talking to Berry. 3a. Berry admiring her girdle. 4. *To* my *dear mother and father I dedicate this book with all best love.*

TICKLES, OR THE SCHOOL THAT WAS DIFFERENT

1. 1924 Partridge. 2. Blue. Phyl and Tickles talking. 2a. Floral. 3. Girls walking through woods carried on to spine.

THE GIRLS OF GWYNFA

1. 1924 Warne. 2. Dark green. Embossed lines. 2a. Gilt title. 3. Maisry meeting Pen and her sister from a coach (by Nina K Brisley). 3a. A Puritan maiden going downstairs in secret. 4. *This story of Adventure in a Far Country is dedicated to HUGO and PRIM with all love and best wishes.*

THE ABBEY GIRLS AGAIN

1. 1924 Elsie Anna Wood. Collins. 2. Dark blue. Girl in tunic dancing (by C. Morse) set in orange circle. 2a. Jen in blue dress, with bells and handkerchief. 3. A pillow fight, Jacky-boy in pyjamas watched by Joan or Joy on a bed. 4. *To Madam who teaches us and dances to us and the Pixie who gives us help and wise advice this story is dedicated with thanks for continued friendship.*

THE ABBEY GIRLS IN TOWN.

1. 1925 Rosa Petherick. Collins. 2. Fawn. Girl's head in red circle. 2a. Girl in blazer. 3. Three girls with short hair, drinking tea. 3a. One in a cloche hat waving goodbye. 4. *To Margaret Bayne Todd Camp Fire Girl folk-dancer with love and happy thoughts of vacation school days.*

THE TESTING OF THE TORMENT.

1. 1925 P. B. Hickling. Cassell. 2. Grey. Vertical leaves with an oval picture in the centre. Same as the frontispiece, showing Marsaili as a Camp Fire Girl lighting a candle watched by Torment and Antonia who are seated. 3. Full plate of the same scene. 3a. Tormentilla at door, seeing Penelope crying by her bed.

VEN AT GREGORY'S

1. 1925 Sep. Nina K Brisley. Chambers. 2. Blue. Ven leaning over garden gate and waving. 2a. Phyllida in her fiddler's outfit playing a violin. 3. and 3a. As cover. 4. *To my dear mother and father I dedicate with book with all best love.*

QUEEN OF THE ABBEY GIRLS

1. 1926 E. J. Kealey. Collins. 2. Fawn. Girl's head in red circle. 2a. Girl in blazer. 3. Girls playing cricket; castle in background. 3a. Girls dancing (same as one of *The Abbey Girls* illustrations.) 4. *Dedicated to the memory of the best of mothers and to my father John Oxenham with heartfelt thanks for the*

very real help of a great example in hope and faith by Elsie Jeanette Oxenham.

A CAMP FIRE TORMENT

1. 1926 Enid Brown. Chambers. 2. Dark blue. Gilt lettering. Plain 3. Veronica in skirt, jumper and red 'tammy' lighting a camp fire. Marsaili watching and two more coming to join the circle. 3a. Torment standing with hands in blazer pockets. 4. *Dedicated in gratitude to my sister Marjorie (Maida) who reads my proofs and saves me many precious hours.*

THE TROUBLES OF TAZY.

1. 1926 Oct. P. Tarrant. Chambers. 2. Dark blue. Rippled blue/black with gilt lettering. 3. Four girls sitting on rocks talking. 3a. Tazy playing tennis. 4. *To J.O. and M.B.T. my companions in Haute Savoie with happy thoughts of happy days.* (N.B. John Oxenham and Margaret Bayne Todd.)

PEGGY MAKES GOOD

1. 1927 H. L. Bacon. Partridge. 2. Blue. Peggy looking at two black cats. 2a. A plant. 3. Three girls marooned on island. 3a. Girl in boat, opening basket to let cats out.

JEN OF THE ABBEY SCHOOL

1. 1927 F. Meyerheim. Collins. 2. Blue. Gilt head of girl (Jen?) in circle. 2a. Title and author in gilt. 3. Two fair-haired girls having a picnic, one pouring out tea. 3a. Head and shoulders of girl with dark plaits.

PATIENCE AND HER PROBLEMS.

1. 1927 Molly Benatar. Chambers. 2. Dark blue. Plain with gilt lettering. 2a. As cover. 3. Barbara sitting on fence piping while Patience Joan listens. Mountains in the background. 3a. Barbara in her Camp Fire gown with a candle. 4. *To my dear mother and father with my love and thanks.*

THE ABBEY GIRLS WIN THROUGH

1. 1928 Mills. Collins. 2. Blue. Plain with gilt figure of girl bottom right. 3. Rosamund and Maidlin arriving from a car. 3a. Girls waving. 4. *Dedicated with happy thoughts to my mother and with deep gratitude to my father for the help they have given in more ways than they know.*

THE CRISIS IN CAMP KEEMA

1. 1928. Aug. P. Tarrant. Chambers. 2. Dark blue. Plain

with gilt lettering. 2a. As spine. 3. A Camp Fire girl standing at a fire. A Girl Guide watching, holding her company flag. 3a. The same two girls walking together. 4. *To my sisters Marjorie, Theodora, Erica and my sisters-in-law Daphne and Prim.*

THE ABBEY GIRLS AT HOME
1. 1929 Inder Burns. Collins. 2. Orange. Two girls in circle, one in striped blazer. 2a. Two girls on spine. 3. Rosamund waving goodbye from car to the school. 3a. Two schoolgirls walking. 4. *To my Father and Mother whose teaching has meant so much to me and all of us.*

DEB AT SCHOOL
1. 1929 Aug. N. K. Brisley. Chambers. 2. Red. Plain with gilt lettering. 2a. Plain. 3. Chloe in bathing costume, beckoning to Deb. 3a. Deb with surreptitious box of chocolates .

THE ABBEY GIRLS PLAY UP
1. 1930 Collins. 2. Blue. Plain with gilt girl bottom right. 2a. Title and author in gilt. 3. Cecily-Tom playing her pipe on the Downs. 3a. Maribel and Rosalind watching.

DOROTHY'S DILEMMA
1. 1930 Aug. Nina K Brisley. Chambers. 2. Red. Plain with black lettering. 2a. Plain. 3. Two girls, one standing,

one sitting, beside a pool. 3a. Two girls climbing stairs of a bus.

DEB OF SEA HOUSE

1. 1931 Aug. Nina K. Brisley. Chambers. 2. Red. Plain with gilt lettering. 2a. Plain . 3. Selina and Deb. walking in the snow; one in red other in blue. 3a. Deb and Hilda.

THE ABBEY GIRLS ON TRIAL

1. 1931 C.P.S. Collins. 2. Dark blue. Gilt patterned border. 2a. Title and author. 3. Two girls in a car. 3a. Girl writing.

BIDDY'S SECRET Sub-titled *A Romance of the Abbey girls.*

1. 1932 Sep. N.K.Brisley. Chambers. 2. Blue. Plain with gilt lettering. 3. Ruth with Elizabeth and Margaret walking down steps. 3a. Ruth looking over carved railings.

THE CAMP MYSTERY

1. 1932 T. Howard. Collins. 2. Dark blue. Plain with gold blocks around the edges and for the lettering. 2a. Same at top and base of spine. 3. Two girls having a picnic, one in Guide uniform. 3a. Girl in red cardigan and beret.

THE REFORMATION OF JINTY

1. 1933 Sep. Rene Cloke. Chambers. 2. Red. Plain with gilt lettering. 2a. plain. 3. Theo, Jinty and Kirsten coming out of Pets' Corner. 3a. Jinty holding Roger.

ROSAMUND'S VICTORY Sub-titled *A Romance of the Abbey girls.*

1. 1933 Victor Cooley. Harrap. 2. Blue. Slanting darker blue lines. 2a. Flower sprays. 3. Rena and Lisabel with rucksacks sitting outside a cottage. Rosamund hanging a sign out of the window. 3a Rena and Lisabel in their working clothes.

MAIDLIN TO THE RESCUE Sub-titled *A Story of the Abbey girls.*

1. 1934 (Sep.) Rene Cloke. Chambers. 2. Blue. Plain with gilt lettering. 2a. Same. 3. Rachel and Damaris wearing shorts, sitting on side of a mountain. 3a. Their heads.

JINTY'S PATROL

1. 1934 Newnes. 2. Light blue. An aeroplane on cover. 3. Girl's head against a trellis. A schoolgirl coming to look for her. 3a. Roger begging.

JOY'S NEW ADVENTURE Sub-titled *A Romance of the Abbey girls.*

1. 1935 Sep. Rene Cloke. Chambers. 2. Blue. Plain with gilt lettering. 2a. Same. 3. Joy and Maidlin sitting on cushions in the Abbey. 3a. Joy and the twins, heads only. 4. To *my friend Margaret Linn who has always maintained that Joy's story was not finished.*

PEGGY AND THE BROTHERHOOD.

1. 1936. P. Hickling. GOP. 2. Green. Plain with raised pattern and vertical lines. 2a. as cover. 3. Girl in blazer being greeted by boy dressed as Red Indian. Two girls and another boy seated at table, all with Red Indian head-dresses. Candles on table. 3a. Carries onto spine.

SYLVIA OF SARN

1. 1937 Warne. 2. Pale blue. Plain. 2a. title/author. 3. Megan and Sylvia looking out to sea. 3a. The girls' heads.

DAMARIS AT DOROTHY'S

1. 1937 Alfred Bestall. Sheldon Press. 2. Red. Rose tree and roses. 2a. Title/author. 3. Pip and Patsy lying on sand dunes. 3a. Two girls, one catching a ball.

ROSAMUND'S TUCK-SHOP Sub-titled *A School Story.*

1. 1937 Girls Own Paper Office. 2. Dark green. Plain with embossed vertical lines, gilt lettering. 2a. Same 3. Rena and Lisabel in smocks and leggings, gardening. 3a. Carried to spine, with one of them standing.

MAIDLIN BEARS THE TORCH Sub-titled *An Abbey Story*

1. 1937 The Girl's Own Paper Office. 2. Dark Green. Embossed vertical lines with gilt lettering. 2a. Same. 3. Maidlin and Cecily-Tom in Camp Fire dress, by a fire. Benedicta standing. 3a. Another Camp Fire girl. 4. *To my father John Oxenham to whose unending sympathy and encouragement we owe so much.*

SCHOOLDAYS AT THE ABBEY

1. 1938 Norman Sutcliffe. Collins. 2. Dark green with silver lettering. Plain. 3. Joan, Joy and Jen seated on ground with a cave behind them. 3a. Jandy Mac standing in entrance.

ROSAMUND'S CASTLE

1. 1938 GOP. 2. Orange with gilt lettering. Plain. 2a. Same. 3. Tansy attacking the stag. 3a. Elizabeth and Margaret in bushes behind her. 4. *To my father John Oxenham with love and thanks for his unfailing interest and encouragement.*

SECRETS OF THE ABBEY

1. 1939 Heade. Collins. 2. Green/silver. Plain. 3. Joan, Joy, Janice and Jen discovering a square hole in the wall. 3a. Carried onto spine. 4. *To Dorita Fairlie Bruce with thanks for all the pleasure her Dimsie, Prim and Nancy have given to me and so many others.*

PATCH AND A PAWN

1. 1940 Warne. 2. Red. Plain with a crown in the centre. 2a. Same. 3. Patch in a canoe watched by other children. 3a. Patch on a horse.

STOWAWAYS IN THE ABBEY

1. 1940 Heade. Collins. 2. Green/silver. Plain. 3. Jen in dressing gown, torch aimed at Susie and Timothy Spindle on the steps. 3a. Carried onto spine. 4. *To my father John Oxenham with love and thanks for sympathy and encouragement.*

DAMARIS DANCES

1. 1940 Margaret Horder. OUP. 2. Grey. A hen, a mask and a ribbon in red, as is the title. 2a. Ballet shoes. 3. Elsa looking out to sea/Daphne as a ballerina. 3a. A hen over ballet shoes and a bee. 4. *To my father John Oxenham whose enjoyment of this story chapter by chapter as it was being written gave me courage to go on.*

ADVENTURE FOR TWO

1. 1941 Margaret Horder. OUP. 2. Yellow. Small stage set with two ballet dancers. 2a. Oars against sea and cloud. 3. Table with oars, ballet shoes, reel of cotton, tape measure. 3a. Elsa in slacks and Daphne in a tutu, one each side of a signpost 4. *To my dear father John Oxenham with all happy thoughts of love and gratitude.*

JANDY MAC COMES BACK

1. 1941 Heade. Collins. 2. Dark Green. Plain with silver lettering. 2a. Same. 3. Janice on horse looking down to river.

3a. Continues onto spine. 4. *To my father John Oxenham with love and thanks for encouragement and sympathy which have never failed us.*

PERNEL WINS

1. 1942 Margaret Horder. Muller. 2. Green. Plain. 2a. Title/author. 3. Head of girl looking down onto Joylands. 3a. Title/author. 4. *To Doris and Julian Acland who have been good friends to Pernel.*

MAID OF THE ABBEY

1. 1943 Heade. Collins. 2. Dark green. Plain with silver lettering. 2a. Same. 3. Maidlin listening to Lindy singing to the twins. 3a. Plain. 4. *Dedicated to my sister Maida on the day we bought our little house.*

ELSA PUTS THINGS RIGHT

1. 1944 Margaret Horder. Muller. 2. Orange. A line of costumed ladies from top to bottom. 2a. Title/author. 3. A broken tree with Elsa one side and Nancybell the other. 3a. Title/author. 4. *Dedication to my dear mother and father with all loving and happy thoughts.*

TWO JOANS AT THE ABBEY

1. 1945 Margaret Horder. Collins. 2. Dark green. Plain, silver print. 2a. Same. 3. A large bell with girls dancing

underneath it. 3a. Light continues to spine. 4. *To Kay Glen with thanks for her unfailing kindly interest in the Abbey Girls.*
DARING DORANNE

1. 1945 Margaret Horder. Muller. 2. Green. Plain. 2a. Title/author. 3. Geoffrey Ginger with Doranne peering out to see Maureen and Marcus. 3a. Title/author. 4. *To all friends of Inverkip here called Dunoon.*

AN ABBEY CHAMPION

1. 1946 June Margaret Horder. Muller. 2. Red. Plain. 2a. Title/author. 3. Littlejan dressed as a jester on stage, with others sketched lightly behind her. 3a. Title/author. 4. *To all who have told me they have found friends in the Abbey Girls.*
ROBINS IN THE ABBEY

1. 1947 Margaret Horder. Collins. 2. Dark green. Plain with silver lettering. 2a. As cover. 3. Brown surrounding a pink background with Robin in the abbey watching Rob sketching. 3a. Pink. 4. *To my cousins Agnes and Mabel Dean with love and all very best wishes.*

THE SECRETS OF VAIRY

1. 1947 Nov. Margaret Horder. Muller. 2. Green. Plain. 2a. Title/author in white. 3. Patch, Rosalin, Bill and Roger looking at the castle. 3a. Title/author. 4. *To Margaret Horder with grateful thanks for all the pleasure her pictures have given to me and many others.*

MARGERY MEETS THE ROSES

1. 1947 Victor Bertoglio. Lutterworth. 2. Dark blue. Plain. 2a. Title/author in white. 3. Nancybell watching dancing. 3a. Carried onto spine. 4. *To Elinor M. Brent-Dyer with love and all good wishes.*

A FIDDLER FOR THE ABBEY

1. 1948 Dec. Margaret Horder. Muller. 2. Orange. Plain. 2a. Author/title. 3. Littlejan and Rosalind looking over parapet of castle. 3a. Title/author. 4. *To all the friends I have found through their friendship and mine with the Abbey girls.*

GUARDIANS OF THE ABBEY

1. 1950 Margaret Horder. Muller. 2. Dark red. Plain. 2a. Title/author in purple. 3. Jansy showing Rachel and Damaris the crocus plot. 3a. Ballet shoes. 4. *To my niece Elspeth Wendy with all good wishes and love.*

SCHOOLGIRL JEN AT THE ABBEY
1. 1950 Sep. Frank Varty. Collins. 2. Green with a large house bottom right. 2a. A young Jen in front of the Abbey. 3a. Continues to spine.
STRANGERS AT THE ABBEY
1. 1951 Frank Varty. Collins. 2. Green. Plain. 2a. Title/author. 3. Jen and Rykie cycling to school, abbey behind them, Joan and Joy waving goodbye. 3a. Continues to spine.
RACHEL IN THE ABBEY
1. 1951 M.D.Neilson. Muller. 2. Dark red. Plain. 2a Title/author in gilt. 3. Rachel robed, with Jansy and Littlejan outside the gatehouse. 3a. Carried on to spine.
SELMA AT THE ABBEY
1. 1952 Frank Varty. Collins. 2. Fawn. Plain. 2a. Title/author. 3. Jen holding kitten standing with Selma and Joan. 3a. Carried onto spine.
A DANCER FROM THE ABBEY
1. 1953. F. Varty. Collins. 2. Pale blue. Plain. 2a. Title/author. 3. Mary Damayris dancing. 3a. Standing ballerina. 4. *To Doris Acland with love and all very best wishes from Elsie Jeanette Oxenham.*
THE SONG OF THE ABBEY
1. 1954 May F. Varty. Collins. 2. Grey. Plain. 2a. Title/author. 3. Nanta Rose playing violin against arches of the Abbey and procession of monks, Ambrose and Jehane. 3a. Continues to spine where Elizabeth and Margaret are sitting. 4. *To Alice A. Manning with all good wishes and many thanks for help in many ways.*
TOMBOYS AT THE ABBEY
1. 1957 Frank Varty. Collins. 2. Green. Plain. 2a. Title/author. 3. Jen and Jack climbing a tree watched by 3a. Joan and Joy on spine. 4. *To my great-nieces Deborah and Sara with every good wish and hoping they will grow up to be lovers of books.*
NEW GIRLS AT WOOD END
1. 1957 Frederick Books. 2. Green. Plain. 2a. Title/author in red. 3. Elisabel unconscious on ground. Two girls in smocks,

one on rearing horse. 3a. Title/author. 4. *To my great-nephews Jonathan Matthew and Timothy with every good wish and hoping they will read and love books.*

TWO QUEENS AT THE ABBEY

1. 1959 F. Varty. Collins. 2. Red. Small abbey bottom of front cover. 2a. Title/author. 3. Elizabeth and Margaret, one holding a queen dress and the other a crown. 3a. Two schoolgirls. 4. *To all the friends at Marlposts and to Janet Margaret Argent with love.*

DEB LEADS THE DORMITORY

1. 1992 Woodfield. 2. Dark green. Plain. 2a. Gilt title/author. 3. Lighter green with silhouette of girl's head in white circle. 3a. Title/author in white. 4. *Dedicated to the memory of Daphne Winifred Dunkerley and Benjamin Robin Dunkerley.*

A DIVIDED PATROL

1. 1992. R. Bayley. Woodfield. 2. Blue. Plain. 2a. Title and author in gilt. 3. Pale blue, pink lettering. Photograph of a group of Guides in oval. 3a. Lettering along spine.

NOTE

A booklet describing all the first edition Oxenham books, plus their illustrations but without their dustwrappers, is available from: Sue Sims 21 Warwick Road, Pokesdown, Bournemouth BH7 6JW, UK. SAE please for details and cost or e-mail sue@sims.abel.co.uk.

APPENDIX 4

READING ORDER

Thanks to the way Elsie Oxenham took characters from books already written as well as going off at tangents with new books, characters and groups, reading order is often little more than a matter of personal preference. My own preference is to read the remote connectors before the main Abbey series so that when one comes across a character or characters about whom there has obviously been another story, it is easier to understand how they fit in.

The main Abbey series with connectors indented
1. *Girls of the Hamlet Club*
2. *The Abbey Girls*
3. *The Girls of the Abbey School*
4. *Schooldays at the Abbey*
      Adventure in the Abbey   Both are short
      Mistakes in the Abbey   annual stories set at the
                                 time of *Schooldays at the*
                                 Abbey

5. *Secrets of the Abbey*
6. *Stowaways in the Abbey*

7. *Schoolgirl Jen at the Abbey*
8. *Strangers at the Abbey*
9. *Selma at the Abbey*
10. *Tomboys at the Abbey*
11. *The Abbey Girls Go Back to School*

Ideally it helps to have read *A School Torment* and *The Captain of the Fifth* first as characters from both appear here.

12. *Jen of the Abbey School*

Fits in before and after No 11

    A Go-Ahead Schoolgirl
    Tickles
13. *The New Abbey Girls*
14. *The Abbey Girls Again*
15. *The Abbey Girls in Town*
16. *Queen of the Abbey Girls*
17. *The Abbey Girls Win Through*
    A Go-Ahead Schoolgirl

These two partly precede *Tickles*

18. *The Abbey Girls at Home*

Has a very faint link with the first Swiss books. Directly precedes *The Abbey Girls Play Up* with characters from both the Swiss and Camp Keema groups.

    The Camp Mystery

19. *The Abbey Girls Play Up*
20. *The Abbey Girls on Trial*
21. *Biddy's Secret*
22. *Rosamund's Victory*
    Damaris at Dorothy's
23. *Maidlin to the Rescue*
    Damaris Dances

(Sequel to *Damaris at Dorothy's*)

24. *Joy's New Adventure*
    A Go-Ahead Schoolgirl

Elisabel and Rena reappear in *Rosamund's Tuck-Shop.*

25. *Rosamund's Tuck-Shop*
    Patch and a Pawn
    The Secrets of Vairy   Also precedes *Rosamund's Castle*

26. *Maidlin Bears the Torch*
    New Girls at Wood End   Follows *Rosamund's Tuck-Shop*. This includes Benedicta who had been in *Maidlin to the Rescue* (where she was not named) so could almost follow that title.

27. *Rosamund's Castle*
    The Girl Who Wouldn't Make Friends   Early story about Robin who has a large part in *New Girls at Wood End*.

    New Girls at Wood End   Follows *Rosamund's Tuck-shop*

28. *Maid of the Abbey*
29. *Jandy Mac Comes Back*
30. *Two Joans at the Abbey*   Follows both *Damaris at Dorothy's* and its sequel *Damaris Dances*.

31. *An Abbey Champion*   Here one can either stay with Abbey titles or go onto more books about the Kanes.

    Adventure for Two   Small references to *Maidlin to the Rescue* and D*amaris Dances*.

    Pernel Wins   The main characters reappear at the beginning of *Daring Doranne*.

    Daring Doranne   Vaguely follows *Adventure for Two*.

    Mistress Nanciebel   Historical novel. Ancestress of a character in the next two titles.

Elsa Puts Things Right
Margery Meets the Roses
The Girl Who Wouldn't
Make Friends

Early story about Robin.
The two main characters
are in *New Girls at Wood
End.*

32. *Robins in the Abbey*
33. *A Fiddler for the Abbey*
34. *Guardians of the Abbey*
35. *Rachel in the Abbey*
36. *A Dancer from the Abbey*
37. *The Song of the Abbey*
38. *Two Queens at the Abbey*

There is a certain amount of overlapping with some of the later Abbey
stories; mainly *Maid/Jandy Mac*; *Two Joans/Robins*; *Fiddler/Guardian*.

The remote connectors:

(Minor connectors are
indented.)

The Woody Dean books
A School Camp Fire

Girls from here appear
very briefly in *The School
of Ups and Downs.*

The School of Ups and Downs
Patience Joan, Outsider

Patience Joan reappeared
in the Swiss group.

The Gregory's books (Also known as the Ven & Gard books)
The Junior Captain
The School Without a Name
Peggy Makes Good

One character was also in
the third *Torment* book.

Ven at Gregory's

Ven reappeared in the
Swiss group.

The Swiss group
The Two Form Captains

The two main characters
were in *The Abbey Girls
Go Back to School* and
others.

The Captain of the Fifth	Also follows *Patience Joan, Outsider.*
The Camp Mystery	Precedes *The Abbey Girls Play Up.*
Patience and Her Problems	Sequel to *Patience Joan, Outsider.*
The Troubles of Tazy	Tazy reappeared in *An Abbey Champion* and a few later Abbey books.
The Torments *The School Torment*	Tormentil was in *The Abbey Girls Go Back to School*
The Testing of the Torment *The Camp Fire Torment* also in The Camp Keema books *The Crisis in Camp Keema* *The Last Night in Camp*	Sadie Sandell was *Peggy Makes Good.* Connecting annual story.
Peggy and the Brotherhood *Freda Joins the Guides* *The Camp Mystery*	Connecting annual story. Follows *The Captain of the Fifth* as well as preceding *The Abbey Girls Play Up.*
The *Rocklands* pair *A Go-Ahead Schoolgirl*	Characters in both met *Tickles* Jen in *Jen of the Abbey School.*

The non-connecting books

The Goblin Island set *Goblin Island* *A Princess in Tatters* *A Holiday Queen*	The links here are characters common to more than one book.

The Twins of Castle Charming
Finding Her Family

Schoolgirls and Scouts
One character is in the last four.
Finding Her Family has nothing to do with the rest of these four otherwise.

The Jintys
The Tuck-Shop Girl
The Reformation of Jinty
Jinty's Patrol
A Divided Patrol

The Debs
Deb at School
Deb of Sea House
Deb Leads the Dormitory

These single stories have nothing to do with each other or with any other books. Listed in order of publication.

The Conquest of Christina
Rosaly's New School
At School with the Roundheads
Expelled from School
The Girls of Gwynfa
Dorothy's Dilemma
    Dicky's Way
    Dicky's Dilemma
    Helen Wins

Annual stories set at the *Dorothy's Dilemma* school and including one of the staff from there.

Sylvia of Sarn

The Inter-Connections

    Girls of the Hamlet Club was the first of the Abbey sequence but by the time *The Abbey Girls Go Back to School* is reached it is obvious that there are previous publications about some of the people the abbey girls met at Cheltenham.

It is clear from *The Abbey Girls Go Back to School* that Karen and Tazy have been to a school in Switzerland. The inclusion of Tormentil Grant in the same story makes the three *Torment* books extremely remote connectors. A twelve-year-old in *A Camp Fire Torment* appeared in *Peggy Makes Good* making another link; this time with one of the Sussex groups.

The only connection between *A School Camp Fire* and *The School of Ups and Downs* is that girls from the former attended a wedding in the latter. Patience Joan Ordway joined the school in which Miss Helen had been the Camp Fire Guardian and *Patience and Her Problems,* the immediate sequel to *Patience Joan, Outsider,* was one of the Swiss books although it didn't appear for another five years after *Patience Joan, Outsider.*

However, some of the Sussex schoolgirls precede Karen and Tazy, so ideally one should learn first how the two Sussex groups led to any stories set in Switzerland.

A different school in Sussex introduced another group of girls plus Barbara, an older one, who was both Camp Fire and a dancer. Barbara, Ven and Patience Joan all met in Switzerland where they became friendly with Karen and Tazy, thus going back very indirectly to the Abbey Girls at Cheltenham. Tazy reappeared in *An Abbey Champion* and some subsequent Abbey books.

Meanwhile two of Patience Joan's cousins who were mentioned briefly in *Patience Joan, Outsider,* go to school in Switzerland in *The Captain of the Fifth* and reappear in *A Camp Mystery* which immediately precedes *The Abbey Girls on Trial*. The elder cousin, Sally Pennyfold, was mentioned in *The Abbey Girls at Home* where Rosamund Kane had met Karen, although *The Abbey Girls at Home* was written five years after *Patience Joan, Outsider* and *The Captain of the Fifth.*

In *The Camp Mystery* Sally's younger sister Gulielma met the main characters from *The Crisis in Camp Keema* and *Peggy and the Brotherhood*. As Maribel from those two eventually married Mike Marchwood, becoming related through that marriage to Jen, there is another link between several different groups.

The two Rocklands books (*A Go-Ahead Schoolgirl* and *Tickles*) may be read more easily than any others in sequence within the *Abbeys*.

Moving from the remote connectors, once Rosamund and Maidlin joined the Abbey Girls, then became adults, they were given their own smaller groups of books and 'new' relatives about whom separate sets of stories were written. Apart from the three *Rosamund* titles there were several about the Kane family. *Margery Meets the Roses* produced Kane cousins and there were offshoots with books such as *Patch and a Pawn* and its direct sequel *The Secrets of Vairy*, both of which also tied in with the Kanes. Later Patch (Patricia) reappeared in *The Song of the Abbey* .

Maidlin was given unknown cousins in *Maidlin to the Rescue* who had been introduced in *Damaris at Dorothy's*. *Damaris Dances* followed those two. Previously in *Maidlin Bears the Torch* Maidlin had befriended Benedicta who had been given an important part to play at Rosamund's wedding as well as being in *New Girls at Wood End* then returning to the abbey in *Rachel in the Abbey* .

At the same time, Daphne Dale, who was destined to become understudy to Mary Damayris, was in *Adventure for Two* making a connection with the *Rosamund* extras and indirectly also providing another small link between the relations of Rosamund and Maidlin. *Mistress Nanciebel,* although a historical novel, produced an ancestress of the modern Nancybell in *Elsa Puts things Right*. Nancybell also connected with *Margery meets the Roses* and the Kanes.

A booklet *The Books of Elsie J. Oxenham* giving another version of the various groups, is available from its compiler Ruth Allen at 32 Tadfield Road, Romsey, Hants., SO51 5AJ for £1.50 plus an A5 stamped envelope (outside UK prices on enquiry)

APPENDIX 5

EJO SHORT STORIES
These are all those discovered by 2002.
They may be found in more than one source.

The first groups are taken from Abbey books.
The Rocklands books

The Girls of Rocklands School	Part of *Jen of the Abbey School*
The Second Term at Rocklands	"
The Third Term at Rocklands	"
The Call of the Abbey School	Part of *Queen of the Abbey Girls*
The Girls of Squirrel House	Part of *The Abbey Girls on Trial*
'New' titles	Where found
The Girls of Rocklands School	*Schoolgirls' Bumper Book* 1925
"	*Schoolgirls' Stories* ND
"	*Schoolgirls' Story Book* 1924
"	*Collins Schoolgirls' Annual* 1924

Jen's Presents	*Schoolgirls' Bumper Book*	1927
"	*Collins Girls' Patrol Book*	ND
"	*Collins Schoolgirls' Annual*	ND
"	*Schoolgirls' Holiday Book*	ND
"	*Our Girls' Story Book*	ND
Treasure from the Snow	*Our Girls' Story Book*	ND
"	*Girls' Outdoor Book*	ND
"	*Schoolgirls' Holiday Book*	c. 1930
"	*Schoolgirls' Yarns*	c. 1930
Secret of the Abbey	*Little Folks*	1921

(Taken from *The Girls of the Abbey School*)

The GIRLS of ROCKLANDS SCHOOL

Elsie J. Oxenham

New Abbey Stories

Adventure in the Abbey	*Collins Girls' Annual*	1955
"	*Girls' Own Story Book*	ND
"	*Girls' Own Book*	ND
Mistakes in the Abbey	*Girls' Own Book*	ND
"	*Collins Girls' Annual*	1956
"	*Girls' Story Omnibus*	ND

Short stories distantly connected to the *Abbey* series

Camp Keema Finds a Guardian	*Girls' All-Round Book*	1929
"	*Nelson's Budget for Girls*	ND
Peggy-Perfect Goes to School	*Little Folks*	1931
The Missing Link	*Little Folks*	1929
Peggy Plays a Part	*British Girls' Annual*	1925
The Bungalow Baby	*British Girls' Annual*	1926
Christmas Quarantine	*Schoolfriend* (paper)	1922

(The last three were later joined together and made into the book *Peggy Makes Good.*)

Stories assumed to have been extra chapters to various books but not included in them on publication.

The Last Night in Camp	*Hulton's Girls' Stories*	1929

(Connects with *Crisis in Camp Keema*.)

Freda Joins the Guides	*Girls' All-Round Book*	1931
	Nelson's Budget for Girls	ND

(Connects with *Peggy and the Brotherhood.*)

Peggy and the
Brotherhood

By
ELSIE JEANETTE OXENHAM

Author of " The School Camp Fire," " The Abbey Girls,"
" The Abbey Girls Again," etc.

Illustrated by J. MILLS

Stories extended into books after having been used as long serials.

Peggy & the Brotherhood	*Girls' Own Annual*	1936
Patch & a Pawn	*Girls' Own Annual*	1939
Patience Joan, Outsider	*Little Folks*	1922
Tickles & the Talking Cave	*British Girls' Annual*	1923
The Testing of the Torment	*Little Folks*	1925

Stories which have nothing to do with the *Abbey* series

The Honour of the Guides	*Hulton's Girls' Stories*	1933
One Good Turn	*Hulton's Girls' Stories*	1928
The Guides & Roger	*Hulton's Girls' Stories*	1926
Jinty of the Girl Guides	*Hulton's Girls' Stories*	ND

(All from the *Jinty* books.)

St Margaret's Schooldays Weekly (paper)		1928

(The first part of *Deb at School*.)

The Silence of Dorothy Cheney	*Little Folks*	?
Dicky's Way	*British Girls' Annual*	1928
Dorothy's Dilemma	*Little Folks*	?
Dicky's Dilemma	*British Girls' Annual*	1926
Helen Wins	*Bumper Book for Girls*	1934

(The last two are placed in the same school as *Dorothy's Dilemma*
and *Dicky's Dilemma* is thought to be an unused chapter taken from
that title.)

Honour Your Partner	*British Girls' Annual*	1922
Dancing Honour	*British Girls' Annual*	1921

(These two are both set in the same school which is not one which
appears anywhere else.)

Single stories not related to each other or to any others.

Muffins & Crumpets	*Bumper Book for Girls*	1926
"	*Stories for Schoolgirls*	ND
"	*Budget for Girls*	ND
Aunt Jane's Piano	*The Quiver*	1908

BIBLIOGRAPHY

Dates given unless stated otherwise are for the first edition of each book quoted.

Abbeys by M. R. James Litt.D., F.S.A., F.B.A. The Great Western Railway. 1926.

Abbeys, an introduction by R. Gilyard-Beer M.A., F.S.A.

A History of Children's Book Illustration by Joyce Irene Whalley & Tessa Rose Chester. John Murray with the Victoria and Albert Museum.1988.

An Introduction to English Folk Song by Maud Karpeles. Faber revised edition. 1987.

A World of Girls by Rosemary Auchmuty. Women's Press Ltd. 1992.

A World of Women by Rosemary Auchmuty. Women's Press Ltd. 1999.

Behind the Chalet School by Helen McClelland. New Horizon. 1981.

Behind the Chalet School by Helen McClelland. Bettany Press. Revised edition. 1996.

Behold the Child by Gillian Avery. The Bodley Head 1994.

Brother Cadfael's Herb Garden by Rob Talbot and Robin Whiteman. Little Brown and Co. New York 1996.

Cecil Sharp by A. H. Fox Strangeways with Maud Karpeles. 1933.

Children's Fiction, a Handbook for Librarians by Sheila Ray

B.A., F.L.A. Brockhampton Press. 1970.

Childhood's Pattern by Gillian Avery. Hodder and Stoughton. 1975.

Chin Up, Chest Out Jemima! by Mary Cadogan. Bonnington Press. 1989.

Christianity in Somerset. Edited by Robert Dunning. Somerset County Council. 1976.

Cleeve & Muchelney Abbeys by Sue Watling. English Heritage. 1989.

Collecting Children's Books compiled by *Book & Magazine Collector*. Diamond Publishing Group. 1995.

Dictionary of British Book Illustrators by Brigid Peppin & Lucy Micklethwait. John Murray. 1983.

Discovering Abbeys and Priories by Geoffrey N. Wright. Shire Publications. Revised edition.1994.

Dromkeen: A journey into Children's Literature by Jeffrey Prentice & Bettina Bird. The Bodley Head 1987.

Early Children's' Books by Eric Quayle. David and Charles. 1983.

EJO: Her Work by Stella Waring and Sheila Ray. D. S. Waring and S. G. Ray. 1985 and revised edition. 1997.

Elinor M. Brent-Dyer's Chalet School. Armada. 1989.

England's Dances by Douglas Kennedy. 1949.

English Abbeys by Hugh Braun Faber and Faber Ltd. 1971

English Folk Dances by Violet Alford. 1923.

English Monastic Life by Abbot Gasquet. 3rd edition.. Methuen and Co. 1905.

English Monasticism Yesterday and Today by E. K. Milliken M.A. George G. Harrap & Co. Ltd. 1967.

Folly Annual Christmas 1995 and 1999.

From Brown to Bunter by P. W. Musgrave. Routledge and Keegan Paul plc. 1985.

Girls Will Be Girls by Arthur Marshall. Hamish Hamilton. 1974.

Great-Grandmama's Weekly by Wendy Forrester. Lutterworth Press. 1980.

Highways and Byways in Buckinghamshire by Clement Shorter. MacMillan & Co. 1910.

Highways and Byways in Somerset by Edward Hutton. Macmillan & Co. 1924.

Highways and Byways in Sussex by E.V.Lucas. Macmillan & Co. reprint 1928.

Intent Upon Reading by Marjorie Fish. Brockhampton Press. 1961.

J.O. by Erica Oxenham 1942. (Longman, Green & Co 1942)

Lighting the Fire by Allison Thompson. The Squirrel Press. 1998.

Medieval Craftsmen / Painters by Paul Binski. Second edition. British Museum Press. 1994.

Medieval Craftsmen / Scribes and Illuminators by Christopher de Hamel. Trustees of the British Museum. Revised edition 1993.

Memories of Tin Town by Professor Brian Robinson M.Sc., Ph.D., D.Sc. J.W. Northend Ltd.

Minehead, Porlock and Dunster by C. E. Larter and Herbert W. Kille. Homeland Handbooks ND.

My Own Schooldays by Angela Brazil. Blackie and Son Ltd.1925.

Old Minehead and Around by Hilary Binding. The Exmoor Press 1983.

Old Watchet, Williton and Around by A.L.Wedlake. The Exmoor Press 1984

Schoolmates of the Long-Ago by Eva Margareta Löfgren. Symposium Graduate. 1993.

Scotland's Dances by H. A. Thurston. 1954.

Scrapbook of J.O. by Erica Oxenham. (Longman, Green & Co) 1946.

Step Change edited by Georgina Boyes. Francis Boutle Publishers. 2001.

Tales Out of School by Geoffrey Trease. Heinemann Educational Books Ltd. Revised edition. 1964.

The Anne of Green Gables Treasury by Carolyn Strom Collins and Christina Wyss Eriksson. Viking Penguin Inc. 1991.

The Book of the British Camp Fire Girls. 1925.

The Book of the Camp Fire Girls. 1922.

The Book of the Camp Fire Girls. Revised edition. 1962.

306

The Book of the Camp Fire Girls. Revised edition. 1966.

The Chalet School Revisited by Helen McClelland. Bettany Press. 1997.

The Country Dance Book by Cecil Sharp.

The Encyclopaedia of Girls' School Stories by Sue Sims and Hilary Clare. Ashgate Publishing Ltd. 2000.

The English Abbey by Fred H. Crossley F.S.A.. B.T.Batsford Ltd. Reprint 1942.

The First Chalet Annual. 1996. (and subsequent years).

The Heirs of Tom Brown by Isabel Quigley. Chatto and Windus. 1982.

The Lancashire Morris Dance by Maud Karpeles.

The Little Town of Arundel by Francis D. Allison. The Arundel Press 1947.

The Morris Book by Cecil Sharp.

The Nesbit Tradition 1945 - 1970 by Marcus Crouch. Ernest Benn Ltd. 1972

The Oxford Companion to Children's Literature by Humphrey Carpenter & Mari Prichard. Oxford United Press. 1984.

The Schoolgirl Ethic by Gillian Freeman. Allen Lane. 1976.

The Storytellers by Simon Appleyard This England Books. 1991.

The Sword Dances of Northern England by Cecil Sharp.

Treasure Seekers and Borrowers by Marcus Crouch. The Library Association. 1962.

Three Centuries of Children's Books in Europe by Bettina Hürlimann. First English Edition. Hamish Hamilton. 1967.

Twentieth Century Children's Writers. The Macmillan Press Ltd. 1978.

What Katy Read by Shirley Foster & Judy Simons. 1995.

Who's Who in Children's Books by Marjorie Fish. Weidenfield and Nicolson. 1975.

Wo-He-Lo The story of Camp Fire Girls 1910-1960. Compiled by Helen Buckler, Mary Fiedler and Martha Allen. Holt, Rinehart and Winston. New York. 1961.

Written for Children by John Rowe Townsend. Penguin Books. Revised edition. 1987.

You're a Brick, Angela by Mary Cadogan and Patricia Craig. Victor Gollancz. 1978.

All issues of *The Abbey Chapter, The Abbey Chronicle, The Abbey Gatehouse* and *The Abbey Guardian* newsletters from their inception.

Also *Folly* and the newsletters/journals relating to Elinor Brent-Dyer and Dorita Fairlie Bruce.

Theses have been written on Elsie Jeanette Oxenham's books and her work and are available via Interloan Libraries.

EJO and Her Work by Sheila Ray and Stella Waring 1985 and revised version 1997.

Aspects of Life and Works of Elsie J. Oxenham by Marjorie Morris 1989

The Use of Social Dance in Literature by Pat Riley 1990

ACKNOWLEDGEMENTS

Theo Dunkerley for permission to produce a biography of her sister Elsie and for providing details about the Dunkerley family as children.

Elspeth Wendy Dunkerley for photographs of her aunt.

Doris Acland who shared all she knew about Elsie as an authoress.

Frances Evered, her son Phillip and his cousin Marion Spiller for information about Cleeve Abbey and Cleeva Clapp.

Margaret Perry for details about Ribby.

Margaret Simey (née Baynes Todd) who, as a girl, knew Elsie.

Polly Whibley for continual support and advice.

Clarissa Cridland for editorial suggestions.

Ealing Public Library for information about John Oxenham and the addresses where the Dunkerley family lived.

The publishers W. & R. Chambers, Frederick Muller, and William Collins for permission to use dustwrappers and extracts from books by Elsie Jeanette Oxenham.

Judges Postcards Ltd. for permission to reproduce postcards.

Country Life and *The Royal Institute of Architects* for additional information about Cleeve Abbey.

All who have provided photographs about places used originally by Elsie Oxenham for her settings. Namely:
Ken Godfrey, Martin Godfrey, Edna Golder, Pauline Harding, Christine Keyes, Mrs Betty North, Margaret Perry & Olga Lock-Kendell, Sheila Ray with Stella Waring, Val Shelley .

Descriptions of first editions
Ruth Allen (dates), Barbara Harris (dustwrappers), Sue Sims (covers/colours).

General thanks to:
Editors of the newsletters/journals
The Abbey Chapter (South Africa). No longer in existence. Polly Whibley, then Valerie Thomson.

The Abbey Chronicle (Great Britain)
Monica Godfrey, then Ruth Allen, latterly with Fiona Dyer.

The Abbey Gatehouse (New Zealand)
Carol Grey, then Jane Webster.

The Abbey Guardian (Australia)
Val Shelley.

Also *Friends of the Chalet School, The New Chalet Club Journal* (both Elinor M. Brent-Dyer), *Serendipity* (Dorita Fairlie Bruce), *Souvenir* (Violet Needham) and *Folly (Fans of Light Literature for the Young)*, all of which have included articles on Elsie Jeanette Oxenham and other relevant authors.

And to everyone who has done research, written articles and provided photographs and illustrations for their newsletters/journals. Also those who kindly let me borrow letters they had had from or about Elsie Jeanette Oxenham over the years. Mainly Doris Acland, Sheila Bender, K. Busby, H. Christie, Regina Glick, Amy Harrison, May Hill, Andrea Hosker, Joan Houseman, D. Leys, Trisha Marshall and A. Roberts.

INDEX

NOTE: this index covers pages 1 to 260. Page numbers in
italics refer to illustrations.

Girls Gone By Publishers

Titles in print and forthcoming titles in 2003

Books by Elinor Brent-Dyer

The Chalet School Series
The Chalet School in the Oberland (Autumn 2003)

Chalet School Connectors
Monica Turns Up Trumps (In Print)

La Rochelle Series
Janie of La Rochelle (In print)

New 'fill-in' Chalet School books completely faithful to the style of Elinor Brent-Dyer
The Chalet School and Robin by Caroline German (In Print)

Books by and about Elsie Jeanette Oxenham

Connected to the Abbey Series
Margery Meets the Roses (Autumn 2003)

Pony Book

Pony Thieves in Cumberland by Julia Cotter (Summer 2003)

Books by Dorita Fairlie Bruce

Nancy and St Bride's Series
The Girls of St Bride's (In print)
Nancy at St Bride's (In print)
That Boarding School Girl (Spring 2003)

Books by Lorna Hill

Marjorie and Patience Titles
Marjorie and Co (Summer 2003)

Books by Antonia Forest

Falconer's Lure (In print)
Run Away Home (Spring 2003)

Books by Gwendoline Courtney

A Coronet for Cathie (Summer 2003)

General Non-Fiction

You're a Brick, Angela! by Mary Cadogon and Patricia Craig (Autumn 2003)

All titles in print may be purchased directly from Girls Gone By Publishers, and we also sell book tokens for our own titles.

For details please send an SAE to Ann Mackie-Hunter or Clarissa Cridland at 4 Rock Terrace, Coleford, Somerset BA3 5NF, UK
or e-mail ggbp@rockterrace.demon.co.uk
or check out our website -
http://www.rockterrace.demon.co.uk/GGBP

We plan to reprint further titles in 2003 by the above and other Authors. Details of these will be announced on our website and in author appreciation society magazines and journals.

Elsie Jeanette Oxenham Appreciation Societies

There are three flourishing Abbey societies in Australia, New Zealand and the UK. Each produces a quarterly or tri-annual A5 magazine.

The Abbey Girls of Australia (newsletter *The Abbey Guardian*)
Details from: Val Shelley, 23 Lagoon Crescent, Bellbowrie, Queensland 4070, Australia

The Abbey Gatehouse
Details from: Barbara Robertson, 39D Bengal Street, Wellington, New Zealand
e-mail: born.robertson@xtra.co.nz

The Elsie Jeanette Oxenham Appreciation Society (UK) (journal *The Abbey Chronicle*)
Details from: Ruth Allen, 32 Tadfield Road, Romsey, Hampshire SO51 5AJ, UK
e-mail abbey@bufobooks.demon.co.uk
website http://www.bufobooks.demon.co.uk/abbeylnk.htm
        http://ds.dial.pipex.com.ct/ejo.html

Elsie Jeanette Oxenham website
There is also an excellent website to be found at
http://www.penrithcity.nsw.gov.au/usrpages/Collect/popular.htm